Lane.

Nora Langhor.

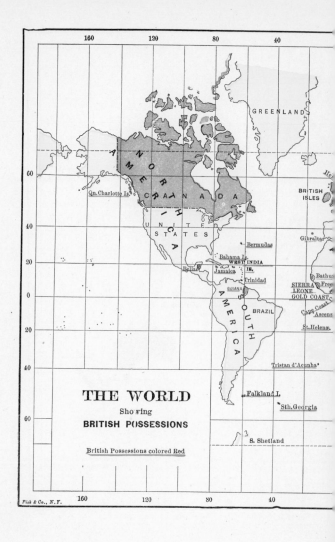

160   120   80   40

GREENLAND

60

Qn.Charlotte Is.

40

UNITED

STATES

20

Bermudas

BRITISH
ISLES

Gibraltar

Bahama Is.
WEST INDIA
IS.

0

Belize

Jamaica

Trinidad

GUIANA

20

BRAZIL

40

60

AMERICA

SOUTH

NORTH

AMERICA

CANADA

He

Bathu
SIERRA Free
LEONE
GOLD COAST

Cape Coast
Ascens

St.Helena.

Tristan d'Acunha

Falkland I.

Sth.Georgia

S. Shetland

THE WORLD

Showing

BRITISH POSSESSIONS

British Possessions colored Red

Fisk & Co., N.Y.

160   120   80   40

PREFACE.

THE object of this little book is to attempt to tell the story of England's history for young folks. Important events have been given in fuller detail than is usual, so as to awaken an interest in them, though no story has been told simply because it is interesting—room having been made for this by omitting much that would be merely burdensome to the memory. Very few dates have been inserted, with the exception of those of the kings' reigns.

PREFACE.

The object of this little book is to attempt to tell the story of England's history for young folks. Important events have been given in fuller detail than is usual, so as to awaken an interest in them, though the story has been told simply because it is information—room having been made for this by omitting much that would be merely irksome to the memory. Very few dates have been inserted, with the exception of those of the kings' reigns.

CONTENTS.

CHAPTER I.

THE BRITONS AND THE ROMANS.

CHAPTER II.

THE ENGLISH CONQUEST.

CHAPTER III.

THE CONVERSION OF ENGLAND.

CHAPTER IV.

THE UNION OF ENGLAND.

CHAPTER V.

THE ENGLISH AND THE DANISH KINGS.

CHAPTER VI.

THE NORMAN CONQUEST.

CHAPTER VII.

THE CONQUEROR AND HIS SONS.

WILLIAM I., 1066. WILLIAM II., 1087. HENRY I., 1100.

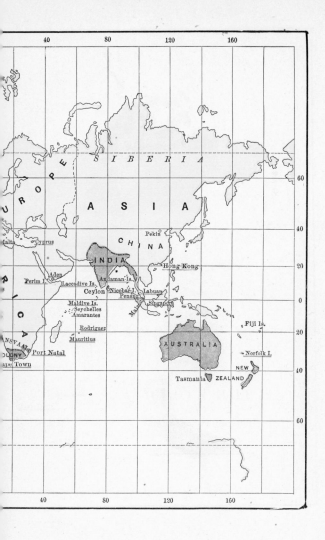

40   80   120   160

S I B E R I A

60

E U R O P E

A S I A

40

Malta   Cyprus

Pekin

C H I N A

20

I N D I A

Hong-Kong

Perim I.   Aden

Andaman Is.

Laccadive Is.

Ceylon   Nicobar I.   Labuan

Penang

Malacca   Singapore   0

Maldive Is.
Seychelles
Amarantes

Rodriguez   Fiji Is.

Mauritius   20

AUSTRALIA

Norfolk I.

TRANSVAAL
COLONY   Port Natal

NEW

Cape Town

Tasmania   ZEALAND   40

A F R I C A

60

40   80   120   160

ENGLISH HISTORY

FOR SCHOOLS

B.C. 55—A.D. 1880

BY

S. R. GARDINER

HONORARY STUDENT OF CHRIST CHURCH, AND PROFESSOR OF MODERN
HISTORY AT KING'S COLLEGE, LONDON

Edition Revised for American Students

NEW YORK
HENRY HOLT AND COMPANY

CHAPTER XIII.

RICHARD II., 1377.

CHAPTER XIV.

THE HOUSE OF LANCASTER.

HENRY IV., 1399.   HENRY V., 1414.   HENRY VI., 1422.

CHAPTER XV.

THE HOUSE OF YORK.

EDWARD IV., 1461.   EDWARD V., 1483.   RICHARD III., 1483.

CHAPTER XVI.

THE FIRST TUDOR KING.

HENRY VII., 1485.

CHAPTER XVII.

THE FIRST YEARS OF HENRY VIII.

(1509–1529.)

CHAPTER XVIII.

LAST PART OF THE REIGN OF HENRY VIII.

(1529–1547.)

CHAPTER XIX.

EDWARD VI. AND MARY.

EDWARD VI., 1547. MARY, 1553.

CHAPTER XX.

THE FIRST YEARS OF ELIZABETH.

(1558–1580.)

CHAPTER XXI.

ELIZABETH'S TRIUMPHS.

(1580–1588.)

CHAPTER XXII.

THE LAST YEARS OF ELIZABETH.

(1588–1603.)

CHAPTER XXIII.

JAMES I. AND THE HOUSE OF COMMONS.

(1603–1614.)

CHAPTER XXIV.

JAMES I. AND SPAIN.

(1614–1625.)

CHAPTER XXV.

CHARLES. I. AND HIS FIRST THREE PARLIAMENTS.

(1625–1629.)

CHAPTER XXVI.

THE UNPARLIAMENTARY GOVERNMENT OF CHARLES I.

(1629–1640.)

CHAPTER XXVII.

THE LONG PARLIAMENT AND THE CIVIL WAR.

(1640–1649.)

CHAPTER XXVIII.

THE COMMONWEALTH AND THE PROTECTORATE.

(1649–1660.)

CHAPTER XXIX.

THE FIRST TWELVE YEARS OF CHARLES II.

(1660–1672.)

CHAPTER XXX.

THE LAST TWELVE YEARS OF CHARLES II.

(1673–1685.)

CHAPTER XXXI.

THE REIGN OF JAMES II.

(1685–1688.)

CHAPTER XXXII.

WILLIAM AND MARY.

(1689–1694.)

CHAPTER XXXIII.

WILLIAM III.

(1694–1702.)

CHAPTER XXXIV.

QUEEN ANNE.

(1702 1714.)

CHAPTER XXXV.

THE REIGNS OF THE FIRST TWO GEORGES TO THE DEATH OF HENRY PELHAM.

(GEORGE I., 1714—GEORGE II., 1727—DEATH OF HENRY PELHAM, 1754.)

CHAPTER XXXIX.

FROM THE BEGINNING OF THE FRENCH REVOLUTION TO THE PEACE OF AMIENS.

(1789–1802.)

CHAPTER XL.

FROM THE PEACE OF AMIENS TO THE BEGINNING OF THE PENINSULAR WAR.

(1802–1808.)

CHAPTER XLI.

FROM THE BEGINNING OF THE PENINSULAR WAR TO THE PEACE OF PARIS.

(1808–1814.)

CHAPTER XLII.

FROM THE PEACE OF PARIS TO THE DEATH OF GEORGE III.

(1814–1820.)

CHAPTER XLIII.

REIGN OF GEORGE IV.

(1820–1830.)

CHAPTER XLIV.

REIGN OF WILLIAM IV.

(1830–1837.)

CHAPTER XLV.

FROM THE ACCESSION OF VICTORIA TO THE FALL OF THE MELBOURNE MINISTRY.

(1837–1841.)

CHAPTER XLVI.

THE MINISTRY OF SIR ROBERT PEEL.

(1841–1846.)

CHAPTER XLVII.

FROM THE BEGINNING OF LORD JOHN RUSSELL'S MINISTRY TO THE END OF THE CRIMEAN WAR.

(1846–1856.)

CHAPTER XLVIII.

THE INDIAN MUTINY.

(1857, 1858.)

DATES OF THE CHIEF EVENTS BEFORE THE CONQUEST.

	A.D.
Landing of the English	449
Landing of Saint Augustine	597
Egbert, King of Wessex	802
The Treaty of Wedmore	878
Cnut, King of all England	1016
Edward the Confessor King	1042
Harold's Reign, and the Battle of Senlac	1066

KINGS AFTER THE CONQUEST.

	A.D.		A.D.
William I.	1066	Henry VIII.	1509
William II.	1087	Edward VI.	1547
Henry I.	1100	Mary	1553
Stephen	1135	Elizabeth	1558
Henry II.	1154	James I.	1603
Richard I.	1189	Charles I.	1625
John	1199	Commonwealth and Pro-	
Henry III.	1216	tectorate	1649
Edward I.	1272	Charles II.	1660
Edward II.	1307	James II.	1685
Edward III.	1327	William III. and Mary II.	1689
Richard II.	1377	Anne	1702
Henry IV.	1399	George I.	1714
Henry V.	1413	George II.	1727
Henry VI.	1422	George III.	1760
Edward IV.	1461	George IV.	1820
Edward V.	1483	William IV.	1830
Richard III.	1483	Victoria	1837
Henry VII.	1485		

OUTLINE OF ENGLISH HISTORY.

FIRST PERIOD.

◆

CHAPTER I.

THE BRITONS AND THE ROMANS.

CROMLECH.

1. **The Britons.**—Nearly two thousand years ago the island now consisting of England and Scotland was called Britain. The people who lived in it were called Britons. They could not read or write, so that, as they did not write any books to tell us about themselves, no-

thing is known about their history till some people
who could write visited the country. There have,
however, been found in the tombs of some of them,
pieces of pottery and other things which they used,
and there are still to be found a few cromlechs, as
they are called, made of huge pieces of rock set
upright with a flat piece to cover them, under which
great men were buried, and which were once covered
with earth which has been taken away. Also in one
or two places there were circles of enormous stones

STONEHENGE.

set up, with other stones lying across on the top,
like the frame of a door. One of the most complete
of those which remain is at Stonehenge on Salisbury
Plain. It is supposed that these were used as
temples. A great part of the country was unculti-
vated and covered with wood. The people had cattle,
and hunted the animals in the woods, but they also
planted barley for food, and made baskets and pottery. Ships came all the way from the east end of
the Mediterranean to buy tin in Cornwall.

2. Britain conquered by the Romans.—The first people who went there who could write down accounts of what they saw were the Romans. Their chief city was Rome in Italy. They had conquered a great part of Europe, and part of Asia and of Africa. Fifty-five years before Christ, Julius Cæsar, a great Roman general, came with an army to Britain. He went back and returned the next year. Afterwards he became emperor, or commander of all the Roman armies, and ruler of the Romans and of all the people whom they had conquered. About a hundred years later, rather more than eighteen hundred years ago, another Roman emperor sent an army to Britain, and after some little time all South Britain, as far as the Firths of Clyde and Forth, was conquered.

3. The Roman Government of Britain.—Before the Romans came, the Britons lived in small tribes, each with a king of its own, and each one often fighting with its neighbours, like the Zulus in Africa now. The Romans did not kill the people they conquered, or drive them out. They treated them very much in the same way as the English, in our own time, have treated the people of India. They made good roads and built towns, and forced the people to live at peace. Wherever we find such a name as street, or anything like it, as Chester-le-Street, Stratton or Stratford, we know there was once a Roman road. Wherever we find chester or caster, as in Winchester or Doncaster, we know that there was once a Roman garrison. The Romans were great builders, and the remains of some of their fortifications are still to be seen. The streets of the towns swarmed with citizens. The richer people built comfortable country houses for themselves to live in. Corn was grown in abundance, and besides the tin mines of Cornwall there were mines of lead and iron. Christian missionaries arrived, and the people became Christian. In some parts the Latin language was spoken, but the conquered people for the most part continued to address one another in their own tongue. On the whole the Romans tried to rule justly. They encouraged trade, and made good laws in their dominions on the Continent, as well as in Britain, so that every man might have what belonged to him. All this was possible, just as it is possible in India, because there was peace in all the lands belonging to the Romans. There were soldiers at the frontier of the empire, to prevent the fierce Germans from bursting in to rob and kill. But inside the Roman frontier no tribe was allowed to fight with another.

4. The Romans leave Britain.—The Roman rule in Britain lasted for about three hundred and fifty years. Then the Roman army went away. The Romans had been attacked by their enemies, and they wanted their soldiers to come home to defend Italy. The Britons were left to take care of themselves. Unfortunately for them, the Romans had not taught them how to fight. They and their fathers had lived so long in peace that they did not know how to keep off an enemy. They were attacked by wild and fierce tribes—the Scots and Picts. At that time the Scots lived in Ireland, though many of them afterwards crossed the sea to the part of Northern Britain where Argyleshire is now, and later on gave the name of Scotland, or the land of the Scots, to the northern part of the island. The Picts lived to the north of the Firths of Clyde and Forth before the Scots came. These Scots and Picts came amongst the Britons, plundering and killing. The Britons had always been defended by the Roman army, and feeling quite helpless they wrote to the Roman general to bring his soldiers back. The general did as he was asked, drove off the Scots and Picts, and then went away for ever. The Scots and Picts returned. A people which cannot defend itself is likely to meet with no mercy.

CHAPTER II.

THE ENGLISH CONQUEST.

1. Coming of the English.—The Britons spoke a language which was the same as that which some of the Welsh, who are descended from them, still speak. The Scots and Picts spoke a language not very different. Beyond the North Sea was a different people living on both sides of the mouth of the river Elbe. They were called Angles, and Saxons, and Jutes, speaking a language which was German, though it was not quite the same as the German spoken in Germany now. It is called Low German, and was more like the Dutch language. The Angles, and Saxons, and Jutes were as fierce as the Scots and Picts. They had small vessels and were hardy sailors. They came across the sea, plundering,

THE
FIRST HOME
OF THE
ENGLISH

NORTHMEN

GOTHS OR JUTES

N S

ENGLISH

Heathby

R. Eider

FRISIANS

R. Ems

R. Rhine

FRANKS

SAXONS

R. Weser

R. Elbe

GERMANS

and burning, and slaying, like the Scots and Picts. In the year 449, some Jutes, under two chiefs, named Hengist and Horsa, landed in the Isle of Thanet. Other chiefs with bands of armed followers landed in other parts of the island. They did not bring law

and order for the Britons as the Romans had done.
They slew or drove away the Britons, and divided
their land amongst themselves. They did not care
to live in towns, as they had always been accustomed
to live in the country. So they either burnt the
towns and left them desolate, or else suffered them
to decay till at a later time they too learned to live
in towns and to trade.

2. Fate of a Roman Town near Pevensey.—A curious example of the way in which the towns were
treated is to be found on the coast of Sussex,
between Hastings and Eastbourne. There is to be
seen the spot where once was the flourishing Roman
city of Anderida. The Roman walls are still there,
firmly built with that mortar which the Romans
knew how to make, and which is harder than even
the stones which it binds together. Inside is a
green flat space with no trace of any building except
in one corner, where are the ruins of a castle built
there long after the days of the Romans. The
Saxon conqueror could not destroy the city wall.
He destroyed the houses inside it. He liked better
to live outside. Two little villages in front of the old
gates of the City tell us by their names the language
to which they belong and what sort of men they
were who came there. To the West is West Ham—
that is to say, the western home of some settler whose
name we do not know. To the East is Pevensey,
the meaning of which name is the Island of Peofn ;
and Peofn, no doubt, was the one amongst the conquerors who fixed his abode there.

3. Gradual conquest of Britain.—These Saxons and

Jutes, and Angles did not conquer the country all
at once.   Like the Britons before the Romans came,
they did not form one people, but lived separately,
each tribe by itself. Many English counties bear the
names of these tribes.   The East Saxons lived in
Essex, the Middle Saxons in Middlesex, the South
Saxons in Sussex.   At first the conquest was not very
difficult.   The south-eastern part of England had
been more civilised by the Romans than the rest of
the country.   It was richer because it was nearer to
the Continent, and the people who lived in it traded
with those who lived beyond the sea.   Its inhabitants were also less warlike than those who lived in
the Western hills, so that the conquest was easiest
here.   In the south-east there had been formed
four small kingdoms, Kent, answering to the modern
county, Sussex, including the modern Sussex and
Surrey, Essex, including the modern Essex and
Middlesex, and East Anglia, including Norfolk, Suffolk, and Cambridgeshire.   In the north and west the
struggle was harder, and the conquerors found it
necessary to join their small tribes together in order
that they might bring a stronger force against the
enemy.   The three larger kingdoms were those of
Northumberland, or the land North of the Humber
as far as the Clyde, of Mercia, occupying the centre
of the country, and of Wessex, the land of the West
Saxons, occupying the country westward from the
border of Sussex.   These three went on fighting
with the Britons.   In 128 years of conflict they had
pushed their frontier as far as the chain of the hills
known as the Pennine range, and thence south-

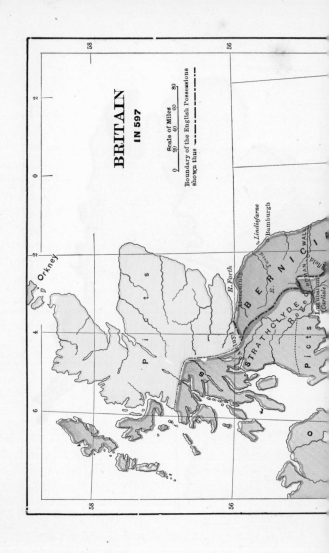

BRITAIN
IN 597

Scale of Miles
0   20   40   60   80

Boundary of the English Possessions
shown thus

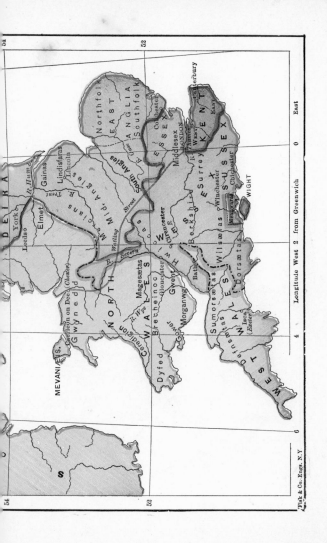

eastward to a spot near Bedford, after which it twisted about irregularly till it reached the English Channel about half way between the mouth of the Exe and Portland. After some further years of struggle the line went from the Pennine Hills southward through the Mendip Hills to the English Channel. Cumberland, Lancashire, Devon, and Cornwall were subdued at a later time. Wales remained independent for many hundred years. In these later and Western conquests many more Britons were saved alive than in the East.

4. The English People and their Kings.—The invaders came to be usually known as Angles or English, though they were sometimes called Anglo-Saxon, that is to say, Angles and Saxons. The country was called England, or the land of the Angles. Each tribe had over it a king, but the king did not do as he pleased. The freemen who made up the tribe met in council and decided whether they would go to war or not. When the king died, they chose a new one out of the family of the last king. Nobody then thought it right that the eldest son of the last king should always reign after his father. A king had to command in battle as well as to sit at the head of the meetings of the freemen. If the eldest son of the king were a child, or a coward, or incapable of ruling from ill health, or from any other cause, the tribe passed him over altogether and chose his uncle or his cousin to be king.

5. Treatment of Criminals.—At these meetings of the people those who had been wronged were listened to. There were no regular judges as there

are now. If a man committed a murder there was no
idea that it concerned anybody to punish him except
the relations of the murdered man. Some time before the English came to the island, the custom had
been that the nearest relation of the murdered man
considered it to be his duty to kill the murderer, like
the avenger of blood, who was the nearest relation,
amongst the ancient Hebrews. Then the relations
of the murderer who had been killed considered it
to be their duty to kill the man who had killed the
murderer. So the blood feud, as it was called, went
on from generation to generation, some one member
of one family being always on the look-out to kill a
member of the other. At last, however, people grew
tired of this constant slaughter, and the custom grew
up that, when a man was murdered, the murderer
came to the relations of the murdered man and gave
them some money to let him off. They brought the
money before the meeting of the people, and then
peace was made between the murderer and the
relations of the man whom he had killed. If a
thief was detected, he had to pay money in the same
way.

3. **The Religion of the English.**—Such an arrangement as this was possible because the English did
not think that it was at all wrong to kill a man.
They were heathens, and their religion taught them
that men were the better, not for being tender and
merciful, but for being strong and bold. Their
gods, they thought, showed favour to them if they
were fierce and masterful, and would only give them
happiness after their death if they died fighting.

They thought that the dead warriors spent their time all day in another world in fighting for amusement.

7. Compurgation and Ordeal.—In other respects the mode of dealing with criminals in those days differed from ours. There were no lawyers and judges as there are now, trained to find out when a man has committed a crime which no one has seen him do. When therefore any one was accused of a murder or a theft, he was asked whether he could bring a number of honest men who lived near him to swear that he was innocent. If he could he was considered to be innocent. This was called Compurgation, because the men joined in purging him, or declaring him to be clean from the fault. If he could not get the men to swear for him he had yet another chance. He might try what was called the ordeal, or judgment of God. He had to walk blindfold over red-hot ploughshares or dip his hand into boiling water. If he missed the ploughshares, or if his hand did not appear to be hurt after three days, he was declared to be innocent. Probably scarcely anybody ever got off in this way, but as only those tried it who had failed to find men who would swear for them, they would all be considered to have bad characters because their neighbours distrusted them. For this reason nobody would feel much surprise if almost every accused person who tried the ordeal failed.

CHAPTER III.

THE CONVERSION OF ENGLAND.

1. A Missionary sent to England by the Pope.—
Soon after the Roman soldiers left Britain, the Roman
Empire came to an end in the West of Europe. Its
place was taken by a number of German nations
who had conquered it. These conquerors, however, were not heathens like the English who
conquered Britain, and the Bishop of Rome had
a great influence over them. He was generally
looked up to, and was called the Pope; that is to
say, the Papa, or Father of Christians. About 150
years after the English began to come into Britain
there was a Pope named Gregory. The English
conquerors were heathens. Long before Gregory
was Pope he had seen some fair-haired boys from
Northumberland in the slave-market at Rome. He
had asked what nation they were of. He was told
that they were Angles. 'Not Angles,' he said, 'but
Angels. Who is their king?' he further asked.
'His name,' said the merchant, who wanted to sell
the boys, 'is Ella.' 'Allelujah,' answered Gregory,
'shall be sung in the land of Ella.' Many years
afterwards, when he had become Pope, he remembered his meeting with the boys. He sent Augustine as a missionary to convert the English.

2. Augustine at Canterbury.—In 597 Augustine landed, on his mission of love, in the Isle of Thanet, where Hengist and Horsa had landed 148 years

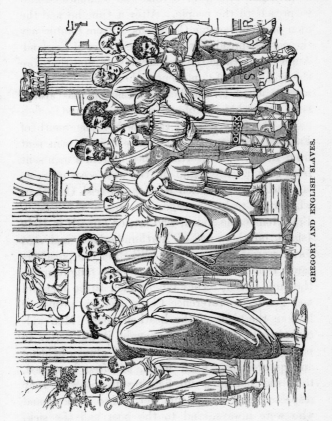

GREGORY AND ENGLISH SLAVES.

before to ravage and to slay. Followed by a band of missionaries, he made his way to the home of the King of Kent, where now is the city of Canterbury, with its grand cathedral rising above the roofs of the houses. Ethelbert, the king, who had married a Christian wife from beyond the sea, allowed him to preach to the people. After a time he and the men of Kent became Christians. From Canterbury the gospel spread over the southern part of England. Augustine became the first archbishop, and therefore the Archbishop of Canterbury, where first Christianity was preached to the heathen English, has always been the archbishop of all Southern England.

3. The Conversion of the North.—The South of England had learned Christianity from a man sent from Rome. The North learned it from a man sent from Iona, a little island off the west coast of Scotland, where was settled a colony of Irish Christians who were zealously eager to preach the gospel. From Iona came Aidan, who settled himself in Holy Island, off the coast of Northumberland, and sent forth swarms of preachers. Whether the preachers came from Rome or from Iona they taught much the same lesson. They taught men to be merciful and gentle, to reverence Christ and his gospel of love in the place of the heathen gods. Men welcomed them because they thought it was better to be meek and forgiving than to be always fighting and quarrelling. Even when, as often happened, they did not give up fighting themselves, they respected men who would not return a blow, and who were always kind to the poor and the sick. One of the kings once gathered his great men together and asked them whether they would be Christians. 'So seems the life of man, O king,' answered one of the chiefs, 'as a sparrow's flight through the hall when a man is sitting at meat in winter-tide with the warm fire lighted on the hearth but the chill rain-storm without. The sparrow flies in at one door and tarries for a moment in the light and heat of the hearth-fire, and then flying forth from the other vanishes into the wintry darkness whence it came. So tarries for a moment the life of man in our sight, but what is before it, what after it, we know not. If this new teaching tell us aught certainly of these, let us follow it.'

4. The Monks.—The new teaching was gradually adopted. But the mass of men did not change their nature because they had learned to pray to Christ. It was much easier to go to church, or to repeat prayers, than it was to live as the gospel taught men to live. Most Englishmen remained as fond of fighting as they were before. There were some, however, who tried hard to make themselves better, to forgive instead of taking vengeance, and to live at peace instead of being constantly at war. Those who tried hardest to do this found that they could not succeed, unless they separated themselves altogether from the people round them. They therefore lived together in houses which were called monasteries. Men who lived together in these monasteries were called monks, and women who lived together were called nuns. They lived very hard lives, not eating or drinking more than was quite necessary, and praying often, as well as working with their hands to procure their daily food. The ruins of many of these monasteries are to be found in England, and people sometimes say that the monks took care to choose very pretty places to live in. The truth is, that they did not care whether the places were pretty or not. They wanted to get away far from the temptations which were to be found where other men lived. They went to places as far as possible from the dwellings of men, where there was a stream of water to give them drink, and trees to give them wood to burn, and a little fertile ground on which to grow corn to eat. Green grass, and corn, with trees and a river, look very pretty to people now who visit them on a holiday, but those who had to live amongst them in those old days had hard work to do to get food enough to live on in such a country.

CHAPTER IV.

THE UNION OF ENGLAND.

1. **What Egbert did.**—The lesson taught by the monks was one which men are slow to learn. The whole of England was full of bloodshed and confusion. The kings were perpetually fighting with one another. Sometimes one, sometimes another would have the upper hand. At last Egbert, the King of the West Saxons, subdued all the others. He was not King of all England in the sort of way that Victoria is Queen of all England. Some of the separate kingdoms still managed their own affairs.

c

But they all looked up to Egbert, and agreed not to fight against him or against each other any more.

2. **The Coming of the Danes.**—Very likely, if this had been all, they would have separated again as soon as Egbert died. But during the lifetime of Egbert a new enemy appeared. A people who were called Danes in England, and were called Northmen or Normans on the Continent, came from Denmark and Norway. They were very much what the ancestors of the English had been when they came with Hengist and Horsa 350 years before. They swept over the sea in light vessels, sailed up the mouths of the rivers, burnt, slew, and plundered, and then sailed away again before they could be caught. The monasteries were their especial prey, for they knew that wealth would be stored up there. Though the monks had once been poor, people who reverenced them had brought them presents, not for themselves but for their churches. They had now gold and silver chalices and crosses, and their books were often bound in jewelled bindings. The Danes knew too that the monks could not fight. They killed the monks like sheep, set fire to the monasteries, and carried off everything that was valuable in them. In some places on the Continent a new petition was added to the Litany : 'From the fury of the Northmen, Good Lord deliver us !'

3. **The Fight against the Danes.**—Egbert, and his son, and grandsons after him, did their best to resist the sea-robbers. Sometimes they won victories, sometimes they were defeated. But on the whole the sea-robbers pressed on. They were

no longer content to plunder and to sail away. They came in swarms and tried to settle in the land, as the English had settled in it before. It seemed as if they would succeed, and as if all England would fall into the power of the Danes.

4. The First Year of Alfred the Great.—At last the Danes met their match. Alfred, the youngest and the noblest of the grandsons of Egbert, was chosen king on his elder brother's death. That brother had left a son who would, in our time, have succeeded to the throne. But a warrior was wanted, and the warrior-uncle was lawfully chosen instead of the boy-nephew. Alfred was at first defeated, and driven to take refuge in Athelney, which was then an island in the midst of the swamps of Somersetshire across which the Great Western Railway now runs with dry ground on either side. After some time, he came out, gathered his countrymen around him, defeated the Danes, and forced them to accept the treaty of Wedmore.

5. Submission of the Danes to Alfred.—By the Treaty of Wedmore in 878 England was divided into two parts by a line which ran from the Thames a little below London to Chester on the Dee. To the south-west of this line the land was English. To the north-east it was Danish. The Danes had not indeed slaughtered all the English in their part, but they had taken the best lands, and they kept all power in their hands. The settlements of the Danes are known by the termination 'by' at the ends of names of places. Such names as Grimsby or Kirkby tell us that a Dane once settled there. 'By' means

ENGLAND AS DIVIDED BY THE TREATY OF WEDMORE, 878.

the place where people lived ; Grimsby is the living-place of Grim. Kirkby is the living-place by the Kirk or church.

6. Alfred's Government.—Alfred seemed to be worse off than his grandfather had been. The Danes acknowledged that he was their over-lord or superior, but they were not likely to be very obedient. He had under him really only a piece of England instead of the whole. Yet that piece was better for him than the whole would have been. In the part that was under him were three of the old kingdoms, Wessex, Sussex, and Kent, a small part of Essex, and half of Mercia. Even if he had been only an ordinary man, we may be sure that these districts would have clung to him for fear of falling into the hands of the Danes. Very few men, however, are as great as Alfred was. People who do not know very much about men are apt to think a man is great because he has done something very great. Those who know most about men know that the best and greatest men are those who not only do great things, but know exactly what they cannot do, and so do not try to do what is impossible, though it may seem easy. Alfred was one of these men. He discovered at once that he could not subdue the Danes in the North, and he contented himself with defending his own part of the country. He set on foot a navy that the Danes might not attack him by sea. He did what was better than this ; he tried his best to make the people better and wiser than they were before. He strove to

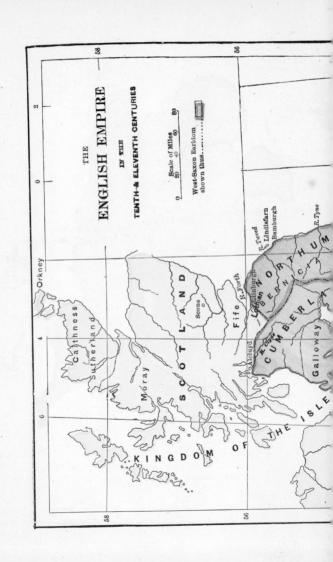

THE

ENGLISH EMPIRE

IN THE

TENTH & ELEVENTH CENTURIES

Scale of Miles
0   20   40   60   80

West-Saxon Earldom
shown thus...........

Orkney

Caithness

Sutherland

Moray

SCOTLAND

Scone

Fife

R.Forth

Edinburgh

Lothian

Alclyd

R.Clyde

CUMBERLAND

Galloway

KINGDOM   OF   THE   ISLE

NORTHUM

BERNICIA

R.Tweed

Lindisfarn

Bamburgh

R.Tyne

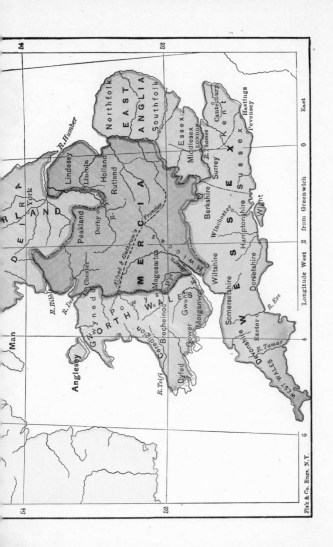

Man

DEIRA

York

R. Humber

Lindesey

Lincoln

R. Ribble

R. Dee

Chester

Peakland

Derby

Rutland

Holland

Northfolk

EAST
ANGLIA

Southfolk

Essex

Middlesex

LONDON

Canterbury

Kent

Hastings

Pevensey

Anglesey

Gwynedd

NORTH
WALES

Powys

Ceredig

Brecheinoc

Gwent

Gwent

Morganwg

Gower

Dyfed

R. Teifi

Magesaetas

MERCIA

Alfred & Guthrum's
Frontier

H W I C C E

Berkshire

Surrey

SUSSEX

R. Thames

Winchester

WESSEX

Wiltshire

Hamptonshire

Wight

Somersetshire

Dorsetshire

WEST WALES

Devonshire

Exeter

R. Tamar

R. Exe

deny himself as much as the monks did. But he did it, not by leaving the world, but by living in the world, and helping his people. No king ever showed forth in his own person the truth of the saying, 'He that would be first amongst you let him be the servant of all,' as Alfred did. He was weak, and subject to a painful disease. Yet he gave himself no rest in doing good. He collected the best laws of his forefathers, added some of his own, and asked his people to accept them. He chose out the best and wisest men for his friends, and set them to teach others. He loved learning and books, not only because he wanted to know more himself, but because he wished to make his subjects know more. He translated books which he thought it would do them good to read, and when he knew anything that was not in the book, he put it into the translation, though it was not in the book itself. When he died he left behind him better laws, better education, a better and higher life altogether.

7. The Submission of the Danes.—The English of the South soon showed that men who are better and wiser are also stronger than the fierce untaught barbarian, whenever they really try to defend themselves, instead of leaving their defence to other people as the Britons did in the time of the Romans. Alfred's descendants who were kings after him, his son Edward, his grandson Athelstan, his great grandsons Edmund and Edred, won by a slow and steady course of victory that northern England which Alfred had given up as beyond his power to conquer. In 954, seventy-six years after England had been divided by the Treaty of Wedmore, the process of reuniting it was completed. The English King came to rule over all England more completely than Egbert had done. Englishmen and Danes were alike subject to his government.

CHAPTER V.

THE ENGLISH AND THE DANISH KINGS.

1. Edgar and Dunstan.—For some years the now united England was at peace. Edgar, the King who reigned after the short rule of his brother Edwy, is called by the chroniclers 'The Peaceful.' He is said to have been rowed by eight kings on the river Dee. The man who really governed in his name was Archbishop Dunstan. He was the first man who ruled England without being a fighting man. The work he had to do was to be done with brains more than with the sword. Dunstan had to keep England united, and to prevent the Danes and the English from quarrelling with one another. This would have been more difficult than it was if the Danes and the English had been as different as Englishmen and Frenchmen. But they were very much alike, and though their languages were not the same, they were not so different that

they could not easily learn to talk to one another.
The Danes were ruder and less civilised than the
English, but they had already become Christians,

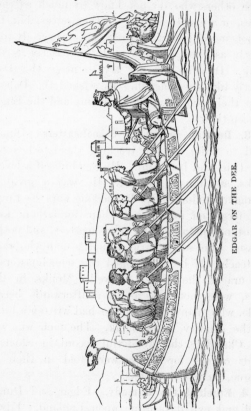

EDGAR ON THE DEE.

and they might be taught, as Englishmen had been
taught, to live as Christians ought to live.

2. **Dunstan and the Danes.**—In trying to make

the Danes and the English live peaceably together, Dunstan avoided one mistake which it is very easy to fall into. Many people are very anxious to improve others who do not know so much as themselves, or are not so good as themselves, but they do not succeed because they want everybody to do exactly as they do, and to think exactly as they think. Dunstan did not try to make the Danes exactly like the English. He wished the Danes to keep their own laws and customs and the English to keep theirs.

3. Dunstan brings in Schoolmasters.—Dunstan tried to unite men by teaching them to love what was true and beautiful. He was himself a lover of books, and music, and art. He was a great encourager of education. In the long wars the English had forgotten much that their forefathers knew. Dunstan sent abroad for schoolmasters, and nothing pleased him so much as to find a man who was fit to teach. If he encouraged the schoolmasters, he encouraged the monks as well. Monks, in those days, were not lazy as they afterwards became. Bede, who many years before had written a history of the country, was a monk. The men who wrote the Chronicle, that wonderful record in which the deeds of our forefathers were told in their own tongue, were also monks.

4. Ethelred the Unready.—Edgar and Dunstan died and evil days came upon England. Edward, the next king, was murdered. Then came Ethelred, rightly named the Unready, or the man without counsel. Fresh Danes from Denmark and Norway came to plunder and conquer England. In some places resistance was made, but the King did nothing to help the people who resisted. His only idea was to give the Danes plenty of money to go away. They went away, and of course they came back again and asked for more money to go away again.

5. Elfheah the Martyr.—There were brave men in England; but the bravest was Elfheah, the Archbishop of Canterbury. He was taken prisoner by the Danes, and set in their midst as they were feasting. They asked him for money. He told them it was not his to give, because he could only find money by taking it from the poor people on the estates belonging to him as archbishop. They grew so angry that they pelted him with beef-bones to make him yield. He would not yield, and at last they killed him with the hard bones. The English Church wisely counted him as a martyr and a saint. Long afterwards, one of his successors, the pure and holy Anselm, was asked whether a man could really be a martyr who did not die for the faith. 'Yes,' he answered, 'he who dies for righteousness dies for the faith.'

6. The Danish Conquest.—Brave men like Elfheah, or like others who fought and died, could not beat off the Danes unless they had a better king than Ethelred. The Danes, this time, wanted to conquer all England. They had a king, Swegen, at their head, who knew how to fight, and when he died his son Cnut, who succeeded him after his death, fought as well as his father. At last Ethelred died and was

succeeded by a brave and vigorous king, Edmund
Ironsides. So fiercely did he fight with Cnut that
the Danish king agreed to share England with the
English king. Not long afterwards Edmund died,
or was murdered, and Cnut got the whole country.

7. The Reign of Cnut.—Cnut's reign was like
Edgar's over again. Dane though he was, he let the
English keep their own laws. He kept peace and
established order with a strong hand. Though he
was himself neither priest nor monk, he reverenced
monks and priests as Dunstan had done. Once
when he was rowing on those broad waters of
the fens which have since been turned into rich
pasture-land and corn-land, he heard the monks
of Ely singing. He bade the boatmen row to the
shore that he might listen to their song of praise
and prayer. At another time he went on a pilgrimage to Rome, that he might see the place which
was reverenced through all the West of Europe
as containing the burial-places of the Apostles
Peter and Paul. He had learnt gentleness and
righteousness since the old cruel fighting-days of
his youth were over. He wrote a letter from
Rome to his subjects. ' I have vowed to God,' he
wrote, ' to live a right life in all things, to rule justly
and piously my realms and subjects, and to ad-
minister just judgment to all. If heretofore I have
done aught beyond what was just, through headiness
or negligence of youth, I am ready, with God's help,
to amend it utterly.'

8. The Sons of Cnut.—Cnut's sons who came after
him were not like their father. They were wild and

headstrong young men, and when they died Englishmen and Danes agreed to send beyond the sea for a son of Ethelred named Edward, who became king, and was afterwards known as Edward the Confessor, a name given by the Church to men of great piety, even when, as in Edward's case, piety was not accompanied by wisdom.

CHAPTER VI.

THE NORMAN CONQUEST.

1. The Normans in France.—Edward had been brought up in childhood in his mother's country— Normandy. Many years before, the Normans, as the Danes were called on the continent, had seized the part of France which is on both sides of the mouth of the Seine, just in the same way as the Danes had seized the North of England. There had been a treaty which, like the Treaty of Wedmore, allowed them to keep the country they had taken. Their chief, Rollo, became Duke of the Normans. The Normans, after two or three generations, learned to speak French and to live as Frenchmen lived. But they did not become subjects of the French king in the way that the Danes in England became subjects of the English king. The French king was weak and could not conquer Normandy. The Norman duke treated him with all respect as his lord. Whenever a duke died, his successor acknowledged

himself to be the French king's man, as was the
phrase.   He then knelt down and, placing his
hands between the French king's hands, swore to be
faithful to him.   But, for all that, he did not obey
him unless he chose to do so, but behaved as if he
were an independent ruler.

A NORMAN KNIGHT.

2. Englishmen and Normans.—In Normandy the
duke had other men who were noblemen or gentlemen, who had their lands from him in the same way
that he had his from the French king.   They did
homage to him and swore to be faithful to him.
These men were called knights, and fought on horse-

back, and were so accustomed to ride that once when some knights came to England and quarrelled with some citizens of Dover, they got on horseback to attack men in their houses, which seems a strange thing to do. They themselves, and the clergy of Normandy, were more intelligent, and cared more for reading and for art than the English did. The English always fought on foot, and only used horses to ride on to the place of battle, getting off when the fighting was to begin. If, however, the Norman knights and clergy were more intelligent than the English were, the Englishmen who were not very rich were more justly treated than men of the same kind were in Normandy. The Norman knight could do almost as he liked with the peasants who lived on his estate, and who sowed and reaped for him, and he had a court of his own in which he could punish them as he pleased. In England the peasants were certainly not so well off as they had been in Alfred's time. Many of them were no longer free men, owning their own land, and gathering in their harvest for themselves, without working for any one else. They had become serfs, that is to say, they were allowed land to till for themselves if they would also work for their lord, and plough, and sow, and reap for him without being paid for their work. Still they could not be punished if they were accused of doing wrong without being allowed to bring their compurgators, who, if they disbelieved the accusations, would be ready to swear that they were innocent. In this way the lord was prevented from ill-treating them, and the poor man was much more justly dealt with in England than he was in Normandy.

3. Edward the Confessor favours the Normans.— Edward might have done great good if he had tried, as Dunstan had tried, to help his English subjects to learn what the Normans knew and they did not know. Instead of doing that, he despised English people and English ways. He did not like to have Englishmen about him. He sent for Normans and promoted them. He actually made one of them Archbishop of Canterbury. He talked French instead of English. All this made the English very angry; and they were headed by a powerful man, Godwin, who was Earl of the West Saxons—that is to say, who ruled the West Saxons under the King. There were two other earls of Mercia and Northumberland who were jealous of Godwin, and Godwin was driven into exile. After a short time he came back and drove out the Normans.

4. Edward's last Days.—After Godwin's death, his son Harold was Earl of the West Saxons, and ruled England in the King's name. Edward had to be content without Normans round him. The thing that he cared for most was the building of the West Minster, the church of the great Westminster Abbey. It was not the one which is now to be seen. It was built with round arches, the fashion of building which had been taught by the Romans, and it was not till afterwards that men began to build with pointed arches. Edward did not live to see it consecrated. He was buried in the church which he had founded.

5. Harold, King of the English.—Edward left no son or brother to succeed him. His brother's grandson, Edgar, known as the Atheling or the Prince, was but a boy, and England could not be ruled by a boy. The great men chose Harold as their king, though he was not of the royal race. Harold would under any circumstances have had a difficult task before him. The earls of Mercia and Northumberland were sure to be jealous of him, and the north of England was not inclined to do much to help a man who came from the south. Though England had long been governed as one country, it was not united in heart as it is now. A man who lived in York did not feel much interest in the safety of men who lived in Exeter or Southampton. Beyond the sea there were still worse dangers. Harald Hardrada, the Norwegian king, was threatening to invade Northern England, and William, Duke of the Normans, the ablest and most warlike of an able and warlike race, threatened Southern England. Harald Hardrada only wanted, as Cnut had done before him, to get as much land or wealth as he could, but William actually claimed to be the true English king. He had no rightful claim at all, but by putting together a number of reasons, none of which was worth anything, he managed to make it seem as though he had a real claim.

6. The Norman Invasion.—Harold, therefore, had hard fighting before him. He heard that Harald Hardrada had landed in Yorkshire. At once he marched north and defeated and slew the Norwegian Harald at Stamford Bridge, near York. On the field of victory he was told that William had landed near Pevensey. He marched hastily southwards. If England had been united, William would certainly have been overcome. But the men of the centre and north of England did not care to fight for Harold. Only the men of the south and his own trained soldiers stood by him. His brother Gurth begged him not to risk a battle, and advised him to lay waste the land between London and Pevensey, so as to starve William out. Harold answered that not a foot of English ground should be desolated by him. He took up his position at Senlac on a chalk ridge a few miles north of Hastings.

7. **The Battle of Senlac.**—The Battle of Senlac, or of Hastings, as it is sometimes called, was one of those battles the winning of which depended on something more than mere bravery. Harold's Englishmen were as brave as William's Normans. But Englishmen thought, as Englishmen have often thought since, that it was best to do exactly as their fathers had done. The old fashion was to fight on foot, packed closely together, with their shields before them, and even a palisade in front of them. An army so defended can resist as long as it stands firm, but it cannot move from the spot where it is, without separating its shields and leaving openings through which the enemy can break in. William's Normans were mostly on horseback. They could move backwards and forwards, or sideways, just as their general wanted them to move. As usually happens, where two armies are equally brave, the ne which had the commander with the strongest

brain prevailed. William's footmen and horsemen tried first to storm the hill and were driven back. They tried again, and by William's orders pretended to fly. Some of the English were simple enough to think that the victory was won. They rushed out in triumph. The Normans swiftly turned back, chased them uphill, and broke through the palisade. The English could resist for hours yet, but they

could not conquer. Slowly and surely the Norman horse pressed along the crest of the hill, strewing the height with corpses as the hay is strewn in swathes before the mower. Harold and his chosen comrades held out longest. Then William called for his archers and bade them shoot into the air. Down came an arrow crushing through Harold's eye. The English King lay slain, and the Normans had gained the victory.

8. The Conquest of England.— It took three years and a half more to conquer England. The English had learned no lesson from their failure at Senlac. They could not unite against William. Sometimes the West resisted, sometimes the North. Each district fought separately, and each was separately overpowered.

CHAPTER VII.

THE CONQUEROR AND HIS SONS.

WILLIAM I., 1066.   WILLIAM II., 1087.   HENRY I., 1100.

1. William the Conqueror.— William is known in history as the Conqueror. But the word did not mean once what it means now. It did not mean a man who obtained his kingdom by a victory in war, but a man who obtained something which he did not possess before, whether he fought for it or not. William claimed to be King of England for certain reasons which, as he pretended, gave him a lawful title. Soon after the Battle of Senlac he was elected king by the great men, and though they were too much in fear of him to refuse to choose him, he could now speak of himself as the lawful King of England, as Edward and Alfred had been before him. He was one of those men who love order and good government whenever they do not come in the way of their own plans. But he would suffer no one to withstand him. 'Stark he

D 2

was,' writes an Englishman of the time, 'to men who withstood him; so harsh and cruel was he that none withstood his will. Earls that did aught against his bidding he cast into bonds. Bishops he stripped of their bishoprics; abbots of their abbacies. He spared not his own brother; first he was in the land, but the king cast him into bondage. If a man would live and hold his lands, need it were that he followed the king's will.'

2. The Normans gain Lands in England.—Even when William did most wrong, he tried to make it seem as though it were rightly done. The fierce horsemen who had charged with him up the hill of Senlac had not come simply to please the Duke. They wanted to be great men in England, to own rich corn-lands and stately homes. If William had not got these things for them they would have turned against him. He therefore set to work to do as they wished, but he made robbery look like the enforcement of the law. He said that he had been the lawful king ever since the death of Edward, and that therefore all Englishmen who had fought against him at Senlac or anywhere else had been fighting against their lawful king, and had forfeited their lands as rebels. He thus got a very large number of estates into his hands, and these he gave away to his Norman followers. Before long, almost all the great estates were in the hands of Normans. The English kept small estates, or became dependent upon the great Norman landowners.

3. William supported both by the Normans and the English.—In this way William was able to do nearly everything that he wished to do. The Norman landowners submitted to him, because, if they had not had a king to lead them, the English would have driven them out. And, strange as it may seem, the English submitted to him not unwillingly. The Norman whom they hated most was not the king, but the landowner with his armed followers, who lived in their midst and was ready to ill-treat them. They would rather have had an English king than a Norman king. But they would rather have a Norman king to keep the Norman tyrants in order than no king at all. William had other schemes for securing obedience. He took care that even the richest of the Norman landowners should not hold much land in any one county, so that his power might be weakened by being unable to bring easily together into one place the men who lived on his estates, and who might be willing to fight for him. In the towns too he built castles, the ruins of which are to be seen now in many places. He filled them with soldiers of his own. One of these was built by him to keep down London, and is known as the Tower of London. He gave lands to the great lords on condition that they would fight for him and bring other fighting men with them. Those who had lands in this way knelt down before him and did homage to him. In order that the lords might be able to bring the proper number of fighting men, they gave pieces of their land to men who did homage to them. William was afraid that those who had done homage to the lords would be more faithful to the lords than to him, and would fight for the lords against himself if they wanted to rebel. So he made all who had lands, either from him or from the lords, swear to him, at a great meeting at Salisbury, that they would be faithful to him. If they broke their oath he could punish them as traitors; whereas if he had not made them swear, they might have said that they must fight for their lords even against the king, because they had sworn to be faithful to them.

4. William's Cruelty.—William did worse things than this to secure his power. He was afraid that the Scots and the Danes might combine to attack the North of England. He therefore resolved to place a barrier between him and them. He pitilessly wasted the whole of the fertile Vale of York through which the North Eastern Railway now runs amidst smiling fields, with the moors on one side and the wolds on the other. Every house was burnt, every blade of corn destroyed. The inhabitants perished or sold themselves into slavery to get food. Of some of them it is recorded that 'they bowed their necks in the evil days for bread.' This means that they had to give themselves up to be slaves, that they might escape starvation.

5. The New Forest.—William's devastation in the north is less generally remembered than his devastation in the south. The Vale of York he wasted in order to defend himself against his enemies. The New Forest he wasted for pleasure. Like all his race he was passionately fond of hunting. It is said of him that 'he loved the high deer as if he had been their father.' There were terrible punishments for those who chased them without his leave. Any one who has ever lived near the New Forest, and knows how poor the soil is, will be quite sure that it never could have been cultivated all over. What William did was to destroy the houses and crops scattered in fertile places. But even that was enough to bring on him the curses of the wanderers whom he had rendered homeless.

6. Domesday Book.—Sometimes a man is blamed as much for things that he does well as for things that he does ill. To us one of his greatest titles to fame is the preparation of Domesday Book, a name which was explained by a writer, about a hundred years later, as meaning the day of doom, or judgment, because when it was appealed to in any dispute it was considered to settle the question. It was a record of the lands of England as well as of the men who owned them, and of the payments due to the king from each of these men. We know how useful such a record must have been. It enabled the king to call upon each man to pay his fair share of taxation and no more. People then, as has sometimes happened since, would have been glad to pay no taxes at all. 'There was not,' they said, 'a single rood of land, nor was there an ox, nor a cow, nor a pig passed by. It is shameful to tell that which he thought it no shame to do.' Worse things even than this were said of him. 'The king and the head men loved much and overmuch covetousness on gold and on silver, and they recked not how sinfully it was gotten, if only it came to them.' With all his hardness William was a lover of justice when justice did not come in the way of his own projects.

He punished thieves and murderers without mercy. It was said that any man might go in his days from one end of the kingdom to the other with his bosom full of gold.

7. William Rufus.—The Conqueror's son, William II., Rufus or the Red King, as he was called, was as able as his father. He never undertook anything in which he failed. He never allowed himself to be stopped by any obstacle which it was possible to overcome. Once he was eager to cross the Channel to put down an insurrection in Normandy. He reached the sea-coast in the midst of a furious storm. The seamen refused to put out in such a tempest. 'Did you ever hear of a king that was drowned?' he said. He forced them to sail, reached the other side safely, and overpowered his enemies. With his father's ability he had none of his father's love of justice. He was desperately wicked with more than ordinary wickedness. Yet even this man owed his throne to the support of the English people. His elder brother, Robert, had inherited the Dukedom of Normandy. The Norman nobles in England wished him to be King of England too. They knew he was soft and irresolute, and would let them do just as they pleased. The last thing which the English people wished was that the Norman nobles should do as they pleased. What they pleased was to oppress their English neighbours. The English therefore rallied in thousands round William, and the Normans sullenly submitted to his rule.

8. William Rufus and Anselm.—After some time

William was brought into conflict with a man whose gentle nature was even stronger than his own violent one. The Conqueror had filled the bishoprics and abbacies with Norman prelates, but had taken care to appoint none who were not distinguished for intelligence. The Red King looked upon the right of appointment as a means of getting money. He hit upon the simple plan of not appointing a successor at all to any bishop or abbot who happened to die. He then took for himself all the money which would have belonged to the bishop or abbot if there had been one. At last he fell dangerously ill. When he was very ill even the Red King had a little conscience, and his conscience told him that he had been doing wrong. The men who were about him begged him to appoint an Archbishop of Canterbury. They urged him to choose Anselm for the post. Anselm was a stranger from Italy who had been at the head of a monastery in Normandy. He was a very learned man, and the holiest and gentlest of men then living. He did not wish to be the Archbishop. He knew that as archbishop he could not live near the king without speaking the truth of him. The plough of England, he said, cannot go straight if you yoke to it a fierce young bull and a quiet old sheep. His remonstrances were in vain. He was dragged to the sick king's bedside and his hands were forced open that the crozier, the mark of the bishop's authority, might be forced into them. Anselm had spoken truly. The Red King recovered, and ceased to have a conscience any longer. Anselm persisted in saying and doing what he thought right, and was forced to leave the kingdom.

9. William's end was sudden. One day his corpse was found in the New Forest with an arrow through his heart. A certain Walter Tyrrell was thought to have done the deed. But no one saw him do it, and it is quite as likely that the murderer was one of the many sufferers who had been driven from their homes when the New Forest was made.

HENRY I.

10. Henry I.—Henry I., the youngest son of the Conqueror, was chosen to succeed him. He married an English wife, a great grand-daughter of Edmund Ironside. Through her the kings of England are descended not merely from William the Conqueror, but also from Alfred and Egbert. Henry, like William, had a quarrel with Anselm.

But after a time the two men were reconciled. Henry, too, put down the great Norman landowners with a heavy hand. His English subjects did not love him. His rule was too stern and his taxation too heavy for that. But they preferred a stern king

MILITARY, CIVIL, AND ECCLESIASTICAL COSTUME.
TIME, HENRY I.

to the tyranny of the Norman landowners. They called him the Lion of Justice, and they served him faithfully for thirty-five years. With their help he overcame his brother Robert, took Normandy from him, and shut him up in Cardiff Castle as a prisoner for life.

CHAPTER VIII.

THE ANARCHY OF STEPHEN'S REIGN AND THE RESTORATION OF ORDER BY HENRY II.

STEPHEN, 1135. HENRY II., 1154.

1. King Stephen.—When Henry died, Englishmen discovered what was the misery from which his hard rule had saved them. Henry's son, William, had been drowned in passing from Normandy to England, and though the barons, that is to say, the great landowners in England, had sworn to accept his daughter Matilda as their Queen, they refused to do so after his death. They chose instead his nephew Stephen. Stephen was not in any way a usurper, as he is sometimes called. There was then no law or custom giving the crown to the eldest son of the last king. The great men had always chosen some one of the royal family. There had never been a queen in England before, and at a time when the king was accustomed to go to battle, most men would think that there ought not to be a queen. Stephen was the man who was the nearest related to Henry. He was a generous and well-disposed man, but he had not the strong will of the three kings before him. He could not keep the barons in order. Soon Matilda came to England and claimed the throne. Some of the barons fought for her, and some for Stephen. In reality very few of them cared either for her or for Stephen. They knew

that, as long as there were two persons fighting for
the crown, they themselves could do as they pleased.

2. **Tyranny of the Nobles.**—What they pleased
to do was ruinous for the English people. They
built strong castles and filled them with armed men.
From these they rode out as robbers, as a wild beast
goes forth from its den. 'They fought among
themselves with deadly hatred, they spoiled the
fairest lands with fire and rapine; in what had been
the most fertile of counties they destroyed almost
all the provision of bread.' Whatever money or
valuable goods they found they carried off. They
burnt houses and sacked towns. If they suspected
any one of concealing his wealth they carried him off
to their castle, and there they tortured him to make
him confess where his money was. 'They hanged
up men by their feet and smoked them with foul
smoke. Some were hanged up by their thumbs,
others by the head, and burning things were hung
on to their feet. They put knotted strings about
men's heads, and twisted them till they went to the
brain. They put men into prisons where adders
and snakes and toads were crawling, and so they
tormented them. Some they put into a chest short
and narrow and not deep, and that had sharp stones
within, and forced men therein so that they broke
all their limbs. In many of the castles were hateful and grim things called rachenteges, which two
or three men had enough to do to carry. It was
thus made; it was fastened to a beam and had a
sharp iron to go about a man's neck and throat, so
that he might noways sit or lie or sleep, but he bore

all the iron. Many thousands they starved with
hunger.' The unhappy sufferers had no one to
help them. Stephen and Matilda were too busy
with their own quarrel to do justice to their subjects.
Poor men cried to heaven, but they got no answer.
'Men said openly that Christ and his saints were
asleep.'

KING HENRY II.

3. Henry II. restores Order.—At last a change
came In 1154, after a reign—if reign it can be
called—of nineteen years, Stephen died. He was

succeeded by Matilda's son, Henry II. Like his
grandfather Henry I., this king was a strong man—
not gentle or merciful, but understanding clearly
that if he wanted to be strong he must gain the
good will of the people, and must put down the
cruel tyrants who were his enemies as much as
theirs. He set himself at once to pull down the
castles. This was enough to restore order, because
when the barons had no longer any strong place to
which they could carry off their victims and their
plunder, they no longer dared to ill-treat their neighbours.

4. Military reforms of Henry II.—When this
was done, Henry set to work to prevent anything of
the kind happening again. There was no army then
as there is now, composed of men who leave their
homes for several years to become soldiers. The
fighting force was composed partly of the great landowners, who had their lands from the king on condition of fighting for him on horseback, and partly
of the men who had only small estates, who were
bound to come out and defend their own homes if
an invader landed in the country or a rebellion took
place. Henry wanted to weaken the great landowners, and offered to excuse them from serving
him as soldiers if they would pay him money. They
were glad enough to be saved the trouble of fighting
for the king, and were well pleased to pay money
instead. In this way they grew less accustomed to
fight, and so less dangerous to the king. On the
other hand, Henry encouraged the men with little
land, and arranged that they should always have

arms, so that they might be ready to defend themselves.

5. Judicial Reforms.— Other reforms, too were made by Henry. The law was improved in many ways. His grandfather had begun to send judges round the country, as they go now to the Assizes in different parts. Henry II. sent them out frequently, and directed them to find out the truth by asking a certain number of men in each county to which they came, who was the true owner of land in dispute, or who had committed murders or robberies. These men were sworn to tell the truth. After a while it was found that they did not always know what the truth was, and wanted to ask some one else. So by degrees after Henry's reign, the custom grew up that they should not say what they thought was true till they had heard the evidence of other people. In this way they gradually grew to be what our jury is, that is to say, a body of men which, after it has heard evidence in Court, declares its belief that something is true. This is called giving a verdict, a word which means ' truly said.' In Henry's time they declared their belief from their own private knowledge, without hearing evidence at all.

6. Union of English and Normans.—These changes were brought about by Henry. There was another change which was going on, with which he had nothing to do. There was no longer a strict line of division between English and Normans. When Henry came to the throne, eighty-eight years had passed since the Conquest, and during that time Normans and English had often married one another. In Henry's reign the upper classes still talked French, and the lower classes, who were almost entirely English by birth, talked English. But no one in the higher classes could say that he was altogether Norman, as he was almost certain to have had an English mother or grandmother.

7. Henry II. and the Clergy.—Henry was very successful in most things, but there was one thing in which he was not successful. The clergy then held the opinion that no clergyman who had committed any crime ought to be tried by the king's courts. He should be tried by special Church courts, and as the Church courts could not put any one to death, if a clergyman committed a murder he was only shut up in a monastery, whilst a layman who committed the same offence, and was tried by the king's court, was hanged. The idea of a clergyman committing a murder happily seems strange now. But now clergymen are men who devote themselves to religious work. Then, everybody who wanted to live otherwise than by manual labour or by fighting became a clergyman. Scarcely any one except the clergy learned to read and write. Many men, therefore, became clergymen who wanted to work with their brains rather than with their hands. Then, as now, some people wanted to use their brains for the purpose of cheating others. Then, as now, some people wanted to use their brains to lead idle lives at the expense of others, and therefore the clergy in Henry the Second's time included a great many idle and wicked men. Henry II. insisted that these men, if they committed crimes, should be tried in his courts.

E

8. Henry II. makes Becket Archbishop of Canterbury.—Thomas Becket had been Henry's chancellor, whose business it was to write letters for him, and look after his affairs. He had been a gay, extravagant man, very zealous in doing all that Henry wished, and Henry therefore now appointed him Archbishop of Canterbury, expecting him to help him in making the clergy submit to be tried in the king's courts.

9. Quarrel between Henry II. and Becket.—As soon as Becket became archbishop he turned against the king, lived very plainly, and gave up all his expensive habits. Becket was the sort of man who was sure to take up any quarrel warmly, and he was not quite without arguments on his side. Henry might ask why a clergyman who had committed a murder should not be punished in the same way as a layman. Becket would answer that a clergyman belonged to a holy order, and ought not to be punished by a lay judge, which is not an answer to which we should pay much attention now. He might also have said that it did not follow that a lay judge would always judge justly. We are accustomed to judges who always do their best to be just. In early times judges often did not care whether they were just or not. Henry himself, when he was out of temper, did not care whether he was just or not. He caused Becket to be accused before his court on a trumpery pretext and had him fined enormously. What the clergy really had to fear was that the king, if once his courts were allowed to judge them, would not be content with punishing those of them who robbed or murdered, but would also punish those who were quite innocent, for the sake of getting their money.   Even Henry, lover of order as he was, was capable of the wildest passion.   Sometimes, when he received news which he disliked, he would throw himself on the floor, and roll about amidst the straw or rushes which then served instead of a carpet, biting them with his teeth in his rage.   But though all this was true, it is also true that Becket was an ambitious man fond of contention, and not at all a gentle and holy saint who cared only for righteous-ness as Anselm had cared for it.

10. Murder of Becket.—At first Henry got the better of the archbishop; Becket refused to submit, and left the kingdom.   After some years the two made peace and Becket returned to Canterbury. Becket again displeased the king.   Henry fell into one of his rages and cried out, 'Who will rid me of this turbulent priest?'   Four knights at once left the house and made their way to Canterbury.   They found Becket, and after using angry words to which he replied no less angrily, they rushed away to arm themselves.   Becket's friends persuaded him to take refuge in the cathedral.   He showed no sign of fear.   When the armed knights were heard approach-ing, he refused to allow his followers to shut the doors.   'No one,' he said, 'should be debarred from entering the house of God.'   Most of those who were with him ran off to hide themselves.   He re-mained quiet and unmoved as the knights dashed in, shouting, 'Where is the traitor?'   'Behold me,' he answered; 'no traitor, but a priest of God.' One of the knights seized on him to drag him out of the cathedral. Becket dashed him to the ground, calling one of the others by a foul name, not such a one as would have proceeded from the lips of Anselm. The knight smote at him with his sword. One of Becket's few faithful attendants thrust his arm

THE PENANCE OF HENRY II.

forward to receive the blow. The arm was almost cut off. Other blows followed, and Becket fell bleeding to the floor. The murderers did not leave him till life was gone. Nothing worse could have

happened for Henry. He who wanted to be a re-
storer of law appeared before the world as a murderer. The great nobles at once took advantage of
his mistake, and rose in rebellion, hoping to be
supported by all who were displeased with Henry's
conduct. Henry at once saw that he must persuade
people that he was sorry for what he had done.
Perhaps, like most people who are passionate, he
really was sorry. He came to Canterbury and knelt
down before Becket's tomb, and told the monks to
flog him as a punishment for his crime His repent-
ance, whether it were real or not, satisfied the people.
They did not want to be ruled over by the great
nobles, and to have again such misery as they had
endured in the evil days of Stephen. Henry's armies
were everywhere victorious, and he once more ruled
England without opposition. But he was obliged to
give up most of his claims over the clergy. Becket
was revered as a priest and a martyr, though there
was very little that was saint-like in him. For
many generations crowds used to flock to Canterbury
to pray at his tomb. The marks on the pavement
are still to be seen which were made by men and
women moving up the church on their knees towards
the place where his body was.

11. Henry's foreign Dominions.—Henry's dominions
were even more extensive beyond the seas than they
were in England. He conquered part of Ireland,
and from his time the English kings counted Ireland
as subject to them. But it was not till the end of
Elizabeth's reign, more than four hundred years
later, that the whole country was really subdued.

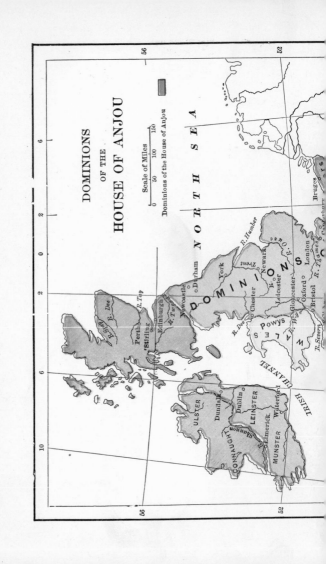

DOMINIONS
OF THE
HOUSE OF ANJOU

Scale of Miles
0   50   100   150

☐ Dominions of the House of Anjou

NORTH SEA

DOMINIONS

R. Tay
R. Dee
R. Esk
Perth
°Stirling
Edinburgh
R. Tweed
Newcastle
°Durham
York
R. Humber
Trent
Chester
R. Ouse
Newark
Leicester
London
R. Thames
Oxford°
Gloucester°
Bristol
R. Severn
R. Wye
R. Dee
Powys
WALES

Bruges

CHANNEL

IRISH

ULSTER
Dundalk°
CONNAUGHT
R. Shannon
Dublin°
LEINSTER
Limerick°
Wexford°
MUNSTER
Waterford°

56
52
56
52
6
6
2
0
2
6
10

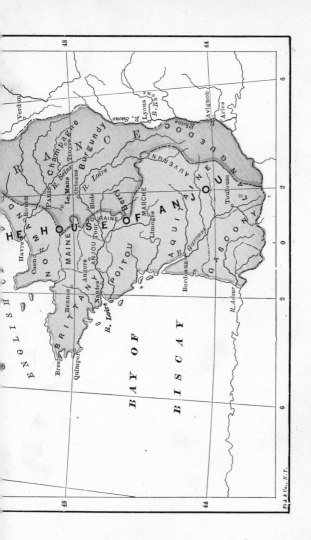

Besides this, Henry, partly by inheritance from his father and mother, and partly by his marriage, ruled over the western part of France from the English Channel to the Pyrenees. From Anjou, which he had from his father, he and his sons are known as the Angevin kings. He had great trouble with his own sons. The elder ones rebelled against him from time to time, and he trusted the youngest, John, more than all. At last there was a war between Henry and the King of France. When peace was made, Henry asked to know who were those of his own subjects who had promised to help the French against him. The list was shown him, and the first name on the list was that of John. He could not bear the revelation. He fell sick and died in a few days. 'Shame, shame, on a conquered king,' were the last words that he spoke. He was succeeded by his son Richard.

CHAPTER IX.

THE SONS OF HENRY II., AND THE GREAT CHARTER.

RICHARD I., 1189.   JOHN, 1199.

1. The Crusades.—Richard I. was hardly an English king. He only visited England twice during his reign, and that was only to get as much money as he could. Early in his reign he went on a crusade. The Crusades had begun in the time of William

Rufus. Christian pilgrims had long been in the habit of visiting Jerusalem to pray at the spots where Our Lord was born, was crucified, and was buried. The Arabs, who before the time of William Rufus, governed Jerusalem, allowed these pilgrims to come and go in peace. Then Jerusalem was conquered by the Turks, who came from the middle of Asia, and did not then rule at Constantinople. These Turks were much more brutal than the Arabs, and ill-treated the pilgrims. A man, called Peter the Hermit, went about Western Europe, calling on all men to take arms and to rescue Jerusalem from the Turks, who as well as the Arabs were Mahometans, or believers in a religion which had been preached by Mahomet. The pope gave his approval, and crowds of men poured out of Western Europe to conquer the Holy Land. The enterprise was called a crusade, because those who went fixed a cross to their dress, as a sign that they counted themselves as the warriors of Christ. Large numbers were starved or killed on the way, but a smaller body of well-armed knights and noblemen followed and conquered Jerusalem. There was a strange mixture of brutality and humility in these men. When Jerusalem was taken there was a horrible massacre of the inhabitants. Not only were grown men and women butchered in cold blood, but innocent children were dashed to death against the walls. The Crusaders set up a Christian kingdom of Jerusalem, and chose one of their number, Godfrey of Bouillon, as the first king. He ruled as king, but he refused to be crowned. He would not, he said, wear a crown of gold where his Saviour had worn a crown of thorns.

2. Richard I. goes on a Crusade.—The Christian kingdom of Jerusalem lasted almost to the end of the reign of Henry II. Then Jerusalem was again conquered by the Mahometans. Before this, very few English had taken part in the crusades. Richard now determined to set out to recover Jerusalem. He was an excellent warrior, fond of adventure, and loving fighting for the sake of excitement and amusement. But he was quarrelsome, and determined not only to do more than any one else, but to make men acknowledge that he did more than any one else. Men like this never succeed. Before he reached the Holy Land he had quarrelled with the King of France. After he reached the Holy Land he quarrelled with the Duke of Austria. He fought bravely and won renown against Saladin, the Mahometan leader. But the men of other nations would not join heartily with him. He could not retake Jerusalem. Once, indeed, he came within sight of it. But he turned proudly and sadly away, and refused to look on the place where a mosque, or building for Mahometan worship, rose on the site which had once been occupied by the temples of Solomon, of Zerubbabel, and of Herod. If he was not worthy, he said, to regain the Holy City, he was not worthy even to look on it.

3. Richard I. returns home.—Having accomplished nothing he returned home. He attempted to pass overland through Austria, but he was recognised and detained. The Duke of Austria handed him over to the Emperor, Henry VI., who ruled over Germany and a great part of Italy, and the Emperor kept him in prison till his mother and his friends ransomed him with a large sum of money. The rest of his life was spent by him in fighting in France. At last he was shot down by a man who aimed at him from a castle wall. The castle was taken before he died, and he ordered his attendants to spare the man to whom he owed his death. There was a nobleness in him besides the bravery, which made him long remembered as *Cœur de Lion*, or the Lion-Hearted. But he had no thought of making the people over whom he ruled better or happier, and England has no cause to be grateful to him.

4. John loses Normandy.—In 1199, Richard's youngest brother John was chosen king in preference to the boy Arthur, who was the son of another brother, Geoffrey, who was dead, and who was younger than Richard, but older than John. John therefore came to the throne in the same way as Alfred and Stephen, and it is only by mistake that some people call him an usurper. John was as wicked as William Rufus, utterly selfish and rapacious. 'He feared not God nor regarded man.' He could be very mean and very cruel. At the beginning of his reign he was afraid lest Arthur, when he grew up, should be too strong for him, and Arthur disappeared. No one told how Arthur was murdered. Some said that John had drowned him with his own hands, but it is not known whether this is true. The King of France at once ordered John, who was Duke of Normandy as well as King of England, to come to Paris to be tried for murder, and when he refused to come, took from him a great part of his lands in France. The lands between the English Channel and the Loire which John had from his father were lost. Only the lands south of the Loire, which John had from his mother, were kept.

5. John's Tyranny in England.—In England John tried to enrich himself by heavy taxes, which he laid on at his own pleasure, and by plundering rich persons. It is said that he threw into prison a rich Jew who refused to give him an enormous sum of money, and pulled out one of the Jew's teeth every day till he paid what was asked. Wealthy noblemen were treated in much the same way. In Stephen's time the great landowners oppressed the people, and the people had therefore supported Henry II., and had made him strong that he might reduce the great landowners to order. John oppressed both great and small, and made them join together against himself. Ready as all classes were to resist the tyrant, it was a long time before they dared to rebel. He brought into England large bodies of foreign mercenaries, or hired soldiers, thoroughly trained for fighting, who would do anything that John ordered them to do as long as they received money from him.

6. John and the Monks of Canterbury.—John fancied that no one could resist him. The monks of Canterbury had the right of electing the archbishop, but as they had always chosen the man whom the king asked them to choose, they had not hitherto had an important part to play in the matter. When the archbishop died, John ordered them to elect his treasurer, the Bishop of Norwich. They chose instead one of themselves, a certain Reginald, and sent him off to the pope to ask for his support. They charged Reginald to hold his tongue till he reached Rome. Reginald, however, was so vain of his election that he chattered about it as soon as he had passed the sea. John was furious when he heard what had happened, and forced the monks to elect the Bishop of Norwich, as if they had never elected Reginald.

7. Stephen Langton chosen Archbishop at Rome.— When Reginald arrived at Rome he found himself in the presence of one of the greatest of the popes, Innocent III. Innocent believed that it would be best for the world if kings and nobles had nothing to do with appointing bishops, and if they could be compelled to keep out of war by submitting their quarrels to the arbitration of the pope. Innocent therefore would not accept the treasurer as archbishop, and he saw that Reginald was too foolish a man to make a good archbishop. He told the monks who had come to Rome with Reginald that they had better choose Stephen Langton, a pious and learned Englishman, to the vacant see. This they did, and Reginald had to return a disappointed man.

8. England under an Interdict.—John was still more furious with the pope than he had been with the monks. He refused to admit Stephen Langton into England, and plundered the clergy. Innocent laid England under an interdict, that is to say, ordered the clergy to put a stop to all the public services of the church. The Holy Communion was no longer to be received, no funeral service was to be heard at the burial of those who died, baptism was only administered in private. To the mass of the people it was horrible to be cut off from attendance upon the services of the Church. It seemed as though the gate of heaven were closed against them. John did not care whether it was closed or not. He took a malicious pleasure in seizing the lands and goods of the clergy who obeyed the pope by shutting up their churches.

9. John excommunicated.—Then Innocent proceeded to excommunicate the king—that is to say, to deprive him of the right of partaking of the Holy Communion. When excommunication had been pronounced, all pious Christians were expected to avoid the society of the excommunicated person. John cared as little for excommunication as he had cared for the interdict, and he treated the clergy more cruelly than ever. Then the pope invited Philip II., King of France, to invade England and dethrone the excommunicated John. Philip was not usually very obedient to the pope, but he found out that it was quite right to obey him when obedience might make him king of England as well as king of France. John had no one to trust but his mercenaries. Almost every Englishman would be on Philip's side. He therefore resolved to make his peace with Innocent. Taking off his crown he laid it at the feet of Pandulph, the pope's legate, and acknowledged that he would thenceforth hold it under the pope, and would pay him a sum of money every year as an acknowledgment of his superiority. He also agreed to acknowledge Langton as Archbishop.

10. Demands of the Barons. —Philip was greatly disappointed. He had to give up the invasion of England. The English nobles were disappointed too They wanted not merely that the clergy should be safe, but that every man, layman or clergyman, rich or poor, should be safe under the protection of the law. When Archbishop Stephen Langton arrived in England, he was large-minded enough to see that it was better for the clergy to join with the laity than to be content with the pope's protection for themselves. The nobles gathered an army together, and the archbishop drew up the demands which the king was to be asked to grant. This time the king had not his mercenaries with him. Sulkily and sorely against his will John swore at Runnimede, an island in the Thames near Staines, to give all that he was asked to give.

11. Magna Carta. —The demands which, in 1215, he swore to grant, are known in history as the Great Charter, or by their Latin name as *Magna Carta*. By them the king engaged to levy no payments from those who held their lands from him, except in certain specified cases, unless they granted money to him themselves. Neither was he to deal with the life and goods of Englishmen at his pleasure. 'No freeman,' he was made to declare, 'shall be seized, or imprisoned, or dispossessed, or outlawed, or in any way brought to ruin; nor will we go against any man nor send against him, save by the legal judgment of his peers or by the law of the land.' The Great Charter contained other articles of the highest value. But the root of the matter lay in these two. The king of England was not to be a man raised up above his fellows to take as much of their money as he pleased, or to imprison them or punish them when he pleased. He was to take their money when they gave it him for public objects, and he was to punish them only when they were adjudged to have committed crimes by the verdict of their fellow-countrymen. Later generations built on these two principles a whole system of law. But it is the Great Charter which is the foundation of it all. The first principle, that the king could not take money when he pleased, made him obliged to take the advice of his subjects, because they would not give him money unless he did as they wished him to do. Gradually in this way the government of the country came to be carried on not as the king wished but as the people wished. The second principle, that the king could not punish those whom he wished has brought it about that we are governed by law, and not by the will of any one man.

12. Final Troubles of the Reign.—It was easier to lay down such principles than to enforce them. John was not inclined to submit to his subjects longer than he could help. He slipped away, got together his mercenaries, turned savagely upon the nobles who had resisted him, and drove them before him. They, in turn, called in foreign help. As he in his necessity had taken the pope to be his supporter, so they in their necessity called upon Lewis, the son of the king of France, to come to be their king. Lewis landed with an army. The pope took

the part of John.   Like some other people, he could
not bear to see a good thing done unless he were the
doer of it.   The fortune of war seemed likely to
decide against John and the pope.   As John crossed
the sands of the Wash, the tide rose and swept away
his baggage, in which was a large quantity of money.
Disappointed, he fell ill and died at Newark in the
autumn of 1216.

CHAPTER X.

HENRY III. AND THE BARONS' WARS.

HENRY III. 1216.

1. **The English People declare for Henry III.**—It
seems strange to us that a Frenchman should have
been invited to reign in England.   The idea that
those who govern a nation should be born in it and
speak its language could not be felt as strongly
then as it is now.   It is true that the mass of men
then, as now, spoke English.   But the nobles and
great men spoke French, and the clergy used Latin
in the services of the Church, and wrote and sometimes spoke in Latin.   Still, especially after Normandy had been lost, the English people were
beginning to feel that they were Englishmen, whatever language they spoke.   The few who followed
John to the last crowned his son Henry as king,
and those who had opposed John after a little time

accepted Henry. Lewis found himself deserted, and was obliged to return to France.

2. Accession of Henry III.—Henry III. was but nine years old. It was the first time that a child had been king of England. If he had had an uncle

WILLIAM MARSHALL, EARL OF PEMBROKE.

or an older cousin he would probably never have ruled. As he had none, men preferred an English child as their king to a grown-up man who was French. The noble William Marshall, Earl of Pembroke, governed the kingdom during the short

F

remainder of his life. The Great Charter was accepted as the law of the land ; but the part of it forbidding the king to tax those who held lands from him without their consent was left out.

3. Henry's Weakness of Character.—When young

KING HENRY III.

Henry became a man, he made a very bad king He was not cruel and violent like his father, but weak and contemptible. He made many promises but never kept them. He was fond of spending money, and he often spent it to no good purpose.

The best thing that he did was to rebuild Westminster Abbey, and to make it very much what it now is. Ever since the days of Henry II. the pointed arches had been used in churches and other buildings in the place of the round arches of the days of the Conqueror and his son. Henry's work in building the great abbey-church was well done. But he could never understand that he had any duty to perform to England. Like Edward the Confessor in many respects, he was like him in this, that he preferred foreigners to Englishmen. Two batches of foreigners were specially favoured by him. First came his mother's relations from Poitou, in the west of France, to the south of the Loire. Then came his wife's relations from Provence, a land on the shores of the Mediterranean, to the east of the Rhone. Whatever there was that Henry had to give away, castles, lands, lordships, and even bishoprics, went to these foreigners. Englishmen, both laymen and clergymen, naturally grumbled at a system which gave all the good things to the foreigners, and left only the crumbs to be picked up by them.

4. **Henry sends Money to the Pope.**—Before long another mischief appeared. The popes, the successors of Innocent III., engaged themselves in wars in Italy. They gave out that they were fighting for the cause of Christianity itself. Henry believed all they said, and allowed them to send men to England to tax the English clergy. As they did not get enough in this way to satisfy them, he himself laid taxes upon both clergy and laity and sent the money to Rome.

5. Growing Influence of Parliament.—To levy these taxes he was obliged to ask the consent of a body which was now beginning to be called Parliament. It had existed under different names, and with some difference in its composition, ever since the English had come into the island. At the beginning of this reign it very much resembled the present House of Lords without any House of Commons. There were in it barons who were landowners with large estates, and also the bishops and the principal abbots or heads of the monasteries. But though parliament was continually asked for money, and though for some time it granted what was asked, the dissatisfaction with a king who squandered English money on foreigners grew deeper every year.

6. Simon de Montfort.—At last the barons and clergy of England found a leader in a man who was, strangely enough, a foreigner by birth. Simon de Montfort, Earl of Leicester, had married the king's sister. He was the first warrior of the day, a man great in capacity as in moral worth. Sir Simon the Righteous was the name by which he was popularly known. Under his guidance a parliament was held at Oxford in 1258, where the barons appeared in arms. By a series of agreements, known as the Provisions of Oxford, the government was taken out of the hands of the king, and placed in the hands of various councils. The arrangement did not last long. The barons had it all their own way in the councils, and the lesser landowners began to fear that they would not get justice from the great ones. Earl Simon

would have done justice if he could, but the barons
were too strong for him.   Their folly made them as
unpopular as the king had been unpopular before,
and Henry almost regained his old authority.

7. **The Battle of Lewes and the Government of
Earl Simon.**—For some time there was agitation and
confusion, with no certain superiority on either side.
The barons were divided between their jealousy of
the king and their jealousy of Earl Simon.   For all
that, Earl Simon was growing in strength.   Some
years before, the freeholders, or men holding land of
their own, whether it was much or little, had been
allowed to choose men to go to parliament to speak
in their name and to ask for the things which they
wanted.   These men are called the representatives
of those who send them, and the representatives of
the freeholders were like the country members of
the present day.   The towns, too, were increasing in
commercial prosperity, and in the habit of managing
their own affairs.   The towns, and especially London,
the greatest of them all, threw themselves on the
side of the earl.   In 1264, he gathered his followers
together, came down upon the king at Lewes, in
Sussex, and utterly defeated him.   At the end of the
day Henry had been made prisoner, and his eldest son
Edward surrendered himself soon after.   For rather
more than a year Earl Simon ruled England.   He summoned the towns to send representatives for the first
time to parliament.   He wished that people of every
kind, the great landowners, the clergy, the small landowners, and the townsmen, should all be able to say
for themselves in parliament what they wanted.   As a

political verse-writer of the day expressed it, the community of the realm was to be consulted, and it was to be known what was thought by the nation as a whole. This is exactly what England tries to do now. Whenever there is a general election, the nation chooses men who can go to parliament and say what the nation itself wishes to have done. Then, after that, it is the business of wise men who make up what is called the government to find out how it is to be done.

8. The Battle of Evesham and the Death of Earl Simon.—Earl Simon meant to rule well; but once more the jealousy of the barons was too strong for him. Young Edward, the king's eldest son, was wise and able beyond his years, and he watched the spread of this jealousy. He resolved to make his escape. One day he suggested to his keepers to ride races for their amusement as well as his own. When their horses were thoroughly tired, he rode off on his fresh one, and was soon out of sight. Most of the barons flocked to his standard. Earl Simon was at Evesham. From the top of the church tower he saw the prince approaching. 'Commend your souls to God,' he said to the faithful few who were around him, 'for our bodies are the prince's.' His little army was overpowered. The earl was slain and his body was shamefully mutilated. After a while all further resistance was overcome. The king's authority was restored, and up to his death in 1272 no man ventured to raise a hand against him.

CHAPTER XI.

(EDWARD I., 1272.)

1. The Rule of Edward I. in England.—Henry's son Edward I., was a very different man from his father. He was great enough and wise enough to carry out the work which Earl Simon had begun. He allowed

KING EDWARD I.

no foreigners to thrust Englishmen out of places of authority on the soil of England. He made no promises with the intention of breaking them. He surrounded himself with the best and wisest counsellors that he could find. Wise as his counsellors were, he did not trust in them alone. He thought, as Earl Simon had thought, that what was intended for the good of all should be submitted to the counsel of all. He did not for a long time summon a parliament in which all classes of men were found; but he summoned just those men who knew anything about the matter he wanted advice on. In this way he became a great lawgiver, because he never made a law without hearing what those people had to say whom the law principally concerned. In his hands England prospered as it had never done before. Edward kept the peace well, and in his days the barons did not dare either to oppress the freeholder and the citizen, or to resist the authority of the king.

2. The Conquest of Wales.—Edward enjoyed the sight of a people living peacefully and orderly. He fancied that the best thing that could happen to people who were not under his rule would be to be brought under it. Of all the Britons who were found on the south of the Solway Firth, at the coming of Hengist and Horsa, those of North Wales only still retained their independence under their own princes, though even there the princes acknowledged the superiority of the English King. Edward resolved to make this superiority felt as a real authority. Two princes in succession resisted the attempt. Edward overpowered them, and united the hills round Snowdon to his English kingdom. He showed his infant son to the Welsh, and offered the child to them as their prince. From that time the eldest son of the English kings has always borne the title of Prince of Wales.

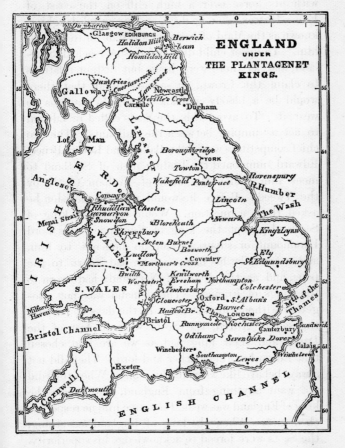

ENGLAND
UNDER
THE PLANTAGENET KINGS.

3. **Edward's Interference in Scotland.**—Wales was a small country, and its conquest was not very hard.

Later in his reign Edward attempted a more difficult task.   Alexander III., King of Scotland, fell
with his horse over a high cliff on the coast of
Fife.   He was taken up dead, and his grand-daughter,
known as the Maid of Norway, was sent for to succeed
him.   The poor child died before she reached Scotland, and as there were none but distant relations
to claim the Crown, it seemed likely that there
would be a bloody civil war to decide who was to
wear it.   To avoid this the Scots called in Edward
to act as umpire between the claimants.   The two
chief competitors were John Balliol and Robert Bruce.
Edward summoned the leading men of Scotland to
meet him under the walls of Norham Castle by
the Tweed.   Before he would give his decision he
asked them a question.   Would the future king of
Scotland accept the king of England as his Lord
Paramount or superior, and do homage to him,
and swear to be his man, as John had sworn to the
pope, and as the dukes of Normandy had sworn to
the kings of France ?   The demand was not altogether without foundation.   In the days of Edward,
the son of Alfred, the Scots were in fear of the
Danes, and their king had, as we are told, chosen
that Edward as their father and lord.   They did not
always behave like very dutiful sons.   When they did
not want anything from England, and when the
king of England was weak, they gave him no respect or
obedience.   When the king of England was strong,
the Scots were forced to acknowledge his superiority.
Henry II. was the last who had enforced the claim.
Richard I. had abandoned it.   The Scots now ac-

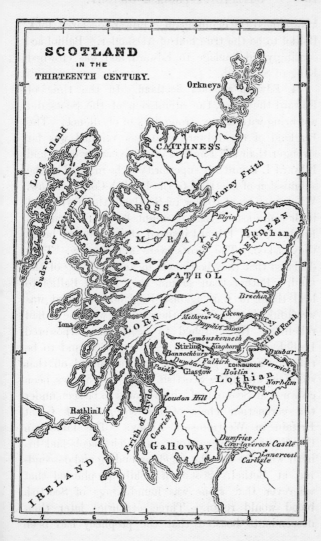

knowledged the claim again. Edward declared John Balliol to be the true heir of Alexander. Balliol accordingly did homage to Edward, and was crowned King of Scotland.

4. Edward subdues Scotland.—In the time of Edward the Elder, the submission of the Scots did not bring with it any strong duty of obedience. The England of the Edward who now reigned was far stronger than the England of those earlier days, and Edward I. meant his superiority to be marked by the submission of Scotland to the English Courts of Law. When men went to law in Scotland, those who lost their cause asked that it might be heard again in England, and Edward insisted that it should be as they asked. The Scots were very angry. They declared that they had never meant anything of the kind. Rather than submit they forced Balliol to lead them in war against England. Edward was wrathful when he heard the news of what he called rebellion. He marched to Scotland, overpowered Balliol, and deposed him. He left Scotland to be ruled by English governors, and he carried off that stone on which the Scottish kings had always been crowned at Scone, and which now is to be seen under the coronation chair of the sovereign of Great Britain in Westminster Abbey. The fable ran that it was the very stone on which Jacob laid his head when he saw the angels ascending and descending at Bethel. Scotsmen boldly prophesied that wherever that stone was found kings of Scottish blood would reign. Three centuries later their descendants boasted that the prophecy had been fulfilled in the accession of a Scottish king to the throne of England.

5. Resistance of William Wallace. — Edward wished to rule Scotland fairly and justly. But it is impossible to rule a nation fairly and justly when it is determined not to be ruled at all. Englishmen were sent to keep order, and many of them ill-treated the Scots. A Scot, named William Wallace, was insulted by some of them. He gathered his friends and attacked them in return. By-and-by all Scotland was in insurrection. Wallace gathered an army and brought it to the north end of a narrow bridge near Stirling. The English despised him, and began to cross over the bridge. When half of them were over, Wallace attacked those who had reached the north bank before the rest could press over the bridge to help them. Wallace gained a complete victory, drove the English out of Scotland, crossed the border and plundered and burnt English houses in North-umberland. Edward and the English were very angry. In Scotland Wallace was regarded as a true patriot. In England he was held to be no better than an infamous robber. Edward again invaded Scotland, where Wallace had few except foot soldiers to oppose to him, and these he gathered together at Falkirk. He formed them in a ring with their pikes stretched out before them. Englishmen had by this time learnt the use of the bow which had done such service to the Normans at Hastings. They boasted that an Englishman's cloth-yard shaft was longer, and his bow stronger, than that of any other nation. On every village green the small landowner learnt to shoot at the butts.   About a century later a great poet pointed it out as the mark of one of these small landowners that ' in his hand he bore a mighty bow.' At Falkirk the flight of English arrows cleared a gap in the Scottish ranks.   The English horsemen dashed in; and the brave Scotsmen died grimly where they stood.   Before long all further resistance was put down.   Wallace's rule was at an end.   He fled, and remained in hiding till he was captured some years later.   It is said that he was betrayed by a Scot named Menteith who gave a signal to the English soldiers by turning the loaf on the table with the bottom uppermost.   For a long time it was held to be an insult to any one of the name of Menteith to turn a loaf the wrong way in his presence.   Wallace was taken to London and brutally executed on Tower Hill as a traitor.   Englishmen and Scotsmen can join now in honouring the memory of one who fought bravely for his native land.   Edward united Scotland with England, and directed that Scottish representatives should take part in the English Parliament.

6. The Confirmation of the Charters.—The English parliament had become, in the midst of the struggle with Scotland, what it has ever since been.   In 1295 the first complete parliament met.   Either then, or at least not long afterwards, the parliament was divided into two Houses.   The barons with the bishops and abbots formed the House of Lords, whilst the men chosen by the counties and towns formed the House of Commons.   Edward found that if he was to expect money from parliament for his wars, he must promise never to take money without the consent of par-

liament, and in 1297 he swore to articles known as the Confirmation of the Charters, in which he promised to levy no more money without a grant from parliament. At the same time that Edward was obliged to give way to parliament, he found himself strong enough to resist the clergy. The pope gave orders that the clergy should not pay taxes to kings, who were only laymen. Edward did not get in a passion as Henry II. had done when Becket displeased him, but quietly let the clergy know that if they did not pay taxes he should not protect them. The consequence was that if a clergyman was robbed the judges refused to punish the thief, and the clergy discovered that it was safer for them to pay taxes. The clergy after this always brought their complaints to the king and the parliament, instead of separating themselves from them. Every one saw that Edward would do his best to do what was just, and the clergy therefore did not find as much support in the people as they had in the time of Henry II. and Becket.

7. **Rise of Robert Bruce.**—Scotland would have nothing to do with Edward's government, however good it might be. The Scots wanted to manage their own affairs without him. The nation found a new leader in Robert Bruce, the grandson of one of the competitors at Norham. Bruce was hardy and audacious. In the church of Dumfries he stabbed Comyn, another of the competitors. 'I doubt,' he said, as he rushed from the sacred building, 'I have slain the red Comyn.' 'I will make sure,' was the reply of one of his followers, who went into the church and completed the murder. It was just the

sort of thing which would rouse Edward's righteous indignation.   Before he could reach Scotland, Bruce had been crowned at Scone, though the ancient stone was no longer there.   Edward's troops, however, were masters of the country.   By his orders, the countess of Buchan, who had placed the crown on Bruce's head, was seized and imprisoned in a cage, like a captive bird, high up on the walls of Berwick.

The Scottish troops were easily routed.   The Scottish leaders were sent to the block or to the gallows.   In 1307 Edward set forth in person to complete his work by the destruction of Bruce himself.   For good or for evil the old man's work was done.   The noblest of our English kings died in Burgh-upon-Sands, near Carlisle.   In England he had been a wise and firm ruler, striving to give to every man his due.   His hand had been heavy upon Scotland, and by all Scotsmen he was long regarded as a bloodthirsty tyrant.   Yet even in his dealings with Scotland he had meant to do well.

CHAPTER XII.

(EDWARD II., 1307.   EDWARD III., 1327.)

1. Edward II. and Robert Bruce.—There have been good kings and bad kings in English history, but Edward II. was the only English king who did not even try to do in some way the work of a king. Edward II. cared for amusements and jests, and

pleasure of every kind, but he let public affairs
alone. He was joking with an unworthy favourite
named Piers Gaveston when he ought to have been
governing England. For a time the English
soldiers whom his great father had trained held

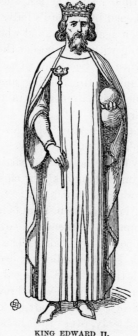

KING EDWARD II.

Scotland down. Bruce fled, through adventure after
adventure, from one Highland hiding-place to another. Whenever he saw a chance, he dashed out
upon the English. But for a long time he was
always forced to fly after a moment's success. There

is a story that, as he lay sleepless on his bed in utter despair of success, he watched a spider springing forward six times to attach its thread to a wall, and failing every time. The seventh time the spider succeeded. Bruce determined to try once more. This time he was at last successful. England was weakened by Edward's folly. The English nobles had risen against him, and when Englishmen were quarrelling with one another they had no time to oppose Bruce in Scotland. One fortress after another was taken, till Stirling alone of all the Scottish fortified towns remained in the keeping of an English garrison.

   2. Bannockburn.— After this even Edward II. could no longer look on carelessly. In 1314 he led a mighty army to the help of the garrison in Stirling. Bruce met him at Bannockburn close by the town. Bruce was as wary as he was bold. 'Well skilled to rule the fight,' he dug pits in front of his army, placed sharp stakes upright in them, and covered them over with turf supported by sticks. The horses of the proud English knights galloping over the ground, broke through the turf and plunged into the pits. The whole army of Edward was thrown into confusion. The Scots fought heartily for their native country. Suddenly, over the brow of a hill, a number of servants appeared, who were mistaken by the dispirited English for another army. Edward and his brilliant array of nobles and knights turned and fled. From that time forward there were many wars between England and Scotland; but Scotland never again ran any serious risk of being conquered.

3. The End of the Reign of Edward II. — For some years longer Edward II. remained on the throne, doing no good to any one. Even his wife joined his enemies, and with general assent dethroned him, and made his eldest son king as Edward III. Not long afterwards Edward II. was brutally murdered at Berkeley Castle.

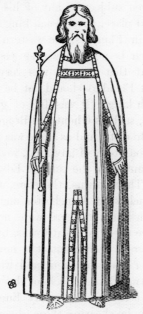

KING EDWARD III.

4. Causes of the Hundred Years War. — In the reign of Edward III. began what is usually known as the Hundred Years' War with France, because, though it did not continue for all that period without

G 2

stopping, fighting stopped very seldom, and then only
for a very few years, till a hundred years were
over. The beginning of the war was caused by two
things. In the first place, the king of England still
possessed lands in the part of France called Gascony,
round Bordeaux, and the king of France coveted a
country where the people talked French, though it
had never been subject to any of his family before.
In the second place, the French king wished to obtain power in Flanders, the western part of that
country which is now known as the kingdom of
Belgium. At that time it was very important to
England that Flanders should not be in the power
of the French king. It was full of great manufacturing towns, such as Ghent and Bruges, where wool
was made into cloth, and as there was no calico made
then, or cotton goods of any kind, woollen cloth was
even more wanted in the time of Edward III. than
it is now. These towns, therefore, were in those
days very much what Manchester and Leeds are in
our time. In England there were no such places.
Not only were there no great towns, but the country
was very different from what it is now. There was
a much larger tract of open land without hedges,
over which strayed large flocks of sheep, just as they
do now in Australia; and many Englishmen lived
and grew rich by shearing these sheep and sending
the wool to be made into cloth in Flanders, as the
Australians now send their wool to be made into
cloth at Leeds, and the Americans and others send
cotton to be made into calico at Manchester.
Englishmen were therefore afraid lest the French

King should conquer these towns, and stop their trade with England.

5. Edward's Claim to the French Throne.—Edward however was not content to fight for the trade with

THE PLANTAGENET KINGS OF ENGLAND.

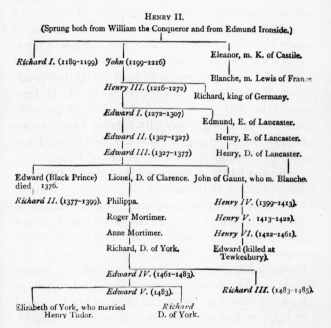

<pre>
                        HENRY II.
  (Sprung both from William the Conqueror and from Edmund Ironside.)

                                      Eleanor, m. K. of Castile.
Richard I. (1189-1199) John (1199-1216)
                                      Blanche, m. Lewis of France.
          Henry III. (1216-1272)
                             Richard, king of Germany.

          Edward I. (1272-1307)
                             Edmund, E. of Lancaster.
          Edward II. (1307-1327) Henry, E. of Lancaster.
          Edward III. (1327-1377) Henry, D. of Lancaster.

Edward (Black Prince) Lionel, D. of Clarence. John of Gaunt, who m. Blanche.
 died   1376.
Richard II. (1377-1399). Philippa.   Henry IV. (1399-1413).
                          Roger Mortimer.   Henry V. 1413-1422).
                          Anne Mortimer.   Henry VI. (1422-1461).
                          Richard, D. of York. Edward (killed at
                                                  Tewkesbury).

          Edward IV. (1461-1483).
          Edward V. (1483).   Richard III. (1483-1485).
Elizabeth of York, who married   Richard
     Henry Tudor.   D. of York.
</pre>

Flanders. He declared that he was himself the lawful king of France, because his mother had been the sister of the last king, whilst the king who now reigned in France, Philip VI., was only the last king's cousin. The French said that a woman could not rule in France; nor could any man have any right to rule there through his mother. What they really cared about was that they should be ruled by a Frenchman, and not by an Englishman. In fact, what was good for France was good for England too. It could only bring harm to Englishmen that thousands of them should kill and be killed in order to make Frenchmen obey a foreigner. They might win battles and be talked of at home; but they were sure to fail in the end. War is sometimes a duty, but a war of this kind is wicked and ruinous. If Edward had been content to fight for the independence of Flanders, he would have been able to have ended his war by a peace which would probably have lasted a long time. By fighting for the crown of France, he engaged in a war which could not end till the English were driven out of France.

6. The Battle of Crecy and the Siege of Calais.— Edward's first victory was in a sea-fight at Sluys, where 30,000 Frenchmen were slain or drowned. After a little time Edward III. gained a still greater victory at Crecy. Just as the English at Senlac continued fighting on foot with axes, though the Normans had long ago learned to fight on horseback, so the French at Crecy (1346) continued to fight on horseback after the English had learned to fight on foot with the bow, though the English knights and gentlemen still fought on horseback. The French indeed had a number of Genoese archers, but the French gentlemen on horseback despised every one who fought on foot. A shower came on and wet the bow-strings of the Genoese archers, so

that they were not ready to use their weapons. Philip VI. called out to his gentlemen to ride in amongst these poor Genoese archers and to cut them down, as if they were mere useless lumber. The English bowmen kept their bows in cases till the rain was over. They were free men long accustomed to shoot strongly and steadily at the mark. Down went those gay and gallant French horsemen before the pitiless shower of arrows, and the English knights charging amongst them completed the victory. The King's eldest son, the Black Prince as he was called, bore himself nobly on that day, boy as he was. Once during the fight some one, who saw him hard pressed, called on Edward to send him aid. ' No,' said Edward, ' let the boy win his spurs.' The spurs were the mark which distinguished the knights from the lower ranks, or from those who were only learning to fight. Not long after the battle of Crecy, Edward besieged Calais. He did not take it for eleven months. When there was no longer anything to eat in the town, the chief citizens came out to beg for mercy, with cords in their hands, to show that they were ready to be hanged. The king showed mercy to them, but he turned almost every Frenchman out of Calais and filled it with Englishmen, so that it remained an English town for more than 200 years.

7. **The Battle of Poitiers.**—Ten years after the Battle of Crecy, the Black Prince won for himself another great victory at Poitiers. Philip VI. had died, and his son John was by that time king of France. He ordered his knights to charge up a lane at the end of which was the small army of the Black

Prince, but he did not know that on either side of the lane there were English archers behind the hedges till the arrows began to fly. As the horses were struck down, those behind fell over them as they lay on the ground in that narrow space. In a moment the proud French army was in confusion. The Black Prince charged, and the victory was complete. King John himself was taken prisoner.

8. Chivalry.—It was the duty of a knight to fight bravely. It was also his duty when the battle was over to treat knights and gentlemen with gentleness and mercy. The word Chivalry, which means that which befits a knight, is still used whenever a man who is strong employs his strength to help those who are weak, more especially to help and protect a woman. After the battle the Prince led John to his own tent, and set him down to the dinner provided for himself. Then he stood behind his chair and waited on him like a servant. Conduct of this kind is the best thing of which we hear in those fierce days. Unfortunately gentleness was not shown to all alike. It was not thought at all necessary to treat kindly any one who was not a knight or a gentleman. The English used their strength to plunder and destroy. Poor French peasants had their cottages burnt, their little store of money carried off, their vine-trees cut down, their corn reaped or trodden under foot. On one occasion, some years later, a town named Limoges, in which the soldiers had refused to surrender, was given over to destruction by the Black Prince himself, and the brave warrior, who was usually so gentle, looked

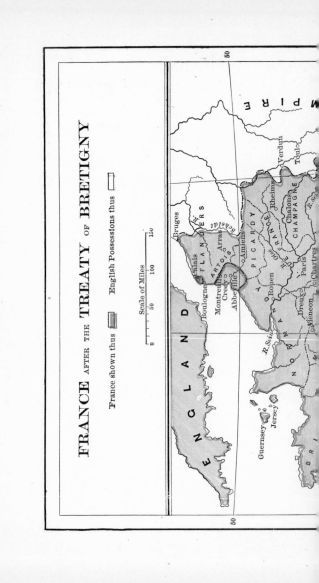

FRANCE AFTER THE TREATY OF BRETIGNY

France shown thus [ ]   English Possessions thus [ ]

Scale of Miles

0   50   100   150

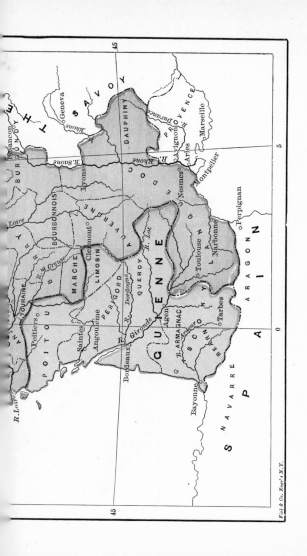

calmly on whilst old men and innocent citizens were brutally slain. In France a bitter hatred arose against the name of Englishman, which has only died out in our own time after 500 years have passed away.

9. The Peace of Bretigny.—Even the better Englishmen themselves felt some shame for the misery they were causing. Once as their army was marching amongst ruined crops and burnt cottages, the black clouds gathered thickly. The lightning flashed and the thunder pealed. To the English it seemed as if the voice of God was heard in condemnation of their wickedness. Edward made peace with France. By the Treaty of Bretigny a considerable part of France was to be his, and Frenchmen were to pay large sums of money to him.

10. The Labourers.—No one is ever the better for robbery. Englishmen had been in the habit of gaining riches by plunder, and money which is got without hard work is usually spent far too easily. The peace put an end to the chance of robbing Frenchmen, but it did not put an end to the expensive habits which had come to all sorts of people in England. Instead of trying to live more quietly and less extravagantly, Englishmen now began to try to get as much as they could from their neighbours. There was one class of people who suffered much. For a long time the land had been cultivated, not by labourers who work for a certain sum of money, but by serfs, or villeins, as they were then called. These villeins were men who had cottages, and lands of their own to cultivate. At one time they had not been badly off. As there was not much money in the country, many of them had paid rent not with money, but with work. They had done a certain number of days' work for their landlord instead of giving him a certain number of pounds or shillings.

KNIGHT OF GARTER. GENTLEMAN. CITIZEN.

For some time, however, most of these villeins had paid money instead of working. It was now found that the landlords who had come back from France tried to make the villeins do more work than they had been accustomed to do, and even to make those of them do work who had not been obliged to work for many years. Besides these villeins there were in the time of Edward III. a great many free labourers who worked for money as they do now. These, too, were hardly treated and forced to work very hard for very little pay.

11. The Black Death.—Whilst the villeins and labourers were grumbling, a terrible disease swept over England. It was called the Black Death, and caused more destruction than any plague which has since destroyed men. We cannot tell exactly how many died, but it is supposed by some that at least one half of the people perished. This fearful death brought some hope to the serfs and labourers who remained alive. It is true that the rich died as well as the poor; but the land did not die. There was just as much work to be done as before, just as much corn to be reaped or sheep to be shorn, and only half as many reapers or shearers to do it. Instead of a master finding more men than he wanted, he could not find enough. The labourers naturally asked for more money than they had had before, and the villeins finding their work was more wanted, were less inclined to give as much of it as they had given before. The landlords, however, chose members of parliament, and the villeins and labourers did not. The landlords, being in Parliament, made there what laws they pleased. One of the new laws made by them was known as the Statute of Labourers. By it any labourer was to be punished who asked for more wages than he had had before the Black Death. No wonder the labourers were very angry at being cheated in this way. A preacher named John Ball went about telling them not only that they had a right to as much as their

labour was worth, but that there ought to be no more
landlords.   He was always repeating two lines—

> When Adam delved and Eve span
> Who was then a gentleman ?

till the villeins and labourers were ready to do anything.

12. **The Last Days of Edward III.**—It was not
only the labourers who were dissatisfied.   War with
France broke out again, and the best leaders of the
English were now dead.   Edward III. lost his senses
in his old age, and was unable either to fight or
govern.   The Black Prince was in ill-health.   There
was a new French king, Charles V., who was too
prudent to fight great battles.   Step by step the
English lost most of the land they had in France.
The English nobles thought it would be a fine thing
to rob the clergy, as they could no longer rob the
French ; and the king's second son, called John of
Gaunt, that is to say, of Ghent, the town in Flanders
where he had been born, cried out loudly that the
clergy should have no more power in England, and
began to turn them out of the offices which they
held in the government.   It seems strange now that
all the offices in the state should be filled by the
clergy, and that a bishop should be Lord Treasurer
to look after the king's money, or Lord Chancellor to decide lawsuits.   But in those days no one
who was not a clergyman knew enough to do anything which needed the exercise of a man's brains,
and there was good sense enough still in England
to remember this.   The Black Prince, sick and
wasted as he was, appeared in parliament and de-

clared against his brother. The Good Parliament, as it was called, turned off some of John of Gaunt's friends who had been getting money by cheating the king and the nation, and put the bishops back into office. But the Black Prince did not live long enough to do more. When he died, John of Gaunt did again as he liked, and soon after Edward III. died also. All the conquests of the early part of the reign had come to nothing, and Englishmen who had set out to rob Frenchmen were trying to rob one another. Warlike glory, when it does not come from self-defence, or from an attempt to protect the weak against the strong, is like the apples which were once fabled to grow by the Dead Sea. Outwardly they were fair to look on, but they turned to dust and ashes in the mouth.

CHAPTER XIII.

(RICHARD II., 1377.)

THE KING AND HIS COUNCIL.

1. **The Insurrection of the Peasants.**—The reign
of Richard II. brought more trouble. He was the
son of the Black Prince, and though he was only ten
years old it was hoped that he would be like his

father when he grew up. At first England was ruled by his uncles, and chiefly by John of Gaunt. The war went on, but every year some French towns were lost, and the English armies, instead of bringing home spoil from abroad, cost much money. Heavy taxes were laid on to pay the expense. If the poor had complained before of their hard treatment from the rich, they complained much more now. The tax-gatherers did not find it easy to collect the money. At last one of them went into the house of Wat Tyler, a Kentish man, and insulted his daughter. Wat Tyler killed the man. Thousands of villeins rose in rebellion. They asked that the new taxes should be put down, and that there should be no more bondage, that is, that no one should be obliged to work for his landlord without being paid. But they did not ask quietly and firmly. They were angry and ignorant, and they did exactly what angry and ignorant men always do. They threw everything into confusion. They burnt the rolls of parchment on which were written the account of the services which they were bound to render to the landlords. They murdered the lawyers who had argued against them in the law-courts that they were bound to render these services. A large body of them, with Wat Tyler at their head, at last reached London. Young Richard was only sixteen, but he rode boldly out to meet them. He promised to free them from bondage. Those to whom he spoke were satisfied, and many went home. But it is impossible to satisfy a whole mob. A yelling crowd rushed through the streets of London, seized on the Archbishop of

Canterbury, and cut off his head. Others of the great lords were put to death in the same way. Young Richard was the only one in the court who was not frightened. Wat Tyler was in Smithfield at the head of thousands of his followers. The boy-king rode up to meet him. Wat Tyler spoke threatening words, and Walworth, the Mayor of London, slew him with his dagger. At once there was a shout for vengeance. Richard rode boldly forward. ' I am your king. I will be your leader,' he said. The peasants had no complaint to bring against the boy. They believed that he would free them from bondage, as he promised once more to do. They went peaceably home as the others had done. Riots, however, and disturbances spread through the country. At last the gentlemen took heart and attacked the peasants. The poor men had no proper arms, no order, no knowledge of war. They were slaughtered in thousands. The king was not allowed to fulfil his promises even if he had wished to do so. The villeins were thrust back into bondage. They were called on to fulfil their task of unpaid work for their landlords, and life seemed to them as hopeless as it had seemed before. But it was not long before better times came. The landlords found out that nothing was to be gained by making men work who did not want to work, and gradually most of the villeins were set free. These freemen who worked willingly for pay worked much harder than the villeins had done when they had been made to work for nothing.

2. John Wyclif.—The landlords had their way, however, for a little time. They had force on their

side.   There was one man in England, however, who
had been for some time trying to teach men that there
is something better than force.   John Wyclif was a
learned priest.   He began by arguing against the
power of the pope in England.   The popes had long

SHIP, TIME OF RICHARD II.

ceased to do any good to England, and all that was
known of them was that they were always asking
for English money, and trying to help their Italian
friends by giving them church offices in England.
In the reign of Edward III. and Richard II. laws
were made by the English Parliament to stop this.

H

Wyclif argued against the pope in this affair. Then he argued against the wealth and power of the clergy. Clergymen, he said, ought to preach and visit the poor. Unless they did their duty they had no right to so much money. Wyclif translated the Bible, and sent out a number of men called the Poor Priests to explain it to the people. The great poet Chaucer, who lived at this time, is thought to have had Wyclif in his mind when he described a good priest, and told how he taught the doctrine of Christ and of his apostles, but followed it first himself. By-and-by Wyclif attacked some of the doctrines which were then believed in the Church. He found people of different kinds to support him. In the first place there were those who learnt to believe what he taught. These people were called Lollards, from a word which means to sing, just as if they had been called Psalm-singers. In the second place he was supported by great noblemen, who were very pleased to hear him say that clergymen ought not to have money unless they did their duty. What Wyclif meant was that the clergymen ought to do their duty. What the great noblemen meant was that they ought to take the clergymen's money away from them, without trying to make them do their duty. For some time Wyclif seemed to be prospering. But there were two things against him. Printing had not yet been discovered, so that Bibles were very expensive, as each copy had to be written out, and even if poor people could have afforded to buy them, they had never been taught to read. Then again, the great gentlemen had been frightened by

the insurrection of the peasants. They had thought
it a fine thing to take away the money of the clergymen because they did not do their duty, without
really caring whether they did their duty or not.
They had now found out that the peasants could ask
gentlemen whether they had been doing their duty,
and whether they really cared for anything except for
money and enjoyment. The consequence was that

SOLDIER WITH HAND-GUN, FIFTEENTH CENTURY.

they did not care to listen any longer to a man like
Wyclif, and that they began to look upon him as a
disturber of the peace. He was prevented from
teaching at Oxford, and forced to go to his parish at
Lutterworth, where he died not long after.

3. Richard II. and his Uncles.—The rest of the
reign of Richard II. was taken up with a long
struggle for power, between the king on the one

side, and his uncles, supported by some of the great
nobles, on the other. Richard, when he reached
manhood, showed that he could sometimes be as
cool and daring as he had been on the day when he
faced Wat Tyler and his mob. 'Tell me,' he
suddenly said to his uncle, the Duke of Gloucester,
'how old I am.' 'Your Highness,' was the answer,
is in your twenty-second year.' 'Then,' said the
king, 'I am surely of age to manage my own affairs,'
and he turned his uncles out of the council. But
he did not know how to use the government when
he had it. His only idea of being a king was that
it gave him plenty of money to spend. His uncles
did not know what to do with power any better than
he did. Sometimes they were strong enough to seize
the government, and to put Richard's chief coun-
cillors to death. Sometimes he was strong enough
to seize the government, and to put his chief
opponents to death. He had one of his uncles,
the Duke of Gloucester, murdered; and had another
great nobleman, the Earl of Arundel, executed.
He seemed to be completely master of England.

4. End of the Reign of Richard II.—At last only
two of the great noblemen who had been Richard's
enemies were left. One of these was Thomas Mowbray, Duke of Norfolk. The other was Henry of
Bolingbroke, Duke of Hereford, the son of John of
Gaunt, and in this way Richard's first cousin. The
king had pardoned them, but he was very well
pleased to hear that they had quarrelled, and that
they intended to settle the quarrel, as men did in
those days, by fighting. The fight was to take place

at Coventry, and Richard was there to see fair play. Just as they were going to begin, the king stopped the fight and banished them both, Mowbray for life, and Bolingbroke for ten years. As they had committed no crime proved against them in any court of law, this was most unjust. Before long, Richard acted more unjustly still. John of Gaunt died, and Richard took possession of his lands, instead of allowing his son, the banished Bolingbroke, to have them. Honesty would have been a better policy. Every man in England who had any property at all, was afraid that if he died his son would be treated in the same way. Bolingbroke understood how many friends Richard had made for him by this act of injustice. He sailed for England and landed in Yorkshire, asking only for his father's lands. Thousands flocked in to support him, and Richard was deserted. Henry then claimed the crown, and Richard, left without support, was obliged to give it up. He was thrown into prison. In those days there was but a short step for kings from the prison to the grave, and, like his grandfather, Edward II., Richard II. was murdered not long after his dethronement.

CHAPTER XIV.

THE HOUSE OF LANCASTER.

(HENRY IV, 1399. HENRY V., 1414. HENRY VI., 1422.)

1. **Henry's Title to the Crown.**—Henry IV., as Bolingbroke was now called, was the first king of the

family known as the House of Lancaster, because
he inherited the duchy of Lancaster from his father,
John of Gaunt. Since the accession of Henry III.,
the custom had established itself, of placing on the
throne the eldest son of the last king, or, if he died

HENRY IV.

in his father's lifetime, as the Black Prince had done,
the eldest son of the eldest son. Still, though the
habit of choosing any one who was thought fit out of
the royal family had gone out, Englishmen did not
consider that the government of a country was to be

looked on as belonging to a king, in the same way that a house or a field belonged to a man. They dethroned Edward II. and Richard II. because they governed badly. When Edward II. was dethroned, they put his eldest son in his place. Richard II. had no children. There was, however, an heir to the crown, nearer than Henry, by right of birth, in Roger Mortimer, Earl of March, who was the grandson of Lionel, Duke of Clarence, a son of Edward III., older than John of Gaunt. Henry IV. therefore reigned not by right of birth, but because parliament had allowed him to take the throne, very much as John had reigned. For this reason he was obliged to act more according to the wishes of parliament than the kings before him had done, because, if he did not, parliament might dethrone him as it had dethroned Richard. In many ways this was a good thing. The king could no longer do as he pleased, as Richard had done, and could not take away men's money or lands or banish them without trial. But parliaments are made of men, and three or four hundred men can do things as wicked and evil as one man can.

2. **Law made for the Burning of Heretics.**—At this time the men who made up the parliament were still frightened lest there should be another rebellion of the peasants. The Lollards were still preaching against the doctrines believed by the church, and those who disbelieved the doctrines of the church were usually the same men who would have tried to free the serfs from working for the landlords without being paid for their labours, and who would have liked to do as much harm to the landlords as they could.

Parliament, therefore, determined to try and put down the heretics—as those were called who taught a belief which was different from that of the church—partly because they thought that heresy was doing harm, and partly because they were afraid lest the heretics should want to take away the property of the gentlemen. For the first time in English history, a law was made directing that heretics should be burnt alive. The bishops and all religious persons were convinced that any one who believed what was false in religion would suffer everlasting torments, even if he made a mistake honestly, and they therefore thought that they were doing a charitable thing in burning those who taught others to believe that which would bring such frightful consequences upon them.

3. Rebellion against Henry IV.—Henry's reign was a troubled one. The great nobles who had done much to place him on the throne were not ready to obey him, and he had to be always ready to fight in order to keep them down. One great house, that of the Percies, was particularly dangerous to him. The head of that house was the Earl of Northumberland. His lands were on the borders which separate England from Scotland. It was his business to see that no Scottish army and no Scottish band of robbers crossed the Tweed, to burn English houses and to kill English men. It was therefore necessary that he should have many armed men under his command, and it was easy to employ these armed men against the king. He made friendship with the Scots, and some of that nation, together with Owen Glendower, a powerful man in Wales, joined him in

a rebellion. A great battle was fought at Shrewsbury, where Northumberland was defeated, and his
son Harry Hotspur was killed. Henry had not
come to an end of his difficulties. Enemy after
enemy opposed him, and he died a sad and worn-
out man, after a reign of fourteen years.

KING RICHARD II. KNIGHTING HENRY OF MONMOUTH IN
IRELAND, 1399.

4. Henry of Monmouth, Prince of Wales.—His son,
Henry of Monmouth, had been knighted by Richard
II. before his father became king. He had fought
bravely at the battle of Shrewsbury. He was full of
frolic, and there are stories about his wild conduct

when he was amusing himself. It is said that he once threatened a judge named Gascoigne, and that Gascoigne sent him to prison. The story used to be believed that, when Henry became king, he praised Gascoigne for doing justice, though he had himself

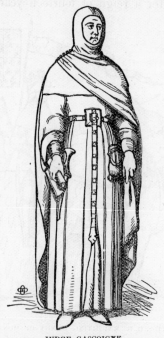

JUDGE GASCOIGNE.

been the sufferer. As however he really dismissed Gascoigne as soon as his father died, it is to be feared that he did not behave as well as has been supposed.

5. **Henry V. makes War upon France.**—The new king, Henry V., resolved to free himself from these

difficulties by imitating Edward III. He thought that if a war was begun with the French the nobles would follow him instead of rebelling against him. He therefore put forward a claim to the crown of France. As he was not the eldest descendant of Edward III., he had no claim which any law-court in the world would have allowed; but it happened that the king of France, Charles VI., was out of his mind, and that his nobles were quarrelling with one another. He was therefore able to set out with more chance of success than Edward III. had had. He was himself a good and upright man in other matters, and a brave and able general. His army was a strong one, and Englishmen, who cared little whether the excuse for the war was good or not, were burning to revenge themselves upon the French for having driven them out of the land in the former war.

6. Siege of Harfleur and Battle of Agincourt.— In 1415 Henry landed, and took Harfleur, after a terrible siege. Sickness broke out in his army and swept away thousands who did not fear the face of an enemy. In spite of this he determined to march from Harfleur to Calais with the few men who remained to him. At Agincourt his way was barred by at least fifty or sixty thousand Frenchmen. Henry had at the highest reckoning but nine thousand men with him, but he had no fear. The battle was fought on October 25, the feast of Saint Crispin and Saint Crispian. The night before, the vigil of the feast, he overheard some one in his camp wishing that a few thousands of the stout men who were idle in England had been with them. 'No,' said the king, 'I would not have one man more.' These words of his have been put into poetry by Shakspere :—

> No, my fair cousin:
> If we are marked to die, we are enough
> To do our country loss ; and if to live,
> The fewer men, the greater share of honour.
> God's will ! I pray thee, wish not one man more.

ARCHERS, FIFTEENTH CENTURY.

> By Jove, I am not covetous for gold,
> Nor care I who doth feed upon my cost ;
> .   .   .   .
> But if it be a sin to covet honour,
> I am the most offending soul alive,
> No, faith, my coz, wish not a man from England.
> God's peace ! I would not lose so great an honour

As one man more, methinks, would share from me
For the best hope I have.   O, do not wish one more
.   .   .   .   .

This day is call'd the feast of Crispian :
He that outlives this day, and comes safe home,
Will stand a tip-toe when this day is named,
And rouse him at the name of Crispian.
He that shall live this day, and see old age,
Will yearly on the vigil feast his neighbours,
And say—'To-morrow is Saint Crispian : '
Then will he strip his sleeve, and show his scars.
Old men forget ; yet all shall be forgot,
But he'll remember with advantages
What feats he did that day.   Then shall our names,
Familiar in their mouths as household words,
Harry the king, Bedford and Exeter,
Warwick and Talbot, Salisbury and Gloster,
Be in their flowing cups freshly remembered.
This story shall the good man teach his son ;
And Crispin Crispian shall ne'er go by,
From this day to the ending of the world,
But we in it shall be remembered :
We few, we happy few, we band of brothers,
For he to-day that sheds his blood with me,
Shall be my brother ; be he ne'er so vile,
This day shall gentle his condition ;
And gentlemen in England now a-bed
Shall think themselves accurs'd they were not here ;
And hold their manhoods cheap whiles any speaks
That fought with us upon Saint Crispin's day.[1]

The battle of the next day was Crecy over again.
The French horsemen, splendid in their bright armour
and their gorgeous array, charged down upon the
little English host.   The ground was wet with rain,
and the horses laboured heavily in the deep mud till
they could move forward no longer.   All the while

[1] The quotation had better be omitted if the class is not sufficiently advanced to understand it.

the English bowmen poured their arrows, their cloth-yard shafts, amongst them, and the English horsemen broke in amongst them to finish their defeat. The ground was strewed with eleven thousand slain Frenchmen, amongst whom were the noblest of the great men of France.

7. The Siege of Rouen.—For the moment there was little to be done. The English army had been large enough to win a victory, but it was not large enough to conquer France. Henry returned to England. Two years later he came back to France. He took town after town. There was a long siege of Rouen. The townsmen were short of food, and in order that they might have all the food that was left for themselves they thrust out of their gates twelve thousand men, women, and children, who had come in for shelter from the country round. Henry cruelly refused to let them pass. Day by day starvation carried off its wretched victims. Inside the town the misery was almost as great. At last the townspeople were driven by mere famine to surrender, and Henry had gained possession of a town the inhabitants of which hated him and his English.

8. The last Years of Henry V.—Henry cared not whether he was hated or not. The strong, brave, cruel man went on his victorious course, little thinking that his evil deeds were preparing evil, if not for himself, for his children after him. Conquest was easy enough. The mad French king could neither command an army nor rule a state. The French nobles were quarrelling with one another as bitterly as ever. Some years before the most powerful of them, the French king's cousin, the Duke of Burgundy, had murdered the king's brother, the Duke of Orleans. Now the friends of the Duke of Orleans murdered the Duke of Burgundy, and the young prince, the eldest son of the king, looked on with approval whilst the deed was being done. The new Duke of Burgundy joined Henry, in order that he might take revenge for his father's murder. This gave Henry great advantage, and before long a treaty was signed by which Henry and his successors were to be kings of France as soon as King Charles died. It was also agreed that Henry should marry the French king's daughter Catharine. Not long afterwards Henry died, and Charles soon followed him to the grave.

9. The English Rule in France.—The heir to all this bloodshed and glory was an infant, Henry VI. of England. The baby was crowned King of France in Paris, and a great part of France submitted because it could not help it. His uncle, the Duke of Bedford, a brave and able man, the brother of the late king, ruled the north of France in the name of his infant nephew. To the south of the Loire king Charles's son, known as Charles VII., was obeyed. The English however were winning town after town. At last they besieged Orleans. If that were taken Charles would hardly be able to resist much longer. The English believed that they would soon have everything their own way. Happily violence cannot last for ever. Armies might march backwards and forwards amidst blood and corpses for a time, as if to spread death and ruin amongst those whose only wish is to be at peace were the only object worth living for. The time was now coming when this blood should be required at their hands. The England of Henry V., like the England of Edward III., had been very strong because it was better governed, and because men lived better and happier lives in it than elsewhere in Europe. But it had used its strength to oppress and not to help other nations. Therefore it was hated with a bitter hatred, a hatred which would make even the divided French strong to resist. They waited but for a word to rouse them against their tyrants.

10. Joan Darc. — The word came, as it always does, when it was little looked for. Far away in Lorraine there was a young peasant girl, Joan Darc, known usually in England, by a curious mistake, as Joan of Arc. She was pure and simple, and utterly without learning. But she had a warm heart of pity, and as she saw around her the trampling of the English horsemen over the corn-fields, and heard the tales of woe and agony which reached her from every side, her soft woman's breast was melted in pity for the realm of France. The words of hope which rose within her seemed as though they came from without. She fancied that she heard angels' voices bidding her deliver her native land, and telling her to go forth and not to rest till Orleans was saved from the English, and till Charles was crowned at Rheims, and anointed with the holy oil which, as was then believed, had come down from heaven. 'I must go to the king,' she said. 'even if I wear my limbs to my very knees. I had far rather rest and spin by my mother's side, for this is no work of my choosing, but I must go and do it, for my Lord wills it.' Her father and her friends tried in vain to hinder her. At last she persuaded a passing knight to take her to the king. ' My name,' she said, when she was brought before him, ' is Joan the Maid. The Heavenly King sends me to tell you that you shall be anointed and crowned in the city of Rheims, and you shall be lieutenant of the Heavenly King, who is King of France.' Charles had by this time lost all hope of gaining a victory by human means, and he let her do as she wished. A suit of armour was made for her, and she mounted her horse astride like a man, with a banner in her hand. The rude soldiers believed that she was indeed sent from heaven. They followed her where they would follow no one else. At her bidding they burst through the English army before Orleans, and entered the town in triumph.

11. **Capture and Death of Joan.**—From that moment the English lost all chance of conquering France. The French had hope again, and hope gave them the courage which they had lost. The Maid marched to Rheims. There, in her presence, Charles received the crown of France. The Maid had done her work, and would gladly have gone back to her home; but the French soldiers did not think that they could conquer without her, and persuaded her to stay. A baser feeling sprang up in the minds of the commanders. They did not like to hear all the praise given to the Maid and none to themselves. They left her in the midst of a fight

I

to be taken prisoner. The English who took her treated her shamefully. If the French soldiers believed her to be a saint, the English soldiers believed her to be a witch, who had defeated them with the help of the devil. They carried her to Rouen, and accused her of being a heretic, because she said that the voices which had bidden her go forth were sent by God. She was condemned to be burnt alive. She died declaring that the voices were from God. The last word which she spoke amidst the flames was 'Jesus.' An English soldier who was looking on was struck with terror. 'We are lost!' he cried. 'We have burnt a saint!'

12. The Loss of France.—The English cause was indeed lost. They had no longer to fight only against the gay French nobles, but against the whole French people. The Maid had been a peasant girl, and the French people, who had been first in her thoughts, rose as one man against its oppressors. She had had, as she so often said, pity upon the realm of France. In thirty-one years after the death of Henry V. Calais was the only spot in France left to the English king.

13. Weakness of Henry VI.—The English king was Henry VI. Gentle and pious, but without strength or wisdom, he could not even keep England in order, far less recover France. His subjects were in that temper which usually makes people who have done wrong blame every one except themselves. They were displeased when the king married a French wife, Margaret of Anjou, and made peace with France. They were more rightly displeased when Henry, not knowing how to govern, let the affairs of the kingdom be managed by men who used their power to enrich themselves. One of these men, the Duke of Suffolk, was particularly hated. He was accused of all sorts of crimes and banished. As he was leaving England he was dragged out of

KNIGHT, LADY, AND CHILD, TIME OF HENRY VI.

the ship in which he was, and murdered. As in the time of Richard II., the men of Kent were the first to rise. Putting Jack Cade at their head they marched to London. Happily, during the years which had passed since Wat Tyler's rebellion, the peasants had ceased to be serfs. They were now free men, and there was no longer any complaint about bondage. Cade reached London, but his men took to robbing, and he was himself soon after killed.

14. The Wars of the Roses.—Men who wanted better government looked to one of the king's kinsmen, the Duke of York, to help them. He was descended from that Mortimer who came from Lionel, the son of Edward III., who was older than John of Gaunt, the king's great-grandfather. Nobody, however, at first wanted to make the Duke of York king. They merely wanted him to govern instead of the king's favourites. Before anything could be done the king went mad, and the lords in parliament named the Duke of York Protector, or, as we should say, Regent. If Henry had remained mad for the rest of his life, the Duke of York might have gone on ruling in his name. Unfortunately Henry was sometimes mad and sometimes sane, and he was not much wiser when he was sane than when he was mad. The first time he was better he drove the Duke of York away from his presence. A war began, which is known as the Wars of the Roses, because the House of Lancaster had a red rose for its badge or mark, and the House of York a white one. There were many battles fought. Sometimes one side won and sometimes the other. At last the Duke of York claimed to be king by right of birth. The queen was terribly angry, as this would take away the right of her only son. At a great battle at Wakefield the Duke of York was defeated and slain. The queen had his head cut off and put over the gate of York, with a paper crown placed in mockery upon it. He soon found an avenger in his eldest son, Edward. The king's party was defeated in a bloody battle at Towton, and Edward became king as Edward IV.

CHAPTER XV.

THE HOUSE OF YORK.

(EDWARD IV., 1461. EDWARD V., 1483. RICHARD III., 1483.)

SHIP, FIFTEENTH CENTURY.

1. Edward IV. and the Barons.—Edward IV. claimed the throne because he was the heir of an older son of Edward III. than the great-grandfather of Henry VI. had been; but he had had other things besides his birth to help him. In the first place he was a much better soldier than any one who was on the Lancastrian side. In the second place, a very great number of people who did not care whether the king were of one family or another, cared very much to have a king who could really govern and keep order. We are so used to see order kept that it is hard for us to understand how difficult it was to do it in the time of the Wars of the Roses. A few policemen are quite enough to keep many thousands of people peaceable, because only a very few people now think of making a disturbance if they do not get what they want at once. Nobody now is armed as a soldier unless he wears the queen's uniform, and is ready to obey the orders of the officers set over him by the queen. In the time of Henry VI. the great lords had a large number of armed followers, who were usually ready to do anything that their lords told them to do. Whenever there was going to be any fighting the lords gave out liveries, as they were called, which were what we should call soldiers' uniforms. The word *livery* means something delivered, and these liveries were coats delivered to the followers with the lord's particular mark. Coats of this kind are still worn by footmen and coachmen, and do not do anybody any harm. Then, when two or three thousand coats were seen about with the bear and ragged staff worked on the front, people knew that the great Earl of Warwick, who had done so much to help Edward IV. to the throne that he was known as the King-maker, was going to fight somebody. When they saw men with a particular kind of knot worked on their breasts, they knew that the Earl of Buckingham was going to fight somebody. Each great lord thus had a little army of his own to dispose of, and was always ready to employ it. Peaceable persons, therefore, wished very much to have a king strong enough to put down all these little armies, and they thought that a king like Edward, who could win the battle of Towton, was much more likely to be able to put them down than a king like Henry VI. who was usually out of his mind.

2. **The Barons and the Middle Classes.**—If these great lords had contented themselves with marching about and fighting one another it would have been bad enough. What was worse than this was that they used their men to hurt innocent people. A man who had displeased a great lord was pretty sure to meet a band of ruffians. He would then be beaten or wounded, and he would be very lucky if he was not actually killed. If a great man coveted a house belonging to some one else, he sent to take it. A certain John Paston, for instance, lived in Norfolk. One day when he was in London his wife looked out of a window and saw about a thousand men in armour, with guns and bows. They brought with them ladders and long poles with hooks at the end, to pull the house down, and pans with burning coals to set fire to it if they could not pull it down. They set to work first to break down the supports of the room in which the lady was. They then made their way into the house, dragged the lady out by force,

broke open all the doors, and carried off everything
they could find. These men were not common
robbers. They were sent by a lord who unjustly
claimed the house as his own. Many years afterwards the son of this Paston was treated in much
the same way. His wife was left at his house
near Norwich, whilst he was away on business.
This time the attack was made by a duke. He
sent a little army to get for him what he wanted.
The lady stood a siege, but was at last obliged to
let the duke's men in. They destroyed the house
entirely, carrying off even the iron-work. To this
day the ruins of the house are to be seen, to remind
us what sort of things lords and dukes could do at
the time of the Wars of the Roses.

3. Difficulties in the way of getting Justice.—The
strangest thing is that all these things were done
while the courts of law sat as usual. Judges went
round to hold the assizes, and juries gave verdicts
just as they do now. We think it a very excellent
thing that nobody can be punished unless twelve
men, who make up a jury, agree in thinking that he
has really done what he is accused of. But that is
because we know that, though the twelve men may
sometimes make mistakes, they will at least try
honestly to say what they really think. In the days
of the Wars of the Roses they did not try honestly
to speak the truth. They were very often chosen to
be jurymen because they were friends or dependants
of the great landowner of the neighbourhood. If
they had to try one of the great man's friends they
would say that he was innocent, whether he were so

or not. If they had to try one of the great man's
enemies, they would say that he was guilty, whether
he were so or not. Even if the jurymen wished to
say what was true, they were often afraid to do so.
A juryman who set himself against the wishes of the

NOBLEMAN IN ARMOUR, WITH MANTLE OF THE GARTER:
FIFTEENTH CENTURY.

great man would probably be waylaid on the way
home and soundly beaten.

4. Growing Power of the King.—It is easy to
understand why Edward was popular. The gentlemen with small estates, the farmers and husbandmen,
the shopkeepers of the towns, all wanted a king who

could keep order. They did not care much whether Parliament met often or not, because the lords who ill treated them at home were very powerful in Parliament. From the time of Edward IV., therefore, the kings began to be much stronger than they had been for a long time. A writer living about a century before this tells a story which will help us to understand the feeling of the people. He says that the mice met one day in council to determine what was to be done to kill the cat, in order that they might live in safety. One little mouse, however, told them that they were very foolish to wish to kill the cat. He said that he could not deny that the cat ate a good many mice, but she also destroyed a good many rats. If the rats were allowed to multiply, they would kill many more mice than one cat did. A king like Edward IV. was like the cat. The nobles were like the rats. The mass of the people were like the mice. They supported him because he kept the nobles in order.

5. Edward's Deposition and Restoration.—After ten years Edward forgot that he had need to be always on the watch to keep his power. He offended the Earl of Warwick, the King-maker, who, great noble as he was, had helped him to the throne. Warwick was the most powerful of the nobles. In the kitchen of his house at Kenilworth a huge caldron was always on the fire. Any one who pleased might come in and stick his fork into one of the pieces of meat boiling in it, and carry it off. The men who were thus fed at his expense were always ready to fight for him. He now took Henry VI. out of prison, and made him king again. Edward fled across the sea.

Queen Margaret came back to take her poor mad husband's part, and even the Duke of Clarence, Edward's next brother, joined Warwick and married his daughter. Edward, however, was not a man lightly to abandon hope. He was soon back again in England with an army. At Barnet a battle was fought which settled Edward on the throne. Clarence basely deserted the side he had chosen, and returned to his brother. Warwick was killed, Edward marched westward to Tewkesbury, and utterly defeated Margaret. After the battle was over, another Edward, the young son of Henry and Margaret, was brutally murdered. Not long afterwards Henry VI. died in the Tower, no doubt also murdered. In that long fierce struggle for power, justice and mercy were forgotten. Men said afterwards that these murders were committed by Edward's youngest brother, Richard, Duke of Gloucester, and it is very probable, though it is not quite certain, that what they said was true.

6. The Benevolences and the Printing Press.—For the rest of his life Edward reigned in peace. At least there was no more fighting. He ventured to do things which no king had done before. When he wanted money, instead of asking parliament for it, he made the rich men give him what he called a benevolence, because they were supposed to give it willingly, though, in reality, they were afraid to refuse. Once he asked a rich old lady for ten pounds. She told him that as he was so good looking he should have twenty. He gave the old woman a kiss, and she then told him that she would give him forty. It was not often that money was given him with such good will as this.

There was plenty of grumbling, but few wished to resist the king, lest they should have the old misery back again. In this reign one novelty appeared which was of far greater importance than all the victories and defeats of the Wars of the Roses. The art of printing had been invented on the Continent, and Caxton brought it into England. He set up the first printing-press at Westminster. The king and his courtiers came to wonder and applaud. They looked on as men look who watch a pretty toy. They little thought that they were watching the birth of a power which would be stronger than kings and parliaments together.

7. The End of the Reign of Edward IV.—Edward, even in his triumph, was not without his troubles. Victory had set the crown on his head, and others began to look on the crown simply as a great prize, which might be won by fighting for it. His brother Clarence, who had first helped Warwick against Edward, and then Edward against Warwick, fancied, or was believed to fancy, that he might gain the crown for himself. He was imprisoned in the Tower, and there put to death. No one really knows how it was done, but it was afterwards reported that he was drowned in a cask of wine. Edward must have felt himself more lonely in the world than ever. He knew that many of the great nobles hated him, and now his own brother had turned against him. He had tried pleasure in all its forms, and had lived a gay, dissolute life. Such a life, as is always the case, had been sweet to the taste at first, but in the end it was bitter as wormwood. Worn out in body and mind, he became sad and dispirited. At last he died, a worn-out but not an old man.

8. Edward V. and the Duke of Gloucester.— When Edward IV. died he left behind him two young sons, Edward and Richard, and several daughters, the eldest of which was named Elizabeth. His widow, the mother of the children, was Elizabeth Woodville, whom he had married, though she was not of any great family. He had shown much favour to her relations, and the great nobles who had taken his side were not well pleased to see men whom they despised honoured by the king. After Edward's death there were many who wanted to prevent the queen and her relations from having any power. At the head of these was the late king's brother, Richard, Duke of Gloucester. One of his shoulders was higher than the other, and his left arm was shrunk and withered; but he was, in other respects, a handsome man, as his brother had been. He was brave and warlike, a good captain, and a man who was much loved by those amongst whom he lived, as long as they did not try to do him any harm. But he had no mercy or pity for any one who tried to prevent him from doing anything that he wanted to do. Men in those unhappy days had grown used to cruelty and murder, and Richard thought no more of killing those who stood in his way than he would have thought of killing flies. Probably he had had to do with killing Edward, the son of Henry VI., and Henry VI. himself. Probably, too, he had had to do with putting his brother Clarence to death. When he heard that his brother Edward was dead, his first thought was to get the young princes out of the hands of their mother and her relations. He took with him his friend, the Duke of Buckingham, and met the little King Edward V. as he was coming to London accompanied by his mother's brother, Lord Rivers, and by one of his half-brothers. He carried the boy with him and ordered that the other two should be imprisoned. Not long afterwards he had the two prisoners beheaded without any trial at all. Richard, when he arrived in London, was named Protector, to rule in his nephew's name till he became a man.

9. **The Duke of Gloucester, Protector.**—The queen was frightened. She had with her her second son, Richard, Duke of York, and she fled with him to the Sanctuary at Westminster—a place in which criminals were allowed to take refuge, and from which they might not be taken against their will. One of Richard's greatest supporters had been Lord Hastings. Hastings was now tired of supporting him any longer, and Richard determined to get rid of him. One morning the Protector appeared in the Council. 'My lord,' he said to the Bishop of Ely, 'you have good strawberries in your garden at Holborn ; I pray you let us have a mess of them.' He seemed to be in good humour. After a time he went out, and came back looking sullen and angry. He asked what punishment those deserved who contrived his death. Hastings answered that they deserved to die. Richard laid bare his withered arm. 'That sorceress, my brother's wife,' he said,

'and others with her, see how they have wasted my body by their sorcery and witchcraft.' Those present knew that his arm had always been as it was, and were much surprised. Yet they did not dare to say what they thought. 'Certainly, my lord,' said Hastings, 'if they have done so heinously, they are worthy of heinous punishment.' Richard pretended to fly into a rage. 'What!' he said; 'dost thou answer me with ifs and ands? I tell thee they have done it, and that I will make good on thy body, traitor!' He struck the table with his fist, and Richard's men, who were standing outside, rushed into the room. He swore that he would not dine till Hastings was dead. Hastings was dragged out, and his head was cut off at once upon a log of timber lying outside.

10. The Duke of Gloucester becomes King Richard III.—Richard then made the queen give up her youngest son. He and his brother, the king, were lodged in the Tower of London. The Tower was not then a prison, as it afterwards became. It was a palace, in which the kings lived when they wanted to be in safety from their enemies behind its strong walls, whilst when they had no fear they lived at Westminster, in the palace which then stood where part of the Houses of Parliament stands now. Richard next spread a story which was probably true, that the father of the boys had promised to marry a lady before he married their mother. In those days, if a man promised to marry a woman and married somebody else instead, he was not considered to be properly married. Richard therefore

said that Edward IV. had never been properly married to the queen, so that his sons could not inherit the crown. He summoned a parliament, which set aside the young princes, and declared their uncle to be King Richard III.

11. Murder of the Princes.—Richard had been allowed to place himself on the throne for the same reason that Edward IV. had been allowed to make himself king. The great mass of Englishmen wanted some one to keep order, and they did not think that a child could keep order any better than a madman. But it was impossible that they should be very eager to support a man who had been so cruel, and it was not long before he did a deed which was more cruel than anything that he had done before. The two boys in the Tower were not dangerous as long as they were boys, because they were not old enough to govern. But they would soon be men, and then every one who had any quarrel with Richard would be sure to take their part. Richard therefore determined that they should never grow up to be men. He employed Sir James Tyrell to get rid of the boys. Tyrell sent two men to do the wicked deed. These men went into the room where the children were asleep in bed, and smothered them with pillows. For many a year no one knew where the bodies of the murdered princes were buried. At last, nearly two hundred years afterwards, some workmen found at the foot of a staircase two skeletons which, from their size, must have belonged to boys of the age of the two brothers.

12. Richard's Defeat and Death.—Richard soon found out that he had lost more than he had gained by his cruelty. A king was sure to make enemies amongst the great nobles, and they could hope to be able to overthrow him now that he had ceased to be popular. He disappointed the Duke of Buckingham, who had helped him to the Crown, by not giving him all the reward that he had promised him. He was still strong enough to overpower Buckingham, and the Duke was executed at Salisbury. A more powerful enemy than Buckingham came next. Henry Tudor, Earl of Richmond, was descended through his mother from John of Gaunt, and though no one of the House of Lancaster had any claim by right of birth to the throne, he thought that Richard's enemies would be sure to support him whether he had any right or not. He set out from Brittany, where he was then living, and landed in Wales with a small force. By his father he was of Welsh descent, and he was therefore welcomed by the Welsh. One Welshman had sworn to Richard that if Henry came he should not land except over his body. He meant that he would fight till he died rather than allow it, but when Henry appeared he could not find it in his heart to resist a man who was of a Welsh family; and in order to keep his promise literally, he laid himself down on the beach and let Henry step over him. Henry found no more resistance than this for some time. He had not a large army, but neither had Richard. The two rivals met at Bosworth in Leicestershire. Richard had no chance of winning, for in the middle of the battle

K

Lord Stanley with all his men deserted to Henry, and the Earl of Northumberland, who had also come to fight for Richard, locked on without fighting at all. Richard knew that he was lost, and, like a brave man as he was, he plunged into the midst of his enemies, striking out manfully till he was slain. Sir William Stanley, Lord Stanley's brother, picked up his battered crown and placed it on Henry's head. From that day Henry ruled England as Henry VII.

CHAPTER XVI.

THE FIRST TUDOR KING.

(HENRY VII., 1485.)

1. Beginning of the Reign of Henry VII.—The new king was not the kind of man to be very warmly loved. He was cold and reserved, never mixing much in the amusements of the people. But he knew how to keep order, and he had never shocked the feelings of his subjects by murdering any one. He was always ready to put down rebellions when they arose, and he took good care always to have plenty of money, and a large number of cannons. The use of guns in war had been increasing for some time. It is said that guns were first used at the Battle of Crecy, and though this is not quite certain, there is no doubt that they were first used about that time. By the time of Henry VII. every king who went to war had a number of large guns. In this way, more than in any other, the power of the nobles, in all Europe,

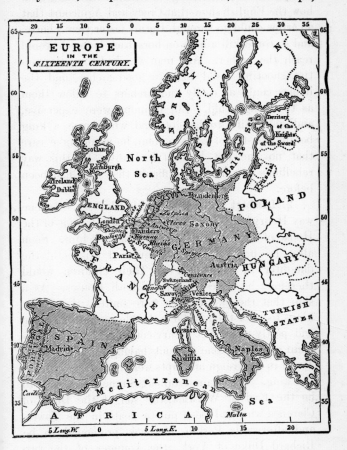

EUROPE
IN THE
SIXTEENTH CENTURY.

came to be much less than it was. When the best way of fighting was on horseback, only those who were

K 2

rich enough to keep good horses and to buy expensive armour could make good soldiers. We have seen
how the English showed at Crecy and Agincourt that
an arrow could go through the air faster than a horse,
and so could kill a man on horseback before he could
reach the archer. Any man who had time to prac-
tise shooting could make a good archer, and the
nobles could as easily find archers to follow them
as the king could. But cannons were expensive,
and not easily to be got, and when once a king
became master of his kingdom, he would take care
that no one but himself had any. In this way
rebellions became more difficult than they had been
before.

2. **Lambert Simnel and Perkin Warbeck.**—In one
way Henry had taken care to make the friends of the
House of York unwilling to rise against him. Soon
after he became king he married Elizabeth, the
daughter of Edward IV. Their children would
therefore be descended from both Houses. As a
sign that the two Houses were united, the Tudor
kings took for their badge a double rose, partly white
and partly red. Yet Henry could not expect to remain on the throne without having to fight for it.
Twice in this reign attempts were made to overthrow
the king. A certain Lambert Simnel pretended to
be the Earl of Warwick, the son of the Duke of
Clarence who had been put to death in the Tower,
and afterwards Perkin Warbeck pretended to be
Richard Duke of York, the younger of the two
murdered princes. Both these impostors were overpowered. Henry contented himself with employing

Simnel, who was but a lad, as a scullion in his kitchen. Warbeck was older, and had imposed upon so many persons that he was more dangerous, and was therefore executed.

3. Henry makes the Nobles obedient.—As Henry did not allow the nobles to possess cannons, he did not allow them to give out liveries, or, as we should say, to put their men into uniform. The habit was dangerous to the peace of the country, because these men in liveries were ready to fight for the noblemen from whom they received them, as modern soldiers are ready to fight for the queen whose uniform they wear. There was a law made against these liveries in the time of Edward IV., but Edward had not been strong enough to see that it was obeyed. Henry took care to carry it out. One day he paid a visit to the Earl of Oxford, a nobleman who had fought heartily for the Lancastrian side, on which Henry was, in the Wars of the Roses. When he left the house the Earl drew up a large number of his servants dressed in his livery to do honour to the king. 'My Lord,' said Henry, 'I thank you for your entertainment, but my Attorney must speak to you.' The Attorney-General brought the Earl before a court and had him fined 10,000*l.* It has often been thought hard to have had him punished after he had done his best to welcome the king. On the other hand, it was well that the king should show that he would not favour his own best friends, and that even those who had served him most must be compelled to obey the laws which had been made in order that the country might be at peace.

4. Henry VII. gathers Money.—Whether this was in Henry's mind or not there can be little doubt that he was very glad to get the 10,000*l.* He loved money, not as a miser loves it, in order to please his eye with the sight of a heap of gold and silver, but because he knew that it made him powerful. At the same time he did not like to cause ill-will by laying on taxes which the poor would have to pay as well as the rich. He thought it wiser to get as much as he could from the rich, and whenever any one of these had broken any law, even if it was unintentionally, the king sold him a pardon instead of punishing him. Then too he revived the system of benevolences which had been invented by Edward IV. There is a story told of his chief minister, Cardinal Morton, that he used to ask rich citizens for money for the king in a way which was known as Cardinal Morton's fork, because if he did not hit a man with one point of his argument, he did with the other. If he heard that the citizen had been living with a great show, and had a fine house and many servants, he would say to him, ' You spend so much money that you are plainly very rich, and can well afford to give the king a good sum of money.' If he found a man who lived very shabbily, and had a small house and few servants, he would say to him, ' You are very economical, and must have saved a great deal, and can well afford to give the king a good sum of money.'

5. The Court of Star Chamber.—Another means which Henry adopted to keep down the nobles was by setting up the Court of Star Chamber. A hundred and

fifty years later this court became very cruel; but when
it was set up by Henry VII. it did much good.   The
nobles oppressed people around them, and prevented
them from getting justice in the courts when the
judges came round for the Assizes.   Juries would be
afraid to give honest verdicts for fear of giving offence
to the noblemen.   The Court of Star Chamber was

CIVIL AND MILITARY COSTUME ABOUT 1496.

made up of one of the judges and some of the king's
officers, who were not the least afraid of any nobleman in England.   When therefore any conspiracy
was heard of, or any riot or disturbance, a nobleman
who took part in it could be brought before this
court and fined and imprisoned as easily as if he had
been a farmer or a blacksmith.

6. Great Power of the King.—Henry VII. thus maintained himself on the throne. He gave to the English people the great thing that they wanted, peace and security. Yet he also gave them what in the long-run is not good for any people, the habit of seeing burdens placed on the rich instead of being placed justly and fairly on all in proportion to their means, and the habit of seeing the king do very much as he pleased. The fact is that now that the nobles were weakened, the people were not accustomed to act together. There were no newspapers to tell them what was going on all over the country, and those who lived in one county scarcely knew anything of what was happening in another. They were therefore content to trust the king, and this made the king strong enough to do a great deal of good. Unfortunately also it made him strong enough to do a great deal of harm, and the English people had afterwards to undergo many hardships to take away from the descendants of Henry VII. the power which they had allowed him to gain.

CHAPTER XVII.

THE FIRST YEARS OF HENRY VIII.

(1509—1529.)

1. Popularity of Henry.—The eldest son of Henry VII., Arthur, Prince of Wales, had died in his father's lifetime. The next brother succeeded as

Henry VIII., and married Arthur's widow, Catharine of Aragon. For some years he and the new queen

lived happily together. Henry VIII. was thoroughly popular. He was strong and active, could leap further and shoot an arrow nearer the mark than any one of his subjects. Bluff King Hal, as he was called, had a ready jest and a hearty word for all men. For some time he left the management of affairs of state to his minister, Cardinal Wolsey. But he had a strong will of his own; and whenever he gave himself the trouble to think about business, he knew better how to contrive to get what he wanted than the cleverest man in his dominions.

2. Wars on the Continent.—During the first years of his reign Henry took part in wars upon the Continent. The kings of France had grown strong since those miserable wars with the English had come to an end, and Spain, which had before been divided into several states, was now united into one state. During the reign of Henry VIII., Francis I., king of France, was almost always at war with Charles I., king of Spain, who was known as Charles V., because he was chosen emperor, and ruled over Germany by that title. Henry was afraid that one or the other would grow too strong, and always took the part of the one who happened to be weakest at the time. Wars conducted in this way were not likely to do good to any one.

3. Condition of the People.—All this while Henry's subjects at home were studying and thinking more than they had been able to do during the Wars of the Roses. In England, as in the rest of Europe, men read more than they had done for centuries, now that printing-presses were at work. Not only did they read more, but they read different things

Instead of studying lives of the saints, and religious books written by priests and monks, they read the old books written by the Greeks and Romans. Instead of thinking how men could best leave their fellow-men and pass their time in a monastery to prepare for heaven, they began to ask how they could best help their fellow-creatures here upon earth. There was certainly much need of thinking about this. It is true that the poor were no longer serfs as they had been in the days of Richard II., but they were very hardly treated. When the king went to war, he hired a large number of men to be his soldiers, and when he finished his war he turned them off. They had forgotten how to work, and unless they were ready to starve, they must procure food in some bad way. They robbed and murdered for a livelihood. The cruel laws of those days condemned every thief to be hanged. Thousands were put to death in the course of this reign, though the robberies and murders went on as before. In some respects the punishments made things worse. If a man committed a robbery he knew that he would be hanged if he were caught, and that he could not be more than hanged if he committed a murder. He therefore usually murdered the man he had robbed, to prevent his living to give evidence against him.

4. The Inclosures.—Another evil came from a change in the management of the land. Landlords found that they could get more money by selling wool than they could by selling corn, and they therefore turned a large quantity of land, which before had been ploughed for corn-land, into pasture-land on which to keep sheep. In this way a large number of men were thrown out of work, because one or two shepherds could look after a very large flock of sheep, whilst it would take several men to cultivate for corn the land on which the sheep were feeding. The men thus thrown out of work were often driven to live by robbery and murder like the discharged soldiery.

5. The Utopia and the Discovery of America.—It was long before remedies were found for these evils. One great and wise man, Sir Thomas More, wrote a book called 'Utopia,' in which he advised that the land should again be sown with corn, and that men should be helped to work that they might be kept out of temptation to rob, instead of being hanged after they had committed crimes. Great improvements cannot be made at once, but it was a good sign that some men were beginning to think how they could be made. As often happens, the way to improvement comes from something which does not at the time seem to have anything to do with it. In the reign of Henry VII., Columbus crossed the Atlantic Ocean and discovered America. As yet England gained no advantage by this. In 1492 Columbus discovered America for Spain. Scarcely any except Spanish ships sailed to the New World. Spaniards alone settled there, and carried to their own country the stores of gold and silver which were dug out of its mines. By-and-by England would have its share in the New World, and more than its share in the trade and commerce which sprung up from the intercourse between the Old World and the New. Men would find that as sailors, merchants, or manufacturers, they could find plenty to do which was as good as keeping sheep, and a good deal better than robbing and murdering.

6. **Beginning of the Reformation.**—Whilst some men were thinking how the poor could be made

ANNE BOLEYN.   THOMAS HOWARD,   CARDINAL WOLSEY.
                    THIRD DUKE NORFOLK.

better and happier, others were thinking about religion. Martin Luther taught in Germany that the religion which men had believed for many centuries was very different from the religion taught in the New Testament. After a little time those who followed Luther were called Protestants. A few people in England thought as Luther taught, but as yet they were not many. There were many more who did not wish to believe otherwise than they had believed before, but who thought that there was need of some change. Very few monks and nuns now lived as well as they had when the monasteries were first founded. Most of them were living idle, useless lives, and cared very little about more than the form of religion. Both they and many of the priests were extremely ignorant. Those who are idle and ignorant usually become vicious as well. Wolsey and the king himself wanted to alter this state of things. They thought that by founding schools and colleges and by spreading learning the clergy would become better.

7. **Henry quarrels with the Pope.**—After Henry had been married for some time he grew tired of his wife, Queen Catharine, and wanted to marry a sparkling young beauty named Anne Boleyn. He suddenly discovered that he had done wrong in marrying his brother's widow, and asked the pope to divorce him from Catharine, and to declare that he had never been lawfully married to her. The pope, Clement VII., could not make up his mind what to do. One of the old popes, when the popes were really great, would have done what he thought right, and would have borne the consequences. Clement was not brave enough for this. He was afraid to make an enemy of Henry, for fear lest Henry should turn Protestant. But he was also afraid of offending Catharine's nephew, the Emperor Charles, who had a large army in Italy. He therefore tried to put off giving any answer as long

as he possibly could. At last he sent orders to Cardinal Wolsey and another cardinal to hear what was to be said on both sides as the pope's legates or representatives. In 1529 their court was opened at Blackfriars. The queen threw herself at Henry's feet. Twice he tried in vain to raise her up. In her broken English she prayed him to have pity on her. She said she was a poor woman and a foreigner. For twenty years she had been his true and obedient wife. In the end she appealed to the pope himself, and declared that she would make answer to the pope only. The legates, however, did not at first take any heed to this, but went on with their inquiry. After a time, however, they gave out that it must be as she asked, and that the trial would be finished at Rome. Henry was very angry. He knew that the pope would be too much afraid of the emperor to decide as he wished.

8. **Fall of Wolsey.**—Wolsey was the first to suffer, as he had been one of the legates. He was turned out of office and his goods were taken from him on the pretence that he had been unfaithful to the king. Not long afterwards he was sent for to answer to a charge of treason. At Leicester, on his way to London, he was taken ill and died. ' If I had served God,' he said, ' as diligently as I have served the king, He would not have given me over in my grey hairs.'

CHAPTER XVIII.

THE LAST PART OF THE REIGN OF HENRY VIII. (1529–1547.)

1. The King's Divorce.—Henry was resolved that whether the pope were willing or not, he would be divorced from Catharine. He first tried to frighten the pope into doing what he wanted. When he found that he did not succeed he got the parliament to pass laws by which all matters relating to the Church were to be settled in England. The king then married Anne Boleyn. Thomas Cranmer, who perhaps believed that the king's marriage with Catharine was really unlawful, was made Archbishop of Canterbury, and held a court at Dunstable, where he pronounced sentence that the king had never been lawfully married at all. The King married Anne. Catharine refused to accept Cranmer's decision. She said that she had always been the king's wife, and that she was his wife still, unless the pope decided against her. 'I would rather,' she said, 'be a poor beggar's wife and be sure of heaven, than queen of all the world and stand in doubt thereof by reason of my own consent.' Henry treated her with contempt, and openly acknowledged Anne as his wife.

2. Henry burns the Protestants, and hangs or beheads the Catholics.—It was no longer possible for Henry even to pretend to be subject in any way to the pope. But he had not the least wish to become a Protestant, or to change either his religion or the religion of the people. He intended to make people more religious in the old way than the pope had been able to do. What he wanted was very much what most people in England wanted. Even those who thought that Catharine had been hardly treated were glad that the country should no longer be obliged to submit to the pope, who was an Italian foreigner. But they thought that the Church should be just as it had always been, and that no one should be allowed to teach Protestantism, which they considered to be heresy, and to be therefore certain to bring those who believed it to hell after they died. During the remainder of the reign most people were quite satisfied when Henry had people burnt alive as heretics for being Protestants, and hung others or beheaded them as traitors for saying that the pope was superior to the king in matters of religion.

3. Execution of Sir Thomas More.—The noblest of those who suffered as traitors was Sir Thomas More. He had been the first to think how to make the life of poor men and women happier and better. His own house was a place adorned with every virtue. He brought up his children in a way which was very unusual then. Both at that time and long afterwards it was generally supposed that the only way to drive knowledge into the heads of boys and girls was to flog them frequently and severely. Luther used to tell how he was once beaten at school fifteen times in one day. We hear of a young lady related to the Paston family that ' she hath since Easter the most part been beaten once in the week or twice, and sometimes twice in one day, and her head broken in two or three places.' More knew better. 'I have given you kisses enough,' he wrote to his children, 'but stripes hardly ever.' As is almost always the case, the gentle man was also the strong man, resolved to do his duty, and to die rather than to say what he believed to be untrue. Soon after the king's marriage with Anne Boleyn, parliament passed an act of succession, requiring all persons, asked by the king to do so, to swear that Henry's second marriage was lawful, and that any children which he and Anne might have would be the lawful successors to the Crown. More was sent for from Chelsea where he lived to come and swear. 'Whereas,' we are told, 'at other times, before he parted from his wife and children, they used to bring him to his boat, and he there kissing them bade them farewell; at this time he suffered none of them to follow him forth of his gate, but pulled the wicket after him, and with a heavy heart he took boat.' For some minutes he sat silently musing. There was a conflict in his mind whether he should yield or not. At last he gave a start and cried, 'I thank our Lord, the field is won.' He had trodden temptation under foot. When he came to Lambeth he was asked whether he would swear. He replied that he would willingly swear to acknowledge the children of Anne as lawful successors of the throne, because he believed that the king, with the consent of parliament, could settle this as he pleased. But he would not swear that Anne was Henry's lawful wife, because he did not believe that she was. Upon this answer he was sent a prisoner to the Tower. He had not been there long before another act of parliament was passed, the Treason Act, directing that every one who refused to give the king a title properly belonging to him was to be put to death as a traitor. One of these titles was that of Supreme Head of the Church of England, and this title More thought that he could not honestly give to Henry. He was brought to trial and condemned. He was carried to execution on Tower Hill. He was always fond of a jest, and he was merry and fearless to the end. 'See me safe up,' he said, when he was asked to mount the scaffold; 'for my coming down I can shift for myself.' After he had laid his head on the block he raised it again for an instant, and moved his beard away. 'Pity that should be cut,' he said, 'that has not committed treason.' The axe descended, and the head of the noblest Englishman of Henry's day was severed from his body.

4. **The Translation of the Bible.**—Far more important than anything else that Henry did was the translation of the Bible which he ordeied. He had little idea how great a change he was preparing when he gave orders that the Bible should be printed in English. He thought that people would learn from it to resist the pope, and he did not suspect that they were likely to find in it very different things from those which he himself believed. He little thought that from that book to which he appealed, his subjects would learn a higher faith and a purer virtue than his, and that they would gain a con-

fidence which would make them as determined to
resist kings as they were to resist popes, when
kings or popes ordered them to believe what they
thought was untrue, or to do what they though
was wrong.

5. The Suppression of the smaller Monasteries.—
Henry's habit of convincing himself that he wa
doing something very good when he was really doing
what he wanted to do for some selfish reason, appear
plainly in his dealing with the monasteries. He
wanted money sadly. His life was an expensive one,
and he was fond of gambling. A gambler is always
in want of money, and Henry's case was no exceptio1
to the rule. He suddenly became convinced that
the monks and nuns who lived in the smaller
monasteries were very wicked. Men were sent to
inquire whether it was so, and they reported that it
was quite true. Most probably there were many
monks and nuns who lived very badly. They were
no longer full of burning zeal to lead a monastic life,
as they had been some centuries before, and when a
number of people lead idle lives, they are very likely
to fall into mischief. But there can be little doubt
that the report spoke of them as much worse than
they were. An act of parliament was passed putting
an end to all monasteries which had less property
than 200*l.* a year, and giving all the money to the
king.

**6. Execution of Anne Boleyn and Death of Jane
Seymour.—**Before the seizure of the monasteries
happened, Henry had an heiress if not an heir to the
throne. Catharine's only surviving child, Mary, had

wanted his people to believe as they had always believed. But then he wanted to have their belief explained to them so that they should understand it better. Just before the Pilgrimage of Grace he had sent out such an explanation, and, as might be expected, the explanation was not quite the same as the pope would have given. The chief alteration, however, was in the matter of images. There were in all the churches images of saints, and figures of Christ upon the cross. Before these the people prayed. They were not intended to pray to the stone or wooden images, but only to be reminded by them of those whom they could not see. Ignorant people had, however, come to think of the image itself as something to be prayed to, and which could do them good. The king did not wish images to be destroyed because prayers were offered before them, but he determined to destroy those which were said to perform miracles, because he thought this was done by trickery. When the tricks were found out, they were exhibited to the people and the image was burned. It would have been well if only images had been burnt. One poor man, Friar Forest, was declared to be a heretic because he said that the king ought to be subject to the pope. He was placed in a cradle of chains hung upon a gallows. Underneath were the fragments of a great image which had been brought from Wales. Then Latimer, a brave honest man, who was afterwards to die a martyr's death, preached to him to convince him of his error. When the sermon was over he asked Forest whether he would live or die. 'I will die,' said Forest, boldly. 'Do your worst upon me. Seven years ago you durst not, for your life, have preached such words as these ; and now, if an angel from heaven should come down and teach me any other doctrine than that which I learnt as a child I would not believe him. Take me; cut me to pieces joint from joint. Burn, hang, do what you will, I will be true henceforth to my faith.' Light was set to the chips of the image beneath. Forest was swung over it, and the cruel flames ate his life away.

9. Henry's Tyranny.—Brave men there were on every side who were ready to die rather than say that the thing was true which they believed to be a lie. Since Wolsey's fall Henry had left the management of business in the hands of Thomas Cromwell. Cromwell wished to see England free from the pope, and to make his master all-powerful. He had no mercy nor pity. He covered the land with spies, who told him tales of all that was spoken against the king. No one could think himself safe. Heretics were burnt, and followers of the pope were hung. Nothing planned against him seemed to prosper. Noblemen formed plots against him, but their plots were detected, and they were brought to a traitor's death. One old lady, the Countess of Salisbury, refused to kneel down to place her head on the block. The executioner had to dash at her with his axe, and to cut off her head as she stood. It was a cruel time. At court, it was also a time when men spent money upon gaiety of every kind. Henry wanted money for his amusements, and for

plain and stout. Henry easily found an excuse to divorce her. Anne of Cleves, unlike Catharine of Aragon, took her divorce quietly, and Henry gave her a good pension, on which she lived comfortably for many years. He was savagely angry with Cromwell.

SHIP: TIME OF HENRY VIII.

As everybody hated Cromwell, the moment that it was known that Henry was tired of him he was accused of treason. A bill was brought into parliament to direct that his head should be cut off. The House refused to listen to anything that he might have to say in his own defence, and his tyranny ended on the scaffold. Henry had still some years to live. He married a fifth wife, Catharine Howard, but she, too, lost her head. His sixth wife, Catharine Parr, actually lived longer than he did. Of the last years of Henry's reign there is not much to tell. There was a war with France, and a war with Scotland. The Protestants were kept down by the Six Articles, but some slight changes took place in the services of the Church. The Lord's Prayer, the Creed, and the Commandments were translated into English, then the Litany was sent forth in English, and this was accompanied by other prayers to be used in English. The Mass, or service of the Holy Sacrament, was still said in Latin. When at last the king died, he had prepared the way for a greater change.

CHAPTER XIX.

EDWARD VI. AND MARY.

(EDWARD VI., 1547.   MARY, 1553.)

1. **The War in Scotland, and the new Prayer Book.**—Henry's son, Edward VI., was only a child when his father died. The country was governed by the young king's uncle, Edward Seymour, Duke of Somerset, who was called the Protector. Somerset was not a wise man. He had so many schemes in his head that he had no time to do anything properly. He went to war with Scotland, in order

to make the Scots give their young queen Mary
in marriage to Edward VI. He beat the Scots in
a battle at Pinkie, near Edinburgh, and burnt and
destroyed a great number of houses. The Scots
naturally grew angry, and sent their young queen

EDWARD VI.

to France, where she was married to the king's
eldest son. Somerset had also plenty to do at
home. He had the images which Henry had left
pulled down in the churches. In less than two
years after Henry's death, parliament ordered a new
Prayer Book in the English language to be read in
all the churches, and gave permission to clergymen

to marry, which had not been allowed before. All these changes shocked many people, and there was a rebellion in Devonshire and Cornwall, which was only put down with great difficulty.

2. Seizure of Church Property.—Somerset was not a man likely to gain the confidence of the people. He seems really to have wished to do what he thought right, but he was also very anxious to make himself and his friends rich. Henry VIII. had set the bad example of dividing the lands of the monasteries amongst the lords whom he favoured. When the lands of the monasteries had been divided, the next thing was to take what belonged to the churches. Somerset was building for himself a great house in the Strand in London, which was called Somerset House from his name. In order to make room for it he pulled down a church and blew up a chapel with gunpowder. At the same time, he dug up part of a churchyard and carried away the bodies of the dead to make room for houses and shops.

3. Somerset's Fall.—It was not long before the Protector had fresh difficulties to meet. The rich landowners went on inclosing land to keep sheep on, and turning out the people who used to be busy in ploughing and sowing for corn. There was great ill-feeling, and in Norfolk there was a rebellion headed by Ket, a tanner. His followers pulled down the palings of the inclosures in all the country round. Somerset pitied the men in rebellion, but he did not know how to help them, though he did not like to attack them. The other great men who were about him had no pity at all for the poor.

They sent soldiers to Norfolk under the command of John Dudley, Earl of Warwick, who had no pity, and soon put down the rebellion. Then they took the protectorate away from Somerset, and not long afterwards they accused him of trying to get power again. He was convicted and executed.

EDWARD SEYMOUR,
DUKE OF SOMERSET.

CRANMER.

JOHN DUDLEY,
DUKE OF NORTHUMBERLAND.

4. Northumberland's Government.—The government fell into the hands of the Earl of Warwick, who was soon afterwards made Duke of Northumberland. He was a selfish, wicked man. He pretended to be very pious and to do all he could for the Protestants. A second Prayer Book was sent out which was much more Protestant than the one prepared at the beginning of the reign. He and his friends plundered the country. They put money into their own pockets which ought to have been used to pay the men who had worked for the king. Their evil example was widely followed. ' The people of this country,' said a preacher at this time, ' say that their gentlemen and officers were never so full of fair words and ill deeds as now they be.' To numbers of men in England Protestantism seemed to have brought nothing with it but the villainy and rascality which stained the greedy men who were in power. Yet even in this evil time the new faith was bearing better fruit. Latimer, a bold preacher of righteousness, told great lords to their faces that they ought not only to be ashamed of their wickedness, but that they ought to make restitution to the poor of all that they had taken from them by trickery or violence. In many towns the merchants and shopkeepers gave money to found schools, which should be open freely to the poor.

5. **Death of Edward VI., and Accession of Mary.—** Edward VI. was a sickly lad. He died of consumption before he grew to be a man. Before he died, Northumberland persuaded him to leave the crown to his cousin, Lady Jane Grey, who was a Protestant. He had no more right to leave it to her than Edward the Confessor had had to appoint William of Normandy as his successor. The whole people rallied round Edward's eldest sister Mary. When Northumberland went out to oppose her in the name of Queen Jane, his own men threw their caps into the air and shouted, ' God save Queen Mary !' Mary

entered London in triumph. Jane was sent to the Tower as a prisoner, and Northumberland had his head cut off as a traitor.

LADY JANE GREY

6. The first Years of Queen Mary.—Mary at once put an end to the use of the new English Prayer Book. Many more people in England disliked it than liked it, and the old service which had been used when the English Church obeyed the pope was brought back again. But there were many people in England who were glad to see the old service, who did not wish to submit to the pope. Some of these liked Englishmen to settle their own affairs without having to give way to any one who, like the pope, was not

M

an Englishman, and did not live in England. Others, who had got fields and houses which had once belonged to the monasteries, were afraid lest if they submitted to the pope he would make them give up what they had taken. Mary, however, was determined that the Church of England should again be

QUEEN MARY.

put under the pope, though she knew that she would have to wait some time before she could persuade parliament to allow it. She made up her mind to marry her cousin Philip, who not long afterwards became king of Spain, and was the son of the emperor Charles V. The marriage was very unpopular. There was a rebellion, and though it was put down, the queen was so afraid of another that she had the head of poor innocent Lady Jane Grey cut off, and sent her own sister Elizabeth a prisoner to the Tower. Soon after her marriage, the queen persuaded the parliament once more to acknowledge the pope's authority over the Church, and to make a law by which heretics who refused to accept his belief were to be burnt alive. The members of parliament, however, insisted that the lands which had been taken from the Church should remain the property of those who had possession of them. They were more careful about their own possessions than about the lives of their fellow-subjects.

7. The Protestant Martyrs.—Whilst lords and gentlemen were thinking more of money and land than of religion, there were Protestant martyrs who died as bravely for their faith as Sir Thomas More had died for his. Rowland Taylor, for instance, a Suffolk clergyman, was condemned in London to be burnt, and was sent down to his own county to die. As he left his prison, in the dark early morning, he found his wife and his children waiting for him in the streets. One of his daughters cried out, ' O, my dear father! Mother, mother! here is my father led away!' There were no gas-lamps burn-ing in the streets in those days, and his wife could not see him. ' Rowland, Rowland!' she called out, ' where art thou?' 'Dear wife,' he answered, ' I am here.' He was allowed to stop for a moment, and he knelt down with his family on the stones to say the Lord's Prayer. ' Farewell, my dear wife,' he said, as soon as he had risen from his knees; ' be of good comfort, for I am quiet in my conscience God shall stir up a father for my children.' He was led away to the village in Suffolk where his voice had once been heard in the pulpit. 'Thanked be God,' he said, when he reached the place where the stake rose amidst the faggots which were to burn him, 'I am even at home.' After he was tied to the stake, a wretch threw a faggot at his face. ' O, friend,' he said gently, 'I have harm enough, what needed that?' Light was set to the wood, the flames blazed up around the suffering body, and Rowland Taylor entered into his rest. Many another, as brave and as trustful, shared his fate. Amongst them two bishops, the meek Ridley, and Latimer, the bold preacher of righteousness, were burnt at Oxford. ' Be of good comfort, Master Ridley,' cried Latimer from amidst the flames. 'Play the man; we shall this day light such a candle, by God's grace, in England, as I trust shall never be put out.'

8. The last Days of Mary.—Latimer spoke truly. Cranmer followed him to the stake at Oxford. The best and firmest of the Protestants were marked out for death. It availed nothing. Men turned against a religion which was protected by such means. Mary's government was as weak as it was harsh. To please her husband, Philip, she joined him in a war with France, and the French suddenly attacked Calais. She had left the place without proper means of defence, and the fortress which had been held by England since the days of Edward III. was lost for ever. Not long afterwards Mary died, worn out and dispirited. She knew that her sister

Elizabeth would succeed her, and that her sister
would not burn Protestants. Mary's reign was the
last in which the authority of the pope over the
English Church was acknowledged by an English
parliament.

CHAPTER XX.

THE FIRST YEARS OF ELIZABETH.

(1558—1580.)

*GENEALOGICAL TABLE OF DESCENDANTS OF
HENRY VII.*

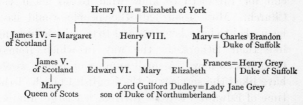

1. **Elizabeth and the Nation.**—When Elizabeth
heard of her sister's death she was sitting under a
tree in Hatfield Park. 'It is the Lord's doing,' she
said: 'it is marvellous in our eyes.' She was to be
Queen of England now, instead of being liable to be
sent as a prisoner to the Tower, and perhaps to have
her head cut off at last. Almost all Englishmen
felt as if they too had been let out of prison. There
were to be no more men and women burnt alive,
nor were Englishmen to be sent abroad to fight for
the King of Spain any longer. Elizabeth was determined that in her time foreigners should not meddle
with the government of England. The King of

Spain and the King of France were both very
powerful sovereigns, and each of them had large
armies, whilst Elizabeth had no regular army at all.
But she knew that as they hated one another more
than they hated her, the King of France would never
allow the King of Spain to conquer England, and that
the King of Spain would never allow the King of
France to conquer England. She therefore believed
that she would be quite safe from either of them.
She made peace with France, and attended to her
own affairs.

2. Elizabeth and the Church.—It was more difficult for Elizabeth to know what to do about the
Church. More than half the people would have
been glad to have been allowed to go on worshipping
like their fathers, in the way in which Roman
Catholics do now. A small number of people would
have liked the services of the English Church of the
time of Edward VI. to be revived. A large number
of people, who came to be called Puritans, would
have been glad to worship as Protestants did on the
Continent, very much in the way in which Dissenters
do now. Elizabeth was afraid to let either the
Roman Catholics or the Puritans have their way.
She wanted to keep the peace, and she was quite
sure that if either of these had all the churches,
those who were not allowed to have the churches
would try to get them by force. She did not think
of letting both have churches to themselves, as is
done now. She was afraid lest there should be
quarrels amongst them, and she therefore wished
that all men should worship in only one way, and

she hoped that they would learn to be friendly with one another, instead of persecuting one another. She found that Parliament was ready to agree with her in this, and so the Prayer Book which had been made at the end of the reign of Edward VI. was altered a little, and ordered to be used in all churches. No other sort of service was to be permitted anywhere. The bishops who had placed themselves under the Pope in Mary's time were deprived of their bishoprics, and new ones were consecrated. There was to be no inquiry to find out what men believed, or any attempt to punish them for believing either the Roman Catholic or any other doctrine. But the Queen expected that every one should go to church.

3. The Reformation in Scotland.—Elizabeth had a rival in Mary Queen of Scots. Mary was very beautiful and very clever. She had been married to the King of France. Whilst she was away, Scotland was ruled by her mother as Regent. A large number of the Scottish people turned Protestant, and insisted on putting an end to the Roman Catholic worship in Scotland, whilst the Scottish nobles wanted to seize the lands of the clergy for themselves. The Regent, to prevent this, sent for some French soldiers. Elizabeth, who was afraid lest, if the French soldiers conquered Scotland, they would try to conquer England too, sent an army to Scotland, and drove the French out. Soon after this the Regent died. Mary's husband died about the same time, and she came back as a young widow to rule in Scotland. Though she was herself a firm Roman Catholic, the Protestants were so many

that she was obliged to allow her subjects to do as
they pleased about religion. Elizabeth was not likely
to be well pleased with having a Roman Catholic
queen so near her, and was therefore not displeased
that the Scottish people differed in their religion
from their own Queen, as this might make them
less ready to help her against England.

4. Mary Queen of Scots in Scotland.—Elizabeth
was the more afraid of Mary because the Queen of
Scots was not merely a Roman Catholic, but claimed
to have a right to be Queen of England as well as of
Scotland. She was the granddaughter of the eldest
sister of Henry VIII.; and she said that, as Elizabeth's mother, Anne Boleyn, had never been properly
the wife of Henry, Elizabeth had no right to the
throne. Elizabeth was therefore not sorry to hear
that Mary before long got into trouble at home.
She married a foolish cousin of hers named Lord
Darnley, and one night the house in which Darnley
was sleeping was blown up with gunpowder. He
managed to escape, but he was killed in the garden
as he was running away. It cannot be said with
certainty whether Mary ordered the murder or not,
but almost every one in Scotland thought that she
did. Her subjects took her prisoner, and shut her
up in Loch Leven Castle. She managed, however,
to escape, and found some friends ready to fight for
her. But she was beaten, and had to fly for her life
to England. When she arrived there, she sent to
ask Elizabeth to help her to the throne again.

5. Mary Queen of Scots in England.—It was not
very likely that Elizabeth would do that. She was

afraid lest the English Roman Catholics might rebel against herself, and set up Mary for their queen. She therefore put Mary in confinement, giving her in charge to the owners of one country house after another, with directions not to let her escape.

6. The Rising in the North.—The captivity of Mary did not bring peace to Elizabeth. The Pope declared the Queen to be a heretic, and ordered her subjects to refuse obedience to her. Many of the English lords were friendly to Mary. The Duke of Norfolk wanted to marry her, and to share her claim to the English throne. In the north of England most of the people, as well as the lords, were longing to see the old religion restored, as in the days of Henry VIII. they had longed to see the monasteries restored. There was a great rebellion, known as the Rising in the North. The rebels trooped into Durham Cathedral, tore up the Bible and Prayer Book, and found a priest to say mass once more. It was the last time that mass was ever said in any one of the old cathedrals of England. But the greater number of the English Catholics refused to fight against Elizabeth. Her troops put down the rebellion without difficulty. She was usually merciful; but she was too frightened to be merciful now, and large numbers of the rebels were pitilessly hanged. Not long afterwards she learned that there was a plot to assassinate her, and that there had been some talk of sending a Spanish army to England, to put Mary in her place. She discovered that Norfolk knew of this, and she had Norfolk tried and executed.

7. Prosperity of the Country.—Englishmen were

the more ready to support Elizabeth because the
country was prospering. There was more trade
than there had ever been before, because Elizabeth
kept her people at peace with other nations.
Men learned to farm better than they had done,
and to manufacture cloth at home instead of buying
it from abroad. The vessels which carried English
productions abroad were very small, no larger than
coasting vessels are now, but they were manned
with hardy seamen. Almost every one had a share
in this increase of wealth. Gentlemen decked
themselves in gorgeous attire, and wore silks and
velvets of brilliant colours. Other ranks profited
in a more sensible way. Meat was eaten where salt
fish had been eaten before, and men were all the
healthier for it. Houses were built with chimneys
instead of holes in the roof, to let the smoke out.
Beds were provided with pillows, which a little time
before had been used only by sick people. In the
reign of Henry VII. the great Earl of Northumberland, when he left one of his houses for a time, took
care to have the glass of the windows taken down
and packed away, because glass was far too rare and
precious to be left to the chance of being broken.
In Elizabeth's time the use of glass was becoming
common. Even for those who had no money to buy
glass or pillows something was done. At first col-
lections of money were made in churches for honest
people who were too old or too sick to work; and
after a time there was a law, known as the Poor Law,
ordering that each parish should provide for all who
were ready to work, but could not find work to do

Nobody was to be allowed to starve, and no one who robbed or cheated was to be able to say with truth that he could not keep himself alive in any other way.

8. Ill-feeling against Spain. — All this prosperity made Englishmen honour Elizabeth. At the same time, they disliked Spain more and more every year. Philip II., the King of Spain, who had been the husband of Queen Mary of England, ruled over many countries in Europe, and did all that he could to prevent any one in them from becoming a Protestant. In the Netherlands he had so many people burnt, and he made his subjects pay such heavy taxes, that at last some of them rose in rebellion. Philip had large and brave armies, and he did his best to put down the rebellion. His soldiers and generals were very cruel, and when they took a town they massacred the men and women in it. But the rebels struggled on, and by-and-by there was a free Dutch Republic which Philip could not conquer. The stories of Philip's cruelty were told in England, and set Englishmen against him. Many Englishmen began to think that it was a righteous thing to attack a king who did such things, and they were not at all sorry that there was plenty to be got by attacking him successfully. Besides the countries which he governed in Europe, he had many lands in America, and in these lands there were rich silver mines, from which a large fleet came with silver for him every year. English sailors paid little respect to Philip. They sailed amongst the West India Islands, which belonged to Spain, and bought and sold though he forbade them. Many of them sold poor negroes, whom they had taken prisoners in Africa, without thinking that they were doing anything wrong. Sometimes they attacked and plundered Spanish vessels. Philip whenever he caught them threw them into prison, and sometimes had them treated very badly, because they were Protestants. Though there was no open war against Spain, many Englishmen hated the Spaniards so, that they thought it would be doing a good work to carry off some of all this wealth to England; and all English sailors believed that it was quite fair to fight the Spaniards in America, whether there was war in Europe or not. One of these sailors was Francis Drake. He was born in Devonshire, and the Devonshire sailors were bold and active men. In 1572 he found his way to the New World, landed at Panama, and seized a large quantity of silver. Before he returned he caught sight of the Pacific, threw himself on his knees, and prayed to God that he might one day sail on that sea, where no Englishman had ever sailed before.

10. Drake's Voyage.— Five years later Drake sailed again from Plymouth. He had with him five vessels, so small that they were manned by no more than 164 men. When he reached the Straits of Magellan he knew no better than to pass through that dangerous passage, where the storm-wind blows in wild gusts in the windings of the channel. It was the only way to the Pacific then known, as it was believed that Terra del Fuego was the northern end of a great continent reaching to the South Pole. When Drake's own vessel, the Pelican, at last entered the open sea, it was alone. The other four little vessels had either been sunk or had been driven back.

Drake was not discouraged. He knew that all Chili and Peru was Spanish, and that nobody there was expecting him or preparing for defence. He sailed

into the harbour of Valparaiso, and found there a huge Spanish ship. The Spanish sailors did not fancy it possible that any English vessel could find its way there, and they made ready to feast the men whom they fancied must be their own countrymen. The English sailors sprang on board and seized the ship. They found in it wedges of gold weighing 400 lbs., which were soon carried to the Pelican. Drake then sailed on to Tarapaca. He found piles of silver bars upon the quay, and tumbled them into his boats. Just as he was going to row away, down came a string of llamas to the quay with another load of silver. Much more was got as Drake sailed up the coast, silver and gold and jewels. At last Drake, having enriched himself and his men, went on towards the north. He fancied that North America would come to an end much sooner than it really does, as no one had made discoveries so far north. When he reached California, he thought that he had gone far enough, and sailed home across the Pacific Ocean and round the Cape of Good Hope. He was the first Englishman who had ever sailed round the world. The Spaniards called him a pirate, and required Elizabeth to deliver him up to them or to punish him, but Elizabeth was proud of his daring, and knighted him. He was now known as Sir Francis Drake.

11. **English Voyages of Discovery.**---Even in those days of fighting English sailors were not all occupied in war and piracy. In the time of Henry VII. a Venetian, named Cabot, was sent out from England, and discovered the coast of Labrador. He was the first man to set foot on the Continent of America, though Columbus had landed on the West India Islands before. In the reign of Henry VIII. the cod fisheries of Newfoundland were visited by English sailors. But the object on which the hearts of adventurous

men was most set was the discovery of a short cut to India and China. In Mary's time Sir Hugh Willoughby sailed round the North of Norway, hoping to reach those wealthy regions in that way, but was frozen to death with all the men in his own ship, though Chancellor, with one of the other ships which had gone with him, reached Archangel, and thus opened a trade with Russia, which at that time did not reach either the Baltic or the Black Sea, and which could therefore only be communicated with through the White Sea. In Elizabeth's time many sailors tried to find their way to India and China through what they called the North-West Passage, which they thought would be found where the northern part of the Continent of America really is, as no one had been further north than the coast of Labrador. Martin Frobisher discovered the strait which leads into Hudson's Bay, and fancied that he had not only discovered the way to India, but had found rich mines of gold. Men were so anxious to find gold that they were ready to believe that it was not far off for the oddest reasons. One reason which Frobisher's men gave for thinking that they would find gold was that they had seen a great many spiders; and they said that 'spiders were true signs of great store of gold.' Frobisher found no gold; but he left his name to the strait which he had discovered; and a few years later the strait which leads into Baffin's Bay was discovered by John Davis, and was named after him. Sir Humphrey Gilbert, Raleigh's half-brother, sailed to found a colony where the northern part of the

United States are now. His men quarrelled with him and with one another, and he had to set sail home. His vessel, the 'Squirrel,' was scarcely more than a boat, being only of ten tons burthen. A storm rose, and one of the vessels which accompanied him came so near that those who were on board could hear what he said. 'Heaven,' he cried out cheerfully, 'is as near by sea as by land.' That night his friends could see the lights of the little 'Squirrel' rocking on the tempestuous waves. On a sudden they disappeared, and neither the brave old man nor his crew were seen again. Other efforts to colonise were made. Raleigh himself sent men to settle in what has from that time been known as Virginia, called after Elizabeth, the Virgin Queen. But they all died or were killed by the Indians. Other explorers followed; but no English colony was permanently settled in America till after Elizabeth's death.

CHAPTER XXI.

ELIZABETH'S TRIUMPHS.

(1580–1588.)

1. The Roman Catholic Missionaries.—Almost at the same time that Drake came back from his voyage some men of a very different kind set foot in England. As Elizabeth had now been Queen for more than twenty years, and young men and women were growing up who had no recollection of the days when the mass had been said in England in Mary's reign, those who believed that the Roman Catholic religion was true were very sad at seeing the number of Protestants increasing. Many earnest men who believed this had gone abroad, and now returned as missionaries. Elizabeth was much frightened. She knew that the Pope had declared her not to be the true Queen of England, and she feared lest, if these missionaries converted many people to be Roman Catholics, they would drive her off her throne and perhaps put her to death. So she and the Parliament made fierce laws against the missionaries. If any Roman Catholic priest converted any one to his faith, or even only said mass, he was to be put to death as a traitor ; because the Protestants believed that nobody could be a loyal subject to the Queen who thought that the Pope had a right to depose her, and they did not doubt that all Roman Catholics thought that. Even the Roman Catholics who were not priests had to pay a great deal of money if they did not go to the Protestant churches, and a great many were put in prison and treated very cruelly.

2. **Throgmorton's Plot and the Association.**—When a number of men are ill-treated, there are usually some who will try anything, however wicked, to revenge themselves on their persecutors. Most of the Roman Catholics bore their sufferings bravely and patiently, but there were some who wanted to murder the Queen and to place Mary Queen of Scots on the throne. One man named Francis Throgmorton formed such a plan. He was found out, and executed. It was discovered that the Spanish ambassador knew of this plot, and Elizabeth at once

ordered him to leave the kingdom. The House of Commons was very eager to prevent any new attempt to kill Elizabeth. The members bound themselves in an Association, engaging that if Elizabeth were killed they would put to death not only her murderers, but also any person for whose advantage she might be murdered. They meant that if Elizabeth were murdered they would kill Mary Queen of Scots. They thought that after this none of Mary's friends would bring her into danger by trying to kill Elizabeth. The paper on which this engagement was written was sent about to all parts of England, and was signed by a very large number of Englishmen. English people do not like assassination, and Throgmorton's plot had much to do with setting a great many people against the Pope.

3. Help sent to the Dutch.—It was not only in England that murders were committed in the name of religion. In the Netherlands, where the Dutch had been fighting bravely against Philip, their great leader, the Prince of Orange, whose great-grandson was one day to come to deliver England, had been murdered by a Roman Catholic. His son was only a boy, and Elizabeth sent soldiers to help the Dutch. She sent to command them a foolish, selfish man, of whom she was very fond, Robert Dudley, Earl of Leicester, the son of that wicked Duke of Northumberland who had ruled England in the time of Edward VI. Besides, she did not pay her soldiers, they came to help. This expedition cost the life of Sir Philip Sydney. He was a young man, but was already well known as a writer of prose and verse, a brave soldier and a courteous gentleman. When he was wounded, a cup of water was brought him to quench his thirst. He saw a common soldier lying in agony near, and bade him drink the water 'Your need,' he said, 'is greater than mine.'

4. **Drake in the West Indies.**—Whilst English soldiers were throwing away their lives uselessly in

ROBERT DEVEREUX,
EARL OF ESSEX.

WILLIAM CECIL,
LORD BURGHLEY.

ROBERT DUDLEY,
EARL OF LEICESTER.

the Netherlands, Drake had sailed for the West Indies with a fine fleet. He attacked and took St. Domingo, and refused to leave it till a large sum of money had been paid. He then sailed to Cartagena and forced the inhabitants to pay him 30,000l. The yellow fever broke out in his ships and he had to sail home. He had taught the King of Spain that,

for all his great navy, his towns were at the mercy
of the bold English sailors.

**5. The Babington Conspiracy and the Execution of
the Queen of Scots.**—Englishmen were growing less
afraid of the King of Spain than they had ever been;
but they were growing more afraid of plots to murder
the Queen. In the year in which Drake came
home there was a new one. Anthony Babington,
with some other young men, most of whom were in
the Queen's service, and who would therefore have
no difficulty in getting near her, proposed to assassinate Elizabeth. The plot was, however, found out
in time, and the conspirators were executed. Their
object had been to put Mary on the throne. Thousands of Englishmen had come to believe that, as
long as Mary lived, Elizabeth's life would never be
in safety. Elizabeth's own ministers thought so too.
They declared that they had found letters written
by Mary in which she gave her approval to the plot.
It is not certain whether this was true or not. At
all events Mary was taken to Fotheringay in Northamptonshire, and was there tried and beheaded.

6. Drake singes the King of Spain's Beard.—Englishmen were almost all now on the side of Elizabeth.
They did not like murderers, and the attempts to
assassinate the Queen made many people turn
against the Church of Rome. Englishmen were
also determined to defend their island against invasion, and they now heard that Philip was going to
send an enormous fleet and army to conquer England, and to make it submit to the Pope. In 1587
Drake was off again. He soon heard that a great

fleet was in Cadiz harbour preparing for an attack upon England. He sailed right into the harbour, in spite of shot from the Spanish batteries, and set fire to the store ships, which were laden with provisions for the fleet. He then steered round Cape St. Vincent, and northward along the Portuguese coast, burning every vessel he could catch. When he reached home he boasted that he had singed the King of Spain's beard. He thought that the great fleet would hardly get a fresh store of provisions together in time to enable it to come to England that year.

7. The Sailing of the Armada.—Drake was right. It was not till next year that the great fleet, the Invincible Armada, as the Spaniards called it, was able to sail. It was intended to go up the Channel, and to take on board a Spanish army commanded by Philip's great general, the Duke of Parma, which was waiting on the coast of Flanders. The Spaniards hoped that if it could succeed in landing them in England, Elizabeth would not be able to make a long resistance. Elizabeth did not fear. She had no regular army, and scarcely any regular navy, but she called on every Englishman who could bear arms to come forward to defend his native land. Scarcely a man refused. The Catholics were as forward as the Protestants. Elizabeth reviewed her troops at Tilbury. ' My loving people,' she said, ' we have been persuaded by some that are careful of our safety to take heed how we commit ourselves to armed multitudes, for fear of treachery ; but I assure you I do not desire to live to distrust my faithful and loving people. Let tyrants fear! I have always so behaved myself that, under God, I have placed my chiefest strength and safeguard in the loyal hearts and good will of my subjects; and therefore am I come amongst you, as you see, at this time—to lay down my life for my God, and for my kingdom, and for my people, my honour and my blood, even in the dust. I know I have the body but of a weak and feeble woman; but I have the heart of a king, and of a King of England too, and think foul scorn that Parma or Spain, or any prince of Europe, should dare to invade the borders of my realm.' Was it strange that when Elizabeth spoke such words as these thousands of her subjects were ready to die in her cause, which was their own as well as hers?

When the news that the Spaniards were indeed on the way, reached England, the warning was carried by lighting up the beacons which then stood on every hill-top to tell by their flames that an enemy was coming, and that every man must gird on his sword to fight for his country.

Night sunk upon the dusky beach, and on the purple sea,
Such night in England ne'er had been, nor e'er again shall be.
From Eddystone to Berwick bounds, from Lynn to Milford Bay,
The time of slumber was as bright and busy as the day;
For swift to east and swift to west the ghastly war-flame spread,
High on St. Michael's Mount it shone: it shone on Beachy Head.
Far on the deep the Spaniard saw along each Southern shire,
Cape beyond cape, in endless range, those twinkling points of fire.

8. The Armada in the Channel.—The commander of the English fleet was Lord Howard of Effingham. He was at Plymouth with a few of the Queen's ships and a number of small merchant vessels, which were ready to fight as well as the Queen's ships. Drake was there too. When the Spanish ships came in sight, the captains were playing a game of bowls. Drake would not hear of stopping the game. 'There is time enough,' he said, 'to finish our game and to beat the Spaniards too.' The huge Spanish ships,

SHIPS OF WAR, TIME OF ELIZABETH.

towering above the waves, swept by in the form of a half moon. When they had passed, the active little English vessels put out, sailing two feet to their one, getting rapidly out of their way, and coming back again as they pleased. The Spanish ships could neither sail away from them nor catch them. Up the Channel sailed the ships of the Armada, firing and being fired at as they went. So high were they that their shot often passed over the heads of the English sailors. One of the Spanish ships blew up, and two or three others were taken. The rest sailed on as they best could, unable to shake off their assailants, like a bear pursued by a swarm of wasps. At last the Spaniards reached the friendly French port of Calais. They had found out that the conquest of England was no child's play.

9. The Armada in the North Sea.—Lord Howard and his captains knew that it would not be safe to leave the Armada long at Calais. Parma and his soldiers were waiting for it in Flanders, prevented from stirring by the Dutch ships which were off the coast, but ready to embark in some large boats which they had got ready, as soon as the Armada came to beat off the Dutch. The English captains determined to drive the Armada out to sea again. They took eight of their own vessels, smeared them with pitch, and let them drift with the tide at night time amongst the enemy's fleet. When these vessels were close to the Spaniards, the few men who had been left on board set them on fire, and, jumping into their boats, rowed away. The sudden blaze in the dark night terrified the Spaniards. The Spanish commander, the Duke of Medina-Sidonia, gave the signal of flight. His men cut the cables by which they were anchored, and sailed away. The wind now rose to a storm. The English fleet followed, hastening their foemen's pace with showers of shot. The Spaniards found it impossible to stop, and the great ships were soon driven past the long low coast on which Parma's army was waiting for their protection in vain. If the wind had not changed a little, they would have been wrecked on the coast of Holland. Every day one or other of their floating castles was either driven on shore or pierced with English shots. Drake was in high spirits. 'There was never anything pleased me better,' he wrote to a comrade, 'than seeing the enemy flying with a southerly wind to the northwards. God grant ye have a good eye to the Duke of Parma ; for with the grace of God, if we live, I doubt not ere it be long so to handle the matter with the Duke of Sidonia as he shall wish himself at St. Mary Port among his orange-trees.' After a few days more even Drake had had enough. He had shot away all his powder, and as he heard the wind howling through his rigging, he knew that no Spaniard would venture back to try what more English sailors might have to offer them.

10. The Destruction of the Armada.—The Armada perished by a mightier power than that of man. The storm swept it far to the north. Of the hundred and fifty sail which had put out from Spain, a hundred and twenty were still afloat when they were left by their English pursuers. But they were in a bad case. Provisions were running short, and large numbers of the men were sick and dying. Masts were split and sails were torn by shot and storm. At last they rounded the Orkneys, and tried to make their way home round Scotland and Ireland. One great ship was wrecked on the Isle of Mull. The natives, savage as they then were, set fire to it and burnt it with its crew. The rest made their way along the west coast of Ireland. Not a few were driven on shore on the high cliffs against which the Atlantic ocean rolls its waves without a break on this side of America. Most of the Spaniards who reached the shore and fell into the hands of the English were put to death. Those who fell into the hands of the Irish were also butchered for the sake of plunder. The greater part were swallowed up by the sea. 'When I was at Sligo,' wrote an Englishman, 'I numbered on one strand of less than five miles in length, eleven hundred dead bodies of men, which the sea had driven upon the shore. The country people told me the like was in other places, though not to the like number.' Fifty-four vessels, with nine or ten thousand sick and suffering men on board, were all that succeeded in struggling home to Spain. Philip was struck to the heart at his failure, shut himself up in his room, and for a time would speak to no one. Yet when the beaten Admiral arrived, he did not reproach him. 'I sent you to fight against men,' he said, 'and not with the winds.' Elizabeth, too, acknowledged that her triumph was not owing to herself, or even to her sailors. She went in state to St. Paul's, to return thanks for the victory which had been gained, and she struck a medal which bore the motto, 'God blew with His wind, and they were scattered.'

CHAPTER XXII.

THE LAST YEARS OF ELIZABETH.

(1588-1603)

1. Continuance of War with Spain.—Elizabeth reigned for fifteen more years after the defeat of the Armada. Spain was unable to protect its trade and its colonies in America. Spanish towns were sacked, and Spanish wealth was carried off to England. The Spaniards were brave men, and fought hard. Drake died in the West Indies, on one of his plundering expeditions.

2. Death of Sir Richard Grenville.—The most heroic death in the whole war was that of Sir Richard Grenville. His little ship, the 'Revenge,' was one of six which were overtaken at the Azores by fifty-three Spanish ships, some of them of enormous size. Five of his comrades fled, as they well might, before such odds. Grenville refused to fly. The little 'Revenge' fought all alone through the whole of the afternoon. Our own living poet has told the story, speaking as if he had been one of that valiant crew.

And the sun went down, and the stars came out, far over the
 summer sea,
But never for a moment ceased the fight of the one and the
 fifty-three.
Ship after ship, the whole night long, their high-built galleons
 came ;
Ship after ship, the whole night long, with her battle-thunder
 and flame,

Ship after ship, the whole night long, drew back with her dead
    and her shame;
For some were sunk, and many were shatter'd, and so could fight
    no more.
God of battles! was ever a battle like this in the world before?

Through the whole of that night the one English
vessel, with but a hundred fighting men to begin
with, fought the fifty-three Spanish ships.

And the night went down, and the sun smiled out, far over the
    summer sea,
And the Spanish fleet, with broken sides, lay round us, all in a
    ring:
But they dared not touch us again, for they fear'd that we still
    could sting.
So they watch'd what the end would be,
And we had not fought them in vain.
But in perilous plight were we,
Seeing forty of our poor hundred slain,
And half of the rest of us maim'd for life
In the crash of the cannonades, and the desperate strife;
And the sick men down in the hold were most of them stark
    and cold
And the pikes were all broken and bent, and the powder was all
    of it spent,
And the masts and the rigging were lying over the side.

The little 'Revenge' could hold out no longer.
Grenville himself, like all his men who remained
alive, was sore wounded, and the Spaniards rushed
on board his ship, and took it.   They carried Grenville to one of their own vessels to die.   His last
words were befitting one who had fought so well.
'Here die I, Richard Grenville,' he said, 'with a joy-
ful and a quiet mind; for that I have ended my life as
a good soldier ought to do, who has fought for his
country and his queen, for his honour and religion.'

3. The Expedition to Cadiz.—After this a great expedition was sent to Cadiz. The command was given to Lord Howard of Effingham and the young Earl of Essex, who was now the Queen's favourite, a dashing young man, who was too vain and impatient to do anything really great. Essex was always wanting to get renown by some great warlike exploit. He was angry when any one said that there had been fighting enough, and that it was time to make peace with Spain. One day, when he was talking in this way, the wise old Lord Burghley, who had been Elizabeth's minister all through the reign, opened a Bible and showed him the words, ' Bloody and deceitful men shall not live out half their days.' On board this fleet was Sir Walter Raleigh, who could do anything he chose to put his hand to. When the fleet reached Cadiz, it found about seventy or eighty armed Spanish ships under the walls, ready to defend the town. The town itself was protected with fortifications, on which guns were mounted. The English fleet dashed in, each captain eagerly trying to thrust his ship into the foremost place. The Spaniards took fright. The soldiers who had been on board their ships hurried on shore 'as thick as if coals had been poured out of a sack.' They set fire to their own ships, and the great Spanish fleet was soon in a blaze. The town was then taken, and plundered and burnt.

4. Essex in Ireland. — As Essex was always asking to be allowed to command an army somewhere, the Queen gave him some work to do which was harder even than the taking of Cadiz.

Ireland had never been really conquered. A small district round Dublin obeyed the English law, but the rest of the people lived in their own way, governed by their own chiefs. Elizabeth had been afraid lest the Spaniards should take it, and she had tried to conquer the Irish chiefs. At one time she took a great quantity of land from them and gave it to Englishmen. The Irish did not like this, and some years after the defeat of the Armada they rose against her and defeated an English army. She therefore sent Essex with a larger army to conquer them. Essex marched about the country, doing nothing which was of any use, and losing most of his men. Then he came back to England suddenly when he ought to have remained in Ireland, and went straight to the Queen in his muddy clothes, without changing his dress after riding, thinking that he would persuade her to forgive him. Elizabeth did not like even her favourite to disobey her, and she sent him away to his own house, ordering him to stop there till there had been an inquiry to find out why he had come away from Ireland. Essex did not like this, and one day he and a few friends mounted their horses and rode into the city, calling on the citizens to rise to protect him. The citizens did nothing of the kind, and Essex was tried upon the charge of treason, and executed.

5. Conquest of Ireland.—After Essex came back Elizabeth sent Lord Mountjoy to conquer Ireland. He succeeded in doing it; and at the end of Elizabeth's reign Ireland was, for the first time, entirely under the English Government. But Mountjoy only conquered the North of Ireland by destroying all the

food in the country. There was a terrible famine, and a large number of the Irish people there died of starvation.

6. The Monopolies.—Elizabeth had very little money. She did not like to ask parliament to tax the people, for fear of making people dissatisfied

QUEEN ELIZABETH IN THE MANTLE OF THE ORDER OF THE GARTER.

with her. At the same time she had a great many favourites whom she wished to reward, and she did it by giving them the monopoly of some article or other; that is to say, by allowing nobody but them to sell it. Of course they charged more for these things than would have been charged if anybody who liked had been allowed to sell them. At last the people got angry, and the House of Commons begged her to put an end to these monopolies. The Queen at once gave way. When she knew that all her people were determined to have a thing, she never resisted them. 'I have more cause to thank you all,' she said to the Speaker of the House of Commons, 'than you me ; and I charge you to thank them of the House of Commons from me, for had I not received a knowledge from you, I might have fallen into the lap of an error, only for lack of true information. I have ever used to set the last judgment-day before mine eyes, and so to rule as I shall be judged to answer before a higher Judge, to whose judgment-seat I do appeal, that never thought was cherished in my heart that tended not to my people's good. Though you have had, and may have, many princes more mighty and wise sitting in this seat, yet you never had, or shall have, any that will be more careful and loving.'

7. **Elizabeth's Death.**—This was the last time that Elizabeth spoke to her people. In 1603 she died, after a long reign of forty-five years. She had many faults, but she was a great queen. She found England divided and weak, she left it united and strong. Englishmen were proud of their country. As we look back to that time we are able to see that if they were fierce and cruel in their revenge upon Spain, the victory was one for which all the world was the better. Spain was a land of tyranny, where no man dared to speak a word against the king or the church. England was not so free as it is now,

but it was much freer than any other country in
Europe was then.   It was a land where men, if they
did not want to overthrow the government, might
speak as they pleased, and think as they pleased.
Great writers and great poets arose at the end of
Elizabeth's reign.   Shakspere, the greatest of them
all, expressed the feeling which taught Englishmen
that their well-being lay in the unity among themselves which sprang from their devotion to the
queen, when he wrote :—

> This England never did—nor never shall—
> Lie at the proud foot of a conqueror,
> But when it first did help to wound itself.

SECOND PERIOD.

CHAPTER XXIII.

JAMES I. AND THE HOUSE OF COMMONS.

(1603—1614.)

1. Accession of James I.—James I., the king who succeeded Elizabeth, came from Scotland. He was the son of Mary Queen of Scots who had been be-headed at Fotheringay, and the great-grandson of the eldest sister of Henry VIII. For the first time the same king ruled over Scotland as well as England ; though each country, for a long time after-wards, kept its own laws and its own Parliament.

2. The Hampton Court Conference.—Many people expected that when the new king arrived he would make many changes which Elizabeth had been unwilling to make. Amongst these, the Puritans thought that he would do something for them. They did not want to separate from the Church of England, and to have churches or chapels of their own. Those of them who were clergymen asked to be allowed to leave out parts of the service which they

thought it wrong to make use of. They were unwilling to wear surplices, or to make the sign of the
cross when they baptised children, or to allow a ring
to be placed on a bride's finger at her marriage;
because they thought that these things were super-
stitious. They also wanted a few other changes to
be made in the Prayer Book. James sent for some

JAMES I.

of them to come to Hampton Court to talk with him
and the bishops. He really wanted to hear what
they had to say, but unfortunately he was a very
impatient man, and he fancied that every one who
differed from him was a fool. He therefore got very
angry, and refused to help the Puritans. The only
good thing that came of this conference was an
order which was given for a new translation of the

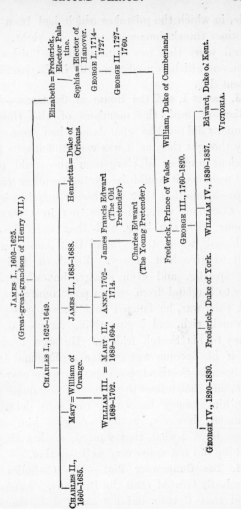

THE HOUSES OF STUART AND HANOVER.

JAMES I., 1603–1625.
(Great-great-grandson of Henry VII.)

CHARLES I., 1625–1649.

Elizabeth = Frederick, Elector Palatine.

Sophia = Elector of Hanover.

GEORGE I. 1714–1727.

GEORGE II. 1727–1760.

William, Duke of Cumberland.

Henrietta = Duke of Orleans.

JAMES II., 1685–1688.

James Francis Edward (The Old Pretender).

Charles Edward (The Young Pretender).

Frederick, Prince of Wales.

GEORGE III., 1760–1820.

CHARLES II., 1660–1685.

Mary = William of Orange.

WILLIAM III. = MARY II. 1689–1702.   1689–1694.

ANNE, 1702–1714.

GEORGE IV., 1820–1830.

Frederick, Duke of York.

WILLIAM IV., 1830–1837.

Edward, Duke of Kent.

VICTORIA.

Bible, in which the mistakes which had been made in former translations were to be set right. After several years this new translation was finished, and is the one which is used generally in England at the present day.

3. James I. and the House of Commons.—When Parliament met, the members of the House of Commons did not like what James had been doing. They thought that, as it was very difficult to find a sufficient number of clergymen who could preach good sermons, it would be better to allow them all to preach, whether they would wear surplices or not. The Commons were, therefore, not in a very good humour with the king, and they were the more displeased when they found that James wanted them to give him money. Elizabeth had been very sparing, and even stingy, but when James came to England from such a poor country as Scotland then was, he fancied that he was going to be extremely rich, and began giving away estates and money to his Scotch friends. He soon found out that if his income was greater in England than it had been in Scotland, his expenses were also much more, and that unless the House of Commons would give him money he would run into debt. The Commons, however, would not give him money unless he did what they wanted, so that they and the king did not agree very well together.

4. The Gunpowder Plot.—The Catholics were more badly treated than the Puritans. James promised that if they did not make disturbances he would not make them pay the fines which they were bound to pay by law, but he soon broke his promise. One of their number, named Catesby, resolved to blow up with gunpowder the Lords and Commons, when they came to hear the king's speech at the opening of Parliament. In this way, both James himself, and the men who refused to alter the laws which directed the persecution of the Catholics,

GUNPOWDER CONSPIRATORS.

would be punished. Catesby expected that James's sons would be blown up with their father, and he intended, after this had been done, to take James's little daughter Elizabeth, who was being educated in Warwickshire, and to bring her up as a Catholic Queen. If Catesby had succeeded, he would probably have been murdered, or executed for his crime long before he could get near the child; but he was too angry to think of this. He let some other Catholics into the secret, one of whom was Guido Fawkes, or, as he is commonly called now, Guy Fawkes. These men hired a house next to the one in which Parliament was to meet, and began to break a hole in the wall which separated the buildings, in order to carry the gunpowder through it to a place under the floor upon which the king would be standing. They were not accustomed to such hard work, and they were in despair at the slow progress they were making, when suddenly they heard a rustling sound. One of them went to see what was happening, and found that a woman was moving coals from a coal-cellar near, and that the cellar was to be let. As they found that it ran underneath the Parliament room they at once took it. There was no longer any necessity for them to break through the wall. They brought into the cellar several barrels of gunpowder and covered them over with faggots and pieces of wood.

5. **Discovery of the Plot.**—The plotters wanted more money than they had got, because they wished to buy horses and armour to enable them to seize the little Elizabeth as soon as the explosion had taken place. They therefore let into the secret some rich men who would be likely to give them money. One of these had a brother-in-law in the House of Lords, and did not wish that he should be blown up with the rest. He therefore let him know what was being done, and the information was carried to the government. On the night before Parliament was to meet, Guy Fawkes went down to the cellar to

be ready to set fire to the powder in the morning. He was made a prisoner, and his companions fled into the country. Some were killed but most of them were taken and executed.

6. The English Government of Ireland.—At the end of Elizabeth's reign, Ireland had been for the first time brought completely under the power of the English government. For some few years the English tried to do their best for the native Irish, and to give to those who wished to live quietly lands which they might have for their own, whilst those who could do nothing but fight were sent abroad to fight in foreign armies. Some of the chiefs who had ruled the Irish tribes before Ireland had been conquered did not like to see the English having so much power in the country, and settling matters where they had been themselves accustomed to have everything their own way. One of their number, O'Neill, Earl of Tyrone, had a quarrel with another Irishman. He was summoned to Dublin that his case might be heard, and behaved so rudely to the Lord Deputy, Sir Arthur Chichester, who governed in the king's name, that he was ordered to go to England to give an account of his actions. He was afraid that if he obeyed he would never be allowed to come back again, and, with another Irish Earl, he fled to Spain.

7. The Colonisation of Ulster.—The two earls who had fled had been chiefs over six counties in Ulster. Chichester advised that the lands of these counties should be given to the Irishmen who lived on them, and that, when they were all satisfied, the land which remained should be divided amongst new colonists from England and Scotland. The English government did not take his advice. The best land was given to Englishmen and Scotchmen, and what remained was granted to the Irish, who were thus thrust out of their old homes. The new colonists were much more industrious than the Irish, and they soon made Ulster more fertile than the Irishmen would have done for a long time to come; but it was very cruel to the Irish, and it would not be easy to make them forget the treatment which they had received.

8. The Great Contract and the Impositions.— These troubles made it necessary to keep up a larger army in Ireland than before. The expense caused by this made James run into debt even more than he had done at the beginning of his reign. In 1610, therefore, he asked Parliament to agree to a scheme which was known as the Great Contract, by which he was to receive a large increase of income on condition of his giving up a number of rights which were burdensome to his subjects. The House of Commons, on its part, asked him to give way on another question of great importance. In order to get more money, he had made the merchants pay duties on goods taken out of the kingdom or brought into it, besides those payments which had been granted to him by Parliament. These duties being put on or imposed by the king himself, were called Impositions. The judges said that the king had a right by law to do this. The House of Commons said he had not. An agreement was very nearly come to about both the Great Contract and the Impositions. But, after all, the king and the House of Commons quarrelled. The king wanted more money than the Commons were ready to give, and he dissolved the Parliament in an ill-temper.

9. The Addled Parliament.—At last James summoned another Parliament. But that Parliament said just the same about the Impositions as the one before it had said. The king dissolved it after it had sat for only a few weeks. It is known as the Addled Parliament, because it did not produce a single new law.

CHAPTER XXIV.

JAMES I. AND SPAIN.

(1614–1625.)

1. James's Favourites.—James had quarrelled with his Parliaments because he wanted to have everything his own way, and did not care about the things about which his subjects cared. In managing the affairs of government, too, he did not like to take good advice. He thought it best to have a young man near him who was clever and amusing, and who would do everything for him, without wanting to have a way of his own. The first young man whom he chose for this purpose was a Scotchman named Robert Carr, whom he made Earl of Somerset. After some time, the new earl was accused of committing a murder, and, though it is not quite certain whether he had done so, there can be no doubt that his wife had planned the crime. At all events, both he and his wife were tried and condemned to death, and, though James pardoned them, they never came near the court again. The next favourite was George Villiers, who was soon made Lord Buckingham, and some years afterwards Duke of Buckingham. He was a gay young man, fond of dancing and riding, and was able to amuse the king with his talk. James gave him very large landed estates, so that he soon became very rich, though when he first came to court he was so poor that he had to borrow money to buy himself a suit of clothes fit to appear in. Nobody was appointed to any office who did not first come to Buckingham to ask for his favour, so that though he was at first kind and affable, he soon became conceited, and used to speak roughly to men who did not treat him with very great respect indeed. This was very bad for the king, as men who were fit to give him good advice did not like to be humble to Buckingham.

2. The Spanish Marriage Treaty.—James knew that he would be obliged to send for another Parliament unless he could get money in some other way. One plan he had for getting money was to marry his son Charles to Maria the daughter of Philip III., king of Spain. She was known as the Infanta, a title given to the daughter of the Spanish kings. Philip offered to give a large sum of money when the marriage took place, but he asked that Catholics in England should be allowed to worship in their own way without punishment. Englishmen were still so angry about the Gunpowder Plot that James would hardly have been able to do this if he had wished it, and, though the marriage was talked of for some time, it did not seem likely that it would ever be really brought about. The English people did not at all like to see their king friendly with Spain, as they had not forgiven the Spaniards for all that had happened in Elizabeth's time, and they thought that if the king of Spain got a chance he would be as ready to meddle in England as his father, Philip II., had been before him.

3. **Raleigh's Voyage.**—One of those who hated Spain most was Sir Walter Raleigh. At the beginning of the reign he had been accused of a crime of which he had not been guilty, and had been condemned to death. But James had shut him up in prison in the Tower instead of having him executed. He now declared that if James would let him out he would go to a gold mine in South America near the Orinoco and bring home a large store of gold. James, who wanted gold, let him go, but told him that he must not go to any of the lands belonging to the king of Spain, and that if he did he should be beheaded, as he might be, without any new trial, because he had been already condemned. Raleigh sailed, and when he reached the mouth of the Orinoco it was arranged that some of his ships should go up the river to look for the mine, and that others should stay at the mouth to prevent any Spanish ships coming in. None of the sailors would go up unless Raleigh would stay to guard the mouth, as

they said that they could not trust any one else not to sail away if danger came. He was therefore obliged to leave the search for the mine to one of his sons and to his friend Captain Keymis. When Keymis had nearly reached the place where the mine was, he found a Spanish village on the bank where he had not expected to find it. He landed his men, and after a sharp fight they forced their way into the village, though they were obliged to set fire to it before the Spaniards could be driven out. Young Raleigh was shot down in the midst of the fight. His comrades never reached the place where the mine was. The Spaniards, who had taken refuge in the woods, fired at the English from behind the trees whenever they attempted to move, and at last Keymis was obliged to re-embark his men in the boats and to make his way sadly down the stream of the mighty river. Raleigh learned from his old friend that all his prospect of success and his hope of life itself was at an end. He lost his temper, and threw all the blame on poor Keymis, who had done his best. 'It is for you,' he said, 'to satisfy the king since you have chosen to take your own way. I cannot do it.' The old sailor could not bear this unmerited reproach. He went back to his cabin, and thrust a knife into his heart. A boy, who opened the door half an hour afterwards, found him dead.

4. Raleigh's Return and Execution.—Raleigh's first thought after this failure was to try to persuade the captains of his fleet to join him in attacking some Spanish ships in order to get gold or silver to

take home to the king. The captains thought
that this would be piracy, and said that they did
not want to be hanged. Raleigh had to come home.
He was seized and thrown into prison. So hateful
were the Spaniards in England that James did not
venture to allow him to be heard in public in his
own defence. Almost every man in England was
ready to applaud a bold sailor who had hurt nobody
but the Spaniards. Raleigh was now the most
popular man in the country. He ascended the
scaffold with a jest on his tongue. The crowd was
thick, and he saw one of his friends trying with difficulty to push his way through it. 'I know not,'
Raleigh called out, 'what shift you will make, but
I am sure to have a place.' When he knelt down
to lay his head on the block some one told him that
he ought to have laid his face towards the east.
'What matter,' he answered, 'how the head lie, so
that the heart be right.' The axe descended, and
his voice was silenced for ever.

5. **James I. and the Thirty Years War.**—A war
broke out in Germany, called the Thirty Years War,
in which the German Catholic princes were on one
side and many of the German Protestant princes on
the other. The principal of these latter was Frederick, who ruled over the Palatinate, a country of
which the chief town was Heidelberg. Frederick
had married James's daughter Elizabeth. He was
defeated, and part of his dominions were seized by a
Spanish army which had come to help his enemies.
Englishmen were very anxious that the Spaniards
should not remain in possession of Frederick's land,

lest he and his Protestant subjects should be compelled to change their religion. James agreed with his people, because he did not want his daughter and her children to be driven out of their home. He sent ambassadors to a great many kings and princes to beg them to stop fighting, but they paid no attention to him. He therefore summoned another Parliament, and asked for money that he might be able to pay an army to defend the Palatinate, if he went to war. As, however, he had made up his mind to send some more ambassadors before going to war, the Parliament only gave him a little money, and waited to see what he would do if the ambassadors did not succeed in persuading the Catholics to leave the Palatinate alone.

6. The Monopolies and Lord Chancellor Bacon.— The House of Commons complained bitterly of many things at home. James had granted a great many monopolies as Elizabeth had done. He had done it partly to reward his friends, but much more to encourage the introduction into England of new manufactures. Those, however, who had got these monopolies behaved very harshly and violently to men who tried, without the king's leave, to make the things which they thought that no one but themselves ought to make. The House of Commons complained, and James was obliged to put an end to these monopolies. The House of Commons then found fault with other matters. Great officials, in those days, were not paid as they are now with a regular salary, but received presents from people who wanted their help. It was very difficult to prevent people who brought presents to the officials to reward them for doing their duty, from bringing presents to persuade them to do what they ought not to do. At this time Lord Bacon was Lord Chancellor. He was a very wise man, and a great philosopher, but when people brought him presents he was foolish enough to take them without asking himself whether they wanted to bribe him or not. In many cases these people hoped that he would decide in their favour in some matter which he had to settle as a judge. He used to take their money, though afterwards he decided against them if they were in the wrong. Some of these people were very angry, and complained to the House of Commons. The House of Commons impeached the Lord Chancellor, that is to say, accused him before the House of Lords. Bacon was condemned to lose his office, and was punished in other ways besides.

7. The Loss of the Palatinate.—At last James found out that his ambassadors could not save the Palatinate merely by talking. He therefore asked Parliament to give him more money in order that he might be able to pay an army to defend that country. The Commons were quite ready to give him money, if he would promise to declare war against Spain. They knew that the Spaniards had sent the first army to attack the Palatinate, and they thought that if Spain were attacked and beaten at sea, as it had been in the days of Sir Francis Drake, the king of Spain would not be able to get any more gold or silver from his mines in America, and would therefore not be able to help to pay the armies of the German Catholics. They therefore wanted a war with Spain, and they were much displeased that James was again asking the king of Spain, who was now Philip IV., to give his sister, the Infanta, to the Prince of Wales. Englishmen did not at all wish to have a Roman Catholic queen in England when Charles came to be king. James, on the other hand, wanted to remain at peace with Spain and only to make war on the German Catholics. He became very angry with the House of Commons, and dissolved this Parliament. As Parliament had not given him any money, he was unable to pay an army, and before the year 1622 was over the Palatinate was conquered by the Spaniards and their friends.

8. Prince Charles's Visit to Madrid.—By this time Buckingham was even on better terms with Charles than he had been with his father, and he now persuaded Charles to visit Madrid to make love to the Infanta. In those days Princes scarcely ever visited foreign countries, because they were afraid of being seized and kept in prison to make them give up something or another which belonged to them. Buckingham persuaded Charles that the king of Spain would take a visit from him as so great a compliment that he would give him back the Palatinate to show how pleased he was. The two young men put on false beards to conceal themselves, called themselves Tom Smith and Dick Smith, and set out for Spain. When they reached Madrid the king pretended to be very pleased to see them. In reality he was very sorry that they had come. His sister had told him that she would not marry Charles, because the English Prince was a Protestant. At the Spanish Court the king and the royal family lived in a very formal way. Charles was not allowed to see the Infanta privately. One day he heard that she was in a garden, and jumped over a wall to talk to her. To his surprise she shrieked and ran into the house. Philip tried to make Charles break off the marriage by asking him to grant liberty to the English Catholics to worship without being punished for it. Charles promised anything he was asked to promise, without thinking whether he would ever be able to keep his word. At last Philip told Charles that he must go back to England and do what he had engaged to do, and that then, if he really did it, the Infanta should be sent after him to be his wife. The Infanta, not very willingly, agreed to this. She got an English grammar and dictionary, and began studying the language which she would have to use here. Charles however thought that he was being treated with contempt. He came back to England, and refused to marry the Infanta unless her brother would give back the Palatinate. The king of Spain said that he could not do this, and the marriage was no more thought of. The Infanta put her English grammar and dictionary away. A few years afterwards she married a German Catholic Prince, the son of the Emperor, and was probably a great deal happier than if she had come to live as Charles's wife, amongst the English Protestants.

9. End of James's Reign.—James called another

Parliament which voted him money, and which would have been very well pleased if he had at once gone to war with Spain. He told the members that he was ready to fight to recover the Palatinate, but he must first send some more ambassadors to find out what allies he was likely to have. Before the Parliament came to an end, it learned that James wanted to marry his son to Henrietta Maria, the sister of Louis XIII., king of France. Englishmen would have been much better pleased to hear that Charles was going to marry a Protestant lady. To give some little satisfaction, both James and Charles promised that they would not engage to the king of France to give freedom of worship to the English Catholics. After the session of Parliament had come to an end, James found that the king of France would not give up his sister unless both James and Charles would engage to let the Catholics worship freely. Rather than be disappointed in this marriage as they had been disappointed in Spain, they both engaged to do this, and so broke their promise to the Parliament. They were therefore afraid to summon Parliament again till the marriage was actually over, when it would be too late for any one to grumble. This was the more disastrous because they had already made some preparations for war, and had arranged that 12,000 English soldiers should go under Count Mansfeld, a German officer, to conquer the Palatinate. As Parliament was not sitting to vote money, the poor men were sent off without pay and without food in the middle of winter. When they arrived in Holland they were put in large boats to be taken up the rivers. It began to freeze hard, and the ice prevented the boats from moving. If the kind Dutch had not brought them bread and cheese, the soldiers would have been starved to death. As it was, they had nothing but a little straw with which to cover themselves, and they fell so ill with the bitter cold that in two or three weeks only 3,000 men of the 12,000 were able to march. They were not enough to conquer the Palatinate, and the whole expedition was a failure. About this time James died.

CHAPTER XXV.

CHARLES I. AND HIS FIRST THREE PARLIAMENTS.

(1625–1629.)

1. **The First Parliament of Charles I.**—Charles I. now summoned Parliament and asked for money for the war. The Commons knew that the young king did everything that Buckingham asked him to do, and that Buckingham had managed the sending out of Mansfeld's expedition without food or money. They also suspected that Charles had not kept his promise about the English Catholics. Instead therefore of giving him the large sum of money that he wanted, they gave him very little. Charles said he must have more. They told him that as long as he consulted no one but Buckingham how money

was spent, they could not help him. If he would take the advice of others whom they trusted, they would give more money. Charles was very angry, and dissolved his first parliament.

2. The Expedition to Cadiz.—Buckingham advised Charles to go on with the war whether Parliament gave him anything or not. He got just enough money

CHARLES I.

together to send a fleet and army to Cadiz. When the army landed, instead of attacking the town it marched in another direction to attack some Spanish troops which its commander had heard of. As there were no Spanish troops near, the soldiers only got very hot and tired, and as their commander had forgotten to see that they had any provisions with them, they were very hungry too. They found a large quantity of wine in a Spanish village, and swallowed it so greedily that the whole army was soon drunk, and if there had been an enemy near every man might have been killed. The next day the troops marched back to Cadiz; but the town was too well fortified to be taken. The fleet and army came back to England without doing anything at all. In some books of nursery rhymes is still to be found the following account of this expedition :—

> ' There was a fleet that went to Spain ;
> When it got there, it came back again.'

3. The Second Parliament of Charles I. and the Forced Loans.

—In the next Parliament Buckingham was impeached—that is to say, he was accused before the Lords by the Commons, of making himself rich and ruining the nation. Before the trial was finished, the king dissolved his second Parliament as he had dissolved his first. He was in great difficulty for money. He sent to ask his subjects to give him some ; but scarcely any one would give him anything at all, and it was against the law to make any one give. Somebody however told Charles that though he could not make his subjects give he could make them lend. As he was not likely ever to be able to repay what he borrowed, there was not much difference between lending and giving. Nevertheless he took the advice and ordered all persons with property to pay him money as a forced loan. He threw into prison the chief men who would not pay, and he got a large sum from those who had rather pay than go to prison.

4. The War with France and the Expedition to Rhé.—Charles had good reason to want money. In less than a year after the dissolution of his second Parliament he had quarrelled with France as well as with Spain. The king of France was at war with his Protestant subjects, and was besieging the town of La Rochelle. Buckingham went with a great fleet and army to deliver it. He began by laying siege to a fort on the Isle of Rhé not far from La Rochelle. He could not take it, and came home, having accomplished nothing at all.

5. The Third Parliament of Charles I. and the Petition of Right.—Charles was determined to go on with the war, to deliver La Rochelle. As he had no money left, he summoned a Third Parliament. That Parliament presented to him the Petition of Right, in which they demanded, amongst other things, that he should never levy taxes or forced loans without the consent of Parliament, and never put any man in prison without giving a reason for it, so that the man might have his case tried by the judges; whereas if no reason was given, the judges would not know what he was accused of and could not try the case, so that he might be left in prison as long as the king pleased. Charles was most unwilling to yield to this, but he did at last, and the Petition of Right became law. The London citizens rang the bells merrily, and lit up bonfires in the streets.

6. Murder of Buckingham.—Charles, in return for his grant of the Petition of Right, got the money which he wanted, and gathered another great fleet

and army, with which Buckingham was to drive
off the besiegers from La Rochelle. Buckingham
went to Portsmouth to take the command. There
was scarcely an Englishman who did not hate
him for squandering the money and lives of his
countrymen on these foolish plans which never succeeded. A certain John Felton, who had been
turned out of an officer's place by Buckingham,
fancied that he would be doing God service by murdering him, just as Catesby and Guy Fawkes had
fancied that they were doing God service if they
could murder the king and the Parliament. He
bought a knife, went down to Portsmouth, and stood
outside the door of a room in which Buckingham was
breakfasting. At last Buckingham stepped out, and
stopped for a moment to speak to one of his officers.
Felton struck him hard with his knife in the breast,
saying as he did it, ' God have mercy on thy soul.'
Buckingham staggered forward and fell dead. The
murderer merely slipped away for a short time, but
his hat fell off, and he was soon recognised. It
was not long before he was sentenced to death, and
hanged.

7. **Breach between Charles and the Parliament.**—
Charles had now to try to govern without Buckingham. When Parliament met again there were new
quarrels between it and the king. In the first place
there was a disagreement between him and the Puritans about certain doctrines which they wished to have
taught, whilst he wished that these doctrines should
not be taught. Then there was a disagreement
about the payment of duties on goods going out of

the kingdom and coming in, which were known as
tonnage and poundage, and which had been granted
to the kings and queens before him by their Parliaments for their lifetime.   He had dissolved his
earlier parliaments so soon that they had never had
time to say whether they would grant him these
duties or not.   He had, however, taken them, as if
they had been granted, and as many people had
lately refused to pay he had seized their goods. One
of those whose goods had been seized was a member
of Parliament, and Sir John Eliot, a noble-minded
man and a great speaker in the House of Commons,
advised that the Custom House officers who had
seized this man's goods should be sent for and punished.   The king said they had acted by his orders,
and should not be punished.   He then ordered the
House to adjourn, that is to say, to stop sitting for
a few days.   The House did as he wished once, but
when orders came for a second adjournment, two
strong members, knowing that as long as the Speaker,
whose business it was to keep order in the House,
remained in his seat, the House could not be ad-
journed, stepped forward and held him down by
force in his chair, whilst Eliot asked the House to
vote that any one who preached the doctrines which
the Puritans thought wrong, or any one who paid or
collected the duties without consent of Parliament,
was an enemy to his country.   There was a great
tumult in the House, and just as the members were
shouting 'Aye! aye!' in answer to Eliot's resolution,
the king arrived.   Parliament was dissolved, and
Charles determined that, for some time at least, he

would not summon another. This third Parliament came to an end in 1629. No Parliament was summoned again for eleven years.

CHAPTER XXVI.

THE UNPARLIAMENTARY GOVERNMENT OF CHARLES I.

(1629—1640.)

1. **The Imprisonment of Members of Parliament.**— Charles's first act was to imprison Eliot and some of the other members of Parliament who had taken part in the disturbance. Eliot and the others said that they ought not to be tried in any court except in Parliament itself for that which they had done in Parliament. He and the two who had held the speaker down were sentenced to heavy fines. He refused to pay, and was kept in the Tower till he died. Though Charles knew that he was dying he would not let him go, and would not even allow his body to be removed, after his death, to his home in Cornwall for burial.

2. **Laud's Rule in the Church.**—Church affairs were almost entirely managed by William Laud, who was Bishop of London, and who, in 1633, became Archbishop of Canterbury. He was determined that in every church in England there should be the same ceremonies, and that the clergy should read

the whole of the services as they were in the Prayer Book, instead of leaving out as much as they pleased. One thing which gave great offence to the Puritans was the removal of the communion table to the east end of the churches, instead of allowing it to stand in the middle of the building, as it had done in most churches for many years. People fancied that Laud wanted to make them Roman Catholics again, and, though this was quite untrue, it was very unwise in him to try to make people worship in a way which they thought to be wrong. There was a Court known as the High Commission Court, which had been set up in Elizabeth's reign, before which the clergy were brought who refused to use the whole of the Prayer Book, and who taught things contrary to its doctrines, or were thought by Laud and his friends to do so. Many of these were turned out of their places, and had to leave the country.

3. The Court of Star Chamber.—The Court of Star Chamber, which had been set up in the reign of Henry VII. to keep in order the great lords, was used by Charles I. to punish those who found fault with his government. Some men who had been abusive had to stand in the pillory, which was a piece of wood with a hole in it to fit the neck, and then had their ears cut off. Others who resisted the government were imprisoned or fined. There was no jury in the Court of Star Chamber. It was now composed of two judges and of all the members of the King's Council. As these were the very people who carried out Charles's orders, they really punished in the Star Chamber those persons who had complained against their own proceedings. They were both accusers and judges. No wonder that the Court became very unpopular.

4. Ship Money.—For a few years Charles got on pretty well without money granted by Parliament. He made the merchants pay the duties, and, as he made peace with both France and Spain, he had no more military or naval expense. With peace came a growth of trade, and the duties on goods brought more money to the king than they had ever brought before. Before long, however, he found it necessary to have a fleet. As the Dutch navy had been a large one for many years, and the French too had now a large navy, Charles thought that England ought to have a fleet to defend her coasts and her trade. The proper thing to do would have been to send for Parliament, and to ask it for money for the navy. But the king knew that if Parliament met it would refuse to give money unless he would follow its advice in everything, and he was determined not to do that. One of his lawyers told him that when the country was in danger he had a right to ask the people of the towns on the sea-coast to serve in their ships against the enemy, and he therefore ordered these towns to send him ships. He took care to ask for ships larger than those which were to be found in any of these places except in London. After a little time, he wrote again to say that if they had not got the ships they might give him money instead. The money was paid, and the next year he asked all the counties in England to pay the ship-money, as it was called. He told them that a man who owned sheep with wool on its back in a midland county was just as much interested in having the trade of the country defended as the man who lived in a seaport town, and owned the ship which carried the wool across the sea. This was quite true. The only question was whether either ought to be made to pay without a grant from Parliament.

5. Hampden's Case.—John Hampden, a Buckinghamshire squire, refused to pay. A court composed

A COACH, TIME OF CHARLES I.

of all the twelve judges was called on to say what the law was. Seven out of the twelve declared their belief that the king had a right to levy ship-money. The king thought that this settled all disputes, but most Englishmen thought that Hampden had been right.

6. The Scottish Prayer Book and the Riot at Edinburgh.—Whilst Englishmen were growing discontented, Scotchmen were preparing actually to resist. James had compelled the Scottish Church to submit to bishops, but he had done very little to alter its form of prayer, which was very different from that which was used in the Church of England. Charles now had a new Prayer Book drawn up which was something like the one that was used in England. In 1637 he ordered that this should be read in the churches in Scotland. As soon as the clergyman began to read it in the principal church in Edinburgh, there began an uproar so loud that his voice was drowned. As he did not stop, one woman threw a stool at his head; luckily she did not hit him. The magistrates turned the disturbers out of the church. The people of Edinburgh took up their cause, and the people of Scotland supported the people of Edinburgh. It was impossible to read the new service anywhere in Scotland. Charles threatened, but could do nothing. In the beginning of 1638 the Scots signed a National Covenant, binding themselves to stand up for their religion against all who attacked it. At the end of the year they held a General Assembly, a sort of Church-Parliament, at Glasgow, where they declared that they would have no more bishops, and called on those bishops who had been appointed by Charles to appear before them to be judged for their faults.

7. **Charles's March to the Borders.**—Charles was very angry. He got an army together and marched with it to the Borders. The Scots marched to the Borders too. Charles's army was not very warlike, and he had very little money to pay it with. Before long his money came to an end, and he was obliged to make peace whether he would or no.

8. Wentworth sent for.—After a few months he was again dissatisfied. The Scots said that the treaty of peace meant one thing, and the king said that it meant another. As the Scots would not give way, he determined to make war upon them once more. He sent to Ireland for Wentworth to advise him how to do it. Wentworth had been a member of the House of Commons in the early Parliaments of the reign, and had taken a great part in opposing Buckingham, and in calling out for the redress of grievances. After the Petition of Right had been granted, he took the King's side. He did not like the Puritans, and he did not wish to see the House of Commons having everything its own way. He had been sent to govern Ireland, and had kept order there, and had made the people better off than they had been before. Amongst other things he had taught the Irish to grow flax to be made into linen. But he was a headstrong man, determined to make every one obey him, and he dealt very hardly with those who resisted him. By his violence he had made many enemies in Ireland, and it was not unlikely that he would make many enemies in England. Soon after he arrived Charles made him Earl of Strafford, and for about a year he governed England in Charles's name.

9. The Short Parliament.—Strafford advised the king to summon another Parliament. It was now eleven years since a Parliament had met in England, and Strafford thought that the new Parliament which met in April 1640 would be as angry with the Scots as he was. Instead of that the House of

Commons asked that Charles should promise never to levy ship-money again. They were ready, if he would promise this, to give him money in return, but not so much as he wanted. They then resolved to ask Charles to make peace with the Scots. This both Charles and Strafford were determined not to do, and Charles dissolved the Parliament. It had sat so short a time that it is known in history as the Short Parliament.

10. The Scottish Invasion.—In spite of the dissolution, Charles resolved to make war against the Scots. He had borrowed money before the Parliament had met, and now he tried to borrow more. When no one would lend him money Strafford tried to get it in all sorts of ways. He threatened the Lord Mayor and Aldermen of London with punishment because they would not lend. He talked of seizing by force some silver which was in the Mint, and of coining bad money so as to pay those to whom the king owed money in shillings, each of which would only be worth sixpence. At last he bought a large quantity of pepper, promising that it should be paid for a year later, and selling it at once below its value. The army which was to be paid by the money got by the sale of the pepper was a miserable one. The men did not want to fight the Scots, and were badly drilled. Before the army was ready the Scots crossed the Tweed, marched through Northumberland, beat some of Charles's soldiers at Newburn close to Newcastle, and drove them out of the county of Durham. Charles had to promise to pay money to the Scots till peace was made. As he

could not get the money without Parliament, he
was obliged to summon another Parliament, which
he was not likely to get rid of as easily as he had
got rid of the others.

CHAPTER XXVII.

THE LONG PARLIAMENT AND THE CIVIL WAR.

(1640—1649.)

1. Strafford's Trial.—The Parliament which met
in November 1640 is known as the Long Parliament, because it continued sitting for so many years.
It began by setting at liberty the men whose ears had
been cut off by the Star Chamber. Then it impeached
the king's chief ministers. Strafford and Laud were
sent to the Tower, and other ministers only escaped
the same fate by flying to the Continent. Strafford
was accused before the Lords of a great many
violent actions and the Commons asked that he
should be beheaded as a traitor, saying that it was
treason to the king to try to make him rule without
Parliaments, because this would really hurt him by
making him unpopular. They were particularly
angry with Strafford because they believed that he
had planned to bring over an Irish army to England
to make Englishmen do whatever the king wished.
The Commons were very much afraid of Strafford.
They knew that the English army which had been

beaten at Newburn was still in Yorkshire, and they thought that if Strafford were set at liberty he would be put at the head of that army in order to lead it against themselves. The people of London did not at all want to see an army marching to take possession of their city, and they came to the House of Lords shouting out for justice upon Strafford. The Lords themselves were at first desirous to save Strafford, but they at last made up their mind to condemn him. The king shrank from allowing his most faithful servant to be put to death, and he sent soldiers to seize the Tower, in which Strafford was imprisoned. But the soldiers were not allowed to enter. An angry multitude came to Whitehall, threatening the king and queen. After this Charles gave way at last, and Strafford was executed. 'I thank God,' he said, as he stood on the scaffold, 'I am not afraid of death, but do as cheerfully put off my doublet at this time as ever I did when I went to bed.'

2. Changes in the Law.—All this while, and for some weeks afterwards, Parliament was busy making changes in the law. The king bound himself never to levy ship-money again or to take any duties at the Custom House without consent of Parliament. The Courts of High Commission and Star Chamber were abolished, and several other new laws were made which made it necessary for the king to consult Parliament more than he had done before. Unfortunately Charles did not at all like these changes, and the Commons believed that if he only had the power, he would try to get back his old authority again. All men were therefore much relieved when at last peace was made with Scotland, and the Scottish and English armies were both broken up and sent back to their homes, so that Charles might no longer be tempted to try to employ either of them against Parliament.

3. Ecclesiastical Parties.—The whole of the House of Commons was of one mind in wishing the king to consult his Parliament, and to govern according to law. But there was one subject on which there was no agreement. The bishops had oppressed the Puritans so much in Laud's time that most of the Puritans wished that there should be no bishops at all, and they also wished that the Prayer Book should be altered. On the other hand there were many men in the House of Commons who wished that there should still be bishops in the Church and that the Prayer Book should remain exactly, or nearly exactly, as it was. In the summer of 1641 there were two parties in the House nearly equal, which always voted against one another whenever anything was to be done about the Church. Pym and Hampden were the chief men of those who wanted some change to be made. Hyde and Falkland were the chief men of those who wished things to remain as they were. No one thought it possible that every one should be allowed to do as he thought right, and that there might be some churches where one Prayer Book was used, and some churches where another was used, and other churches, again, where there was no Prayer Book at all.

4. The Rebellion in Ireland.—At the time when

the two parties were growing angry with one another, a rebellion broke out in Ireland. The Irish of Ulster, whose lands had been taken away in James's reign, drove out the English and Scottish colonists who were in possession of those lands. The Irish knew that they had been wronged, and they were ignorant and cruel. They murdered a great many of the colonists, and stripped a great number of men and women of their clothes, leaving them to wander naked through the country in the cold winter nights. The story was bad enough as it really was, but it was far worse as it was told in England. The Parliament resolved that an army must be sent to Ireland. Unhappily when the soldiers arrived they treated the Irish without mercy, and massacred not only men, but even women and children.

5. The Grand Remonstrance and the Attempt on the Five Members.—Pym and his friends in the House of Commons were afraid lest if the king appointed the officers of this army he would be able to use it against Parliament as well as against the Irish. They therefore drew up a long paper called the Grand Remonstrance in which they found fault with all that Charles had done since the beginning of his reign, and asked him never to appoint any ministers except such as Parliament should approve of. They also asked him to allow a number of clergymen to meet to consider what alterations should be made in the Prayer Book. Charles refused to do this, and though the greater number of the Commons were against him, the greater number of the Lords were for him. The mob from the City came to threaten the Lords, and especially the bishops. Charles determined to accuse five members of the House of Commons and one member of the House of Lords as traitors for having resisted his authority. The House of Commons refused to deliver them up, and the king came to the House to take them, followed by three or four hundred armed men. When he reached the House he looked round, and found that the five members were gone. He commanded the speaker to tell him where they were. ' Sir,' said the speaker, ' I have neither eyes to see, nor ears to hear, save as this House shall please to direct me.' The king left the House without discovering where the five members were. The next day he learned that they were in the City, and he went there to take them. The citizens refused to give them up. A few days later the citizens in arms escorted them back to Westminster. Charles left London rather than see the triumph of his enemies.

6. Breach between the King and the Parliament.— For some months the king and the House of Commons argued with one another. The Commons did not trust the king. They thought he would bring foreign soldiers into England to attack them, and they asked him to let the Parliament appoint the officers of the militia. As there was no regular army in England then, the country was defended by men who were drilled for a few days every year, and spent the rest of their time in looking after their farms or keeping their shops. These men were called the militia. If an enemy invaded the country these men were bound to come together to resist him. Up to this time their commanders had been appointed by the king, but the House of Commons were too much afraid of the king to allow these to be appointed by him any longer. Charles would not give up his right of appointing the officers. He went to York and summoned his faithful subjects to join him there.

CAVALIER AND PURITAN.

Nearly half the House of Commons and more than half the House of Lords supported him. Some of these men were ready to fight for him because he was the king, but a great many more fought for him because they did not want to see the Prayer Book altered. At last, in August 1642, he set up his standard at Nottingham, as a sign that he in-

tended to march against Parliament. The civil war
had begun. Those who took the side of the king
were known as Cavaliers, meaning horsemen, or
gentlemen; whilst those who took the side of the

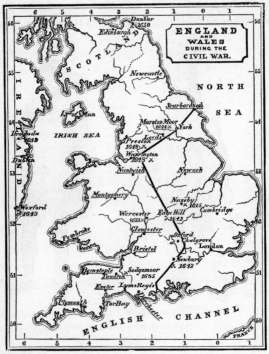

Parliament were nicknamed Roundheads, because
being Puritans they cut their hair short.

7. The Beginning of the first Civil War.—For
some time the King prospered. The first battle was
fought at Edgehill. Neither side gained the victory,
but as the Parliamentarians retreated, the king had

the advantage. He entered Oxford and made it his head-quarters for the rest of the war. Then he marched towards London and reached Brentford. The citizens of London took arms and went to Turnham Green. The two armies looked at one another, but there was no fighting. If the king had taken London the war would have been over, as the London merchants were so rich that the Parliament could not have paid its army without their help. The next year, 1643, sometimes one had the better, and sometimes the other. Hampden was killed on the side of the Parliament, and Falkland on the side of the king. On the whole, however, the king gained more than he lost. The whole of the north and west of England was in his hands. At the end of the year Pym died worn out with anxiety. So little chance did the Parliament appear to have that its leaders invited the Scots to help them. In 1644 the Scots crossed the border and joined an English army. The two forces together completely defeated the king's army in the north at Marston Moor near York. From this time the king began to lose ground.

8. **Presbyterians and Independents.**—Amongst the Puritans themselves there were now two parties. The greater number of the members of the House of Commons who had taken part against the king were Presbyterians. They had ordered that there should be no more bishops in the Church, and that the Prayer Book should not be used any more, but they were not at all willing that congregations should meet to hear doctrines preached of which

the Presbyterian clergy did not approve. There were, however, a few members who were called Independents. These thought that every congregation should settle its own religion for itself, and that every man, or at least every Puritan, should be free to worship God as he thought right. The head of this party was Oliver Cromwell. At the beginning of war he had been a captain in the army and had filled his company with Puritans who were determined to fight for their religion. As the war went on he became a general, and always filled his regiments with men of the same sort. He soon found that these men, though they were all Puritans, were not all agreed about religion. One soldier was a Baptist, another an Independent, another a Presbyterian. Cromwell thought that when he made a man an officer he ought to take the best soldier, without asking what his religious opinions were, provided that he was a good man and a Puritan. He thought too that members of Parliament and persons in office in the State should be chosen in the same way. The Presbyterians did not like this, and thought that people who were not Presbyterians should not be allowed to have office.

9. The Self-denying Ordinance and the New Model. —Most of the generals of the army were Presbyterians, and would rather have made an agreement with the king than have allowed Cromwell to do as he wished in this matter. As they did not want to beat the king too much, they did not beat him at all, and as most people were tired of the war, Cromwell was able to persuade Parliament to pass what was called the Self-denying Ordinance, which forbade any member of Parliament to be also an officer in the army. As the chief Presbyterian generals were also members of Parliament, this made them give up their posts in the army. Cromwell was also a member of Parliament, but he was such a good general that he was allowed to remain as an officer. A new set of officers were appointed. The General was to be Fairfax, and the Lieutenant-General Cromwell. The army after this change was called the New Model.

10. End of the First Civil War and the Negotiations with the King.—The New Model met the king in 1645 at Naseby, and defeated him utterly. The next year his condition was hopeless. He rode off to the Scots and surrendered himself to them. They wanted him to set up a Presbyterian church government in England. As he would not do this they gave him up to the English Parliament, which lodged him at Holmby House in Northamptonshire. He had not been long there when the English army quarrelled with the Parliament. The Presbyterians in Parliament wanted to send the soldiers home without paying them. The soldiers said that they would not go home without being paid, and they also said that they had fought for their religion, and that they would remain armed till they were sure that they would be allowed to worship as they thought right. They marched to London and turned some of the leading Presbyterians out of Parliament. The army was now master of England. Before this it had taken possession of the king, and had lodged him at Hampton Court. The officers offered to allow the worship of the

Church of England to be set up again, provided that no one was compelled to attend it who did not wish to do so, and that full religious liberty was granted to all Protestants. Charles would not hear of this, and soon afterwards he escaped to the Isle of Wight.

11. The Second Civil War and the Execution of Charles I.—Charles was not allowed to remain at large. He was lodged in Carisbrook Castle, near

CARISBROOK CASTLE.

Newport. Persons were sent by the Parliament to negotiate with him. While Charles was arguing with them in a friendly way, he was preparing for a second civil war. In the spring there was an insurrection in his favour in Wales, in Kent, and in Essex. A Scotch army, this time taking his part, invaded the north of England. Charles himself tried to escape from Carisbrook by getting out of a barred window at night, but he found that the bars were too close for him to slip the whole of his body through, and after this he was more closely watched than he had been before. Fairfax put down the insurrection in Kent and Essex. Cromwell put it down in Wales and then marched northwards and caught the Scots at Preston, where he defeated them entirely. The soldiers came back from their victory with anger in their hearts against Charles. They felt that he had tricked them by raising war against them at a time when words of peace were in his mouth. They resolved to bring him to trial. To do this they wanted to find a court to sit in judgment on him. None of the judges would do anything of the kind. Parliament would not make a new court. The soldiers turned out about ninety members of the House of Commons, and those who were left did as they wished and voted that there should be a High Court of Justice to try the king The House of Lords refused to have anything to do with the matter, and they were turned out too. When Charles was summoned before the new court he refused to answer. He said that it had no right to try him. He was nevertheless condemned to death, and his head was cut off on a scaffold outside the windows of his own palace at Whitehall.

CHAPTER XXVIII.

THE COMMONWEALTH AND THE PROTECTORATE.

(1649—1660.)

1. The Commonwealth.—The Government of England was now to be a Commonwealth ; that is to say, there was to be no king.   The country was to be ruled by a few men who were chosen year by year by the body called the Parliament.   In this Parliament, however, there was no House of Lords, and the House of Commons consisted of only about eighty members who had remained sitting, whilst the rest had either left Westminster to fight for the king in the course of the war, or had been turned out at different times by the soldiers.

2. Cromwell in Ireland.—In the first year of the Commonwealth Cromwell was sent to Ireland.   Ever since the rebellion in Ulster, eight years before, Ireland had been full of bloodshed.   It is difficult to say which were most savage, the English or the Irish. Cromwell came to restore peace.   There was a brutal slaughter by his orders of the defenders of Drogheda, and another brutal slaughter, not by his orders, of the defenders of Wexford.   Others carried on the work which he had begun.   Thousands of Irish were driven away from their homes to live as well as they could in the desolate regions of Connaught.   There was peace in Ireland, but peace which was produced by mere conquest without justice was not likely to last long.

3. The War with Scotland.—The next year Cromwell had to lead his army to Scotland. The Scots were shocked at the execution of the late king, and they sent for his son, whom they crowned as Charles II. Cromwell was shut up at Dunbar between the sea and the hills on which the Scottish army lay. He could not fight and he could not get away. One day the Scottish army came down towards him. Early the next morning he fell upon it. ' Let God arise, let his enemies be scattered,' he cried, as his troopers, never conquered yet, plunged into the ranks of their enemies. The Scots turned and fled, and the victory was won. Cromwell gained Edinburgh, but he did not gain all Scotland. In the next year, 1651, a Scottish army, taking young Charles with them, slipped past him and invaded England. They marched steadily southwards, calling on the English Royalists to join them. Cromwell was at their heels, and he caught them at Worcester, where he scattered them to the winds. ' The dimensions of this mercy,' he wrote, ' are above my thoughts. It is, for aught I know, a crowning mercy.' Cromwell was right. As long as he lived, neither Scots nor Royalists ever lifted up their heads again in England. The young king escaped to the Continent. At one time he hid himself in an oak whilst Cromwell's troopers were riding underneath.

4. Expulsion of the Long Parliament.—The eighty members who called themselves a Parliament did not govern England well. They were fond of giving

offices to the friends and relations of the members
and they were hard upon Royalists who did not
bribe them. Cromwell wanted them to dissolve
themselves and to order fresh elections; but he and
they did not agree upon the way in which these

OLIVER CROMWELL.

elections should be held. Besides this, they got
into a war with the Dutch, which he did not like,
because he did not like to see Protestant nations
fighting with one another. One day in 1653 he
came to the house, summoned in a number of soldiers,
turned all the members out and locked the door.

Nobody in England was sorry for what had happened, 'We did not see a dog bark at their going,' said Cromwell not long afterwards.

5. The Barebones Parliament.—Cromwell and the officers invited a number of men to meet together to consider what was to be done. This assembly, which was not a real Parliament, is generally known by the nickname of the Barebones Parliament, after a certain Praise-God Barebones who was a member of it. It did not accomplish anything, but after sitting some months it gave up all its power to Cromwell.

6. Cromwell's First Parliament.—Cromwell was now to be Lord Protector; that is to say, he was to rule like a king without the title. He was to have a Parliament of one House. As soon as the Parliament met, it began to be troublesome, and to want to settle everything in its own way. Cromwell dissolved it and tried to rule without it.

7. Cromwell's Government.—At home Cromwell allowed all Puritans to worship as they liked. But he would not allow the members of the Church of England to meet to pray out of the Prayer Book, because he knew that they wanted to have the young king back to rule over them. Abroad he joined France in a war against Spain. His soldiers took part in a battle in which the Spaniards were beaten, and he received Dunkirk as a reward for the assistance which he gave. At sea Blake, the great sailor, was victorious over the Spaniards. Cromwell could do great things, but he was not liked by the mass of English people. He and the Puritans wanted everybody to be like themselves, and they tried to stop a great many amusements

R

which they thought were wicked, but which are not thought wicked now. Cromwell knew that plots were constantly being formed against him, and he did all that he could to put them down, without caring whether what he was doing was lawful or not. Then too, as he had dismissed his Parliament, he gathered taxes which had never been voted by Parliament at all. Still, he would have been glad to have had a Parliament to support him, and he therefore summoned another.

8. Cromwell's Second Parliament.—This time Cromwell drew up a list of those members who were likely to be troublesome, and would not let them come to the Parliament. As might be expected, those who were left in were more friendly to him than the last Parliament had been. They drew up what was called the Petition and Advice, in which they asked Cromwell to take the title of king, to add a House of Lords to the Parliament, and to renounce the power of excluding from the House of Commons members who had been duly elected. Cromwell refused to take the title of king, but agreed to the rest. When Parliament met again he found himself worse off than before. The House of Commons refused to pay any respect to the new lords, and would not attend to business. Cromwell dissolved his second Parliament as he had dissolved his first. Very few people except the soldiers wished him well, and before the end of 1658 he died. He had tried to do his best as far as he understood it, but England did not like to be governed by a soldier.

9. Richard Cromwell's Protectorate and the restored Commonwealth.—Cromwell's eldest son Richard succeeded his father as Protector. He was a good-natured man who never took any trouble about anything, and had no idea how to govern. He summoned a Parliament, and the Parliament supported him because its members wanted to be ruled by a man who was not a soldier. The soldiers demanded to have the right of naming their own general, so as to make themselves quite independent of Richard. When this was refused, they marched to Westminster, and turned Richard and his Parliament out of doors. They then brought back such of the members of the Parliament which had been turned out by Cromwell some years before as were still living. They soon found that these men were as resolved not to be managed by the soldiers as Richard's Parliament had been, and they turned them out too. They tried to manage the government without a Parliament at all, but it was not long before they found out that people would not pay taxes unless they were voted by a Parliament, and they brought back the members of the old Long Parliament once more.

10. The Restoration.—In Scotland there was an English army commanded by George Monk. He was a silent man, who did not care much about politics, but who knew that Englishmen did not like to be governed by soldiers. He crossed the Tweed and marched for London, without letting any one know what he intended to do. When he arrived he found everything in confusion. After some hesitation he declared for a free Parliament, that is to say, for a Parliament from which no one who might be elected should be kept out by the soldiers, and which should decide matters as it thought right, whether the soldiers liked it or not. The old Long Parliament voted its own dissolution. A new Parliament was chosen, and the young king was invited to come home, and to reign as Charles II.

CHAPTER XXIX.

THE FIRST TWELVE YEARS OF CHARLES II.

(1660–1672.)

1. Character of Charles II.—There was a song which the Royalists had been in the habit of singing, in which every verse ended with the words, 'The king shall enjoy his own again.' Charles thought that his chief object in life was gained if he enjoyed his own. As he afterwards told his brother, he was resolved that whatever happened he would never go on his travels again. He liked pleasure, and his pleasure was usually of a very low and bad kind. He married a Portuguese princess, Catharine of Braganza, but he did not behave at all well to her. He was witty, and was always pleased with the society of amusing people. His subjects called him the Merry Monarch. But he had no idea that it was right for a king to sacri-

fice his time and his jests to do his duty. Indeed,
he never understood that there was such a thing
as duty at all.   It was said of him that

> He never said a foolish thing,
> Nor ever did a wise one.

Yet if he did not do wise acts, he was clever enough

CHARLES II. AND CATHARINE OF BRAGANZA.

to know when it would be hurtful to him to do foolish ones. When he saw that people were determined to have their own way, he did not try to stop
them, as his father would have done.   In this way,

though nobody ever found out any good that he ever did, he managed to die in his bed in England, instead of having his head cut off, like his father, or being driven into exile, as his brother afterwards was. He was not the sort of man to care much about religion. Before he came back he had

TROOPER OF HORSE GUARDS, TIME OF CHARLES II.

secretly acknowledged himself to be a Catholic, and he declared the same when he was dying. But he openly spoke of himself as a Protestant during his whole reign.

2. The Army disbanded and the Judges of Charles I. executed.—When Charles II. landed at Dover he was received with the greatest enthusiasm. 'It is my

own fault,' he said, ' that I have not come back
sooner, for I find nobody who does not tell me he
has always wished for my return.' In reality it
was the fault of the Puritan army. The strongest
feeling amongst Englishmen then was dislike of
an army which had enabled Cromwell to rule over
them. They wanted to be again as they were in
the old days before the Civil War, when there had
been no soldiers in England except the farmers or
shopkeepers, who came out to be drilled for a few
days in the year, and then went quietly to their
work. Charles had therefore no difficulty in sending Cromwell's soldiers back to their homes. Only
three regiments were kept, and these regiments were
the beginning of the present royal army. Some
of the men who had sat in the Court which condemned Charles I. to death, or had taken part against
him very violently, were tried and executed. The
bodies of Cromwell and of two others were actually
dug up and hanged, though they had been dead some
time.

3. Treatment of the Puritans.— About a year after
the King came back a new Parliament was elected.
Scarcely any one was chosen to it who had not taken
part with Charles I. It was therefore known as the
Cavalier Parliament. When people have been very
much frightened, they sometimes think that they
can get rid by force of those who have frightened
them. Englishmen had been very much frightened
by the Puritans in Cromwell's time. Those who
liked the old church service had not been allowed to
have it, and those who did not care at all about

church services had been prevented from amusing themselves as they pleased. The Parliament and the people were, therefore, very angry with the Puritans. The bishops were restored, and the services of the Church of England were again used in all the churches. Laws were passed which were expected to make an end of the Puritans. All of the clergy who were unwilling to use the Prayer Book were turned out of their parishes. But they were not permitted to preach in chapels or even in private houses. No man was to be allowed to gather in his house for purposes of worship more than five persons beyond the members of his own family. Besides this, none of the Puritan clergy who had been turned out were to come within five miles of a town. It was believed that many more of the people who were willing to listen to them in private lived in the towns than in the country, and that, if the Puritan clergy were kept away from the towns, they would not be likely to find a congregation even in secret. The Parliament forgot that even harder laws had been made against the Catholics in Elizabeth's time, without putting an end to them, and that it was therefore not likely that these laws would put an end to the Puritans. The Puritans were very badly treated. They had by this time given up all hope of changing the prayers of the Church of England, and they therefore now only wished to be allowed to worship without punishment in churches of their own. For this reason they were now called Dissenters, because they dissented from the Church, and wanted to separate from it. They were brave men, ready to endure persecution rather than do what they thought to be wrong.

4. John Bunyan.—Amongst these men was John Bunyan, who wrote the 'Pilgrim's Progress' when he was imprisoned in Bedford Gaol for his religion. He was born in Bedfordshire, of very poor parents. As a young man he was irreligious, but he afterwards changed his character entirely. After the Restoration he was greatly persecuted, because he refused to go to church, and preached to congregations of his own. He was thrown into prison, and kept there more than twelve years. He was a tinker by trade, and he provided for himself in prison by making metal tags for the ends of laces. He wrote many religious books, the most famous of which is the 'Pilgrim's Progress.'

5. John Milton.—John Milton, the Puritan poet of England, published the 'Paradise Lost' in the reign of Charles II. He had written many beautiful poems when he was a young man, in the time of Charles I. When the Long Parliament met, he thought it to be his duty to give up writing poems almost entirely, and to write books about the state of the Church. He thought that true religion was only hindered by the ceremonies used in the churches, and that the bishops were making men irreligious by making them use these ceremonies. He therefore wrote very violently against the bishops, and was very glad when the king was defeated. He admired Cromwell very much, and, though he was blind, he was employed in the time of the Commonwealth and Protectorate to write letters in Latin to foreign princes. The Restoration, when it came, made him very sad. After 'Paradise Lost' was finished he wrote a poem about Samson. His own blindness made him think of Samson's blindness at the end of his life; and when he wrote about the Philistines who ill-

GEORGE MONK, DUKE OF ALBEMARLE.

treated Samson, he was thinking of the riotous courtiers of Charles II., who did such wicked things.

6. Lord Chancellor Clarendon.—Soon after the Restoration, Monk was made Duke of Albemarle, but he never had much to do with the Government. The man who managed business for the King at this time was the Hyde who had been one of the chief men of the Royalist party in the beginning of the Long Parliament. He was now made Earl of Clarendon and Lord Chancellor. He had been at the head of those who wished to restore the bishops. He thought that the King ought always to have a Parliament, but that under no circumstances should the Parliament take up arms against the king, whatever he might choose to do. This was what the Parliament itself thought at that time. People are very often inclined to be very violent in condemning things which their enemies do, and which they do not think of doing themselves; and as it had been the Puritans who had fought against the King in the time of Charles I., it never entered into the heads of the Royalists that they themselves might some day want to resist him. They therefore condemned all persons who thought that any king ought ever to be resisted.

7. The First Dutch War.—It was not long before even this Cavalier Parliament found out that the King deserved at least to be blamed. The Dutch were a great commercial people, with ships on every sea. England had now become commercial, and the two nations regarded one another with feelings as unfriendly as those of the owners of two shops which sell the same articles next door to one another. When nations are in a bad temper, they easily find an excuse for quarrelling, and so the English and the Dutch began a war in 1664.

8. The Plague and the Fire of London.—In the hot summer of 1665 a terrible sickness broke out in London called the plague. It was an infectious disease, which had appeared in England several times before, but it had never been so bad as it now was. The streets of London and of all other towns were narrow and dirty, and the upper storeys of the houses were made larger than the lower ones, so that those on one side of the street almost met those on the other, and left little room for fresh air to circulate. This was quite enough to make people ill. There was more sickness and there were more early deaths at that time than now. When any man caught the plague the doctors did not know how to do anything for him. A red cross was painted on the door of his house, and the words, ' The Lord have mercy upon us ! ' were written above it. Then the house was shut up, and nobody was allowed to go in or to come out. Every one who could afford to leave London hurried into the country, leaving the poor to suffer. The dread of catching the plague spread far and wide. ' How fearful,' wrote one who lived at the time, ' people were, thirty, or forty, if not a hundred miles from London, of anything that they brought from any mercer's or draper's shop ; or of any goods that were brought to them, or of any persons that came to their houses. How they would shut their doors against their friends ; and if a man passed over the fields, how one would avoid another.' The deaths became so numerous that it was impossible to bury the dead in the usual way. Carts went about the streets at night, preceded by a man ringing a bell, and calling out, ' Bring out your dead.' The corpses were thrown into a huge pit, because it was impossible to provide coffins for so many. Fires were lit in the streets, under the belief that the heat would keep off the infection. At last winter came, and the plague came to an end with cooler weather. The next year another disaster befell the great city. A fire broke out when a strong wind was blowing, and quickly spread. It burnt for three days. All the City from the Tower to the Temple and from the Thames to Smithfield was absolutely destroyed. The old St. Paul's, the largest cathedral in England, perished in the flames. Great as the suffering caused by the fire was, it did good in the end, for it destroyed the old houses which kept the air out of the streets, so that the plague never came to London again.

9. The Dutch in the Medway.—The Dutch war went on all the while, with plenty of hard fighting at sea, and no very great success on either side. Parliament voted money to keep the fleets ready for fighting. After a little time, even the Royalists in the House of Commons began to suspect that the King spent some of this money on his own pleasures. Both in Parliament and out of it they began to grumble, and to say to one another that if Cromwell had been alive things would have been different. At last a misfortune came which increased their discontent. Negotiations were opened at Breda, in Holland, and the terms of peace were almost settled. Before they were quite settled, Charles took it for granted that there would be no more war, and dismissed most of the sailors, in order to get for himself the money which would have paid them. The Dutch at once sent their fleet up the Thames, where there was no English fleet to meet them. The

Dutch ships sailed up the Medway, burnt three men-
of-war, and carried off a fourth.   For some time they
blockaded the Thames, so that the Londoners could
get no coals.   Charles was obliged to give way to
the Dutch, and peace was made at Breda, as they
wished to have it.

10. The Cabal Ministry.—In 1667, a few weeks

DUTCH FLEET IN THE MEDWAY.

after peace was made, Clarendon fell from power.
The five ministers who had influence after him were
Clifford, Arlington, Buckingham, Ashley, and Lauderdale.   The first letters of their names spelled the
word Cabal, a word which was at that time applied
to any body of men specially consulted by the King
on state affairs.   They are therefore known in
history as the Cabal Ministry.   Lauderdale was a

Scotchman, and was chiefly employed about Scotch business. The others wanted to tolerate other religions than the Church of England, allowing congregations to worship separately in churches of their own. The House of Commons did not want to have toleration at all, and it was much less likely to allow it to the Catholics than to the Dissenters. The Catholics were more disliked and more feared. There was now a very powerful king in France, Lewis XIV., who had very large armies and skilful generals, as well as plenty of money, and people in England thought that he was likely to send his soldiers to England to help the Catholics against the Protestants. Charles himself was first cousin to Lewis, as his mother, Henrietta Maria, had been the sister of Lewis's father, and he had lived a long time in France during his exile. He therefore did not feel at all ashamed to ask Lewis to help him to carry out his plans when his own people were against them, or even to take money from Lewis, to enable him to do as he liked, without having to ask his Parliament for more taxes.

11. The Triple Alliance and the Treaty of Dover.— What Charles now wanted was to be independent of Parliament, and to get as much money as he could. A little time before he had made a treaty with the Dutch and the Swedes, known as the Triple Alliance, by which the three nations bound themselves to join together to stop Lewis from making any more conquests. Not long afterwards Lewis persuaded Charles to break off from his new friends, and to sign the Treaty of Dover, which bound Charles to join

Lewis in making war against the Dutch. Charles was also to declare himself a Catholic, and to receive money from Lewis. Lewis even promised to send French soldiers into England, if Charles thought that he wanted them to put down any resistance from his own subjects. The treaty was to be a profound secret. It was impossible to speak of it openly without producing a general rebellion. Charles did not even tell all of his own ministers. Two of them, Clifford and Arlington, who were Catholics, knew all about it. The others, who were Protestants, only knew that there was going to be a war with the Dutch, and that the King was about to give permission to his subjects to worship as they pleased.

12. The Declaration of Indulgence and the Second Dutch War.—Charles did not after all venture to announce that he was a Catholic, but in 1672 he declared war against the Dutch, and he issued a Declaration of Indulgence, giving orders that the laws against the Catholics and the Dissenters should no longer be put in execution. Parliament was furious. The Commons were much less disposed to respect the King than they had been at the time of the Restoration, twelve years before, but they were quite as much disposed to refuse permission to anybody who was not a member of the Church of England to worship as he thought right. They declared that Charles had no right to refuse to execute the law, and the great body of the people thought so too. Charles did not persist in his own way. He did not want to have another rebellion, to be driven into exile, or to lose his head, as his father had done. He withdrew the Declaration, and the Prayer Book of the Church of England was again the only form of public prayer allowed in the land. Those who wished to join in prayer in any other way had to do it by stealth.

CHAPTER XXX.

THE LAST TWELVE YEARS OF CHARLES II.

(1673–1685.)

1. The Test Act.—Though the Treaty of Dover had been kept a secret, yet people suspected that there was something arranged of which they did not know. They were determined that the Catholics should not become powerful, and a law was made called the Test Act, which required every person appointed to any office either in the army and navy or in the state to receive the Sacrament from a minister of the Church of England. He was also to declare his disbelief in one of the most important doctrines of the Roman Catholic Church, so as to test whether he really belonged to that Church or not. This Act put an end to the Cabal ministry. Clifford and Arlington refused to take the test, and Charles turned Ashley, who had been lately made Earl of Shaftesbury, out of office. There had been a quarrel between them, probably because Shaftesbury had found out the secret of the Treaty of Dover, and had been angry at having been duped.

From this time Shaftesbury did everything in his
power to attack the King. He did his best to
secure toleration for the Dissenters, and to prevent
the Catholics from having any at all. People were
the more afraid of seeing the Catholics in office, because the King's brother James, Duke of York, who

COURT AND CITY COSTUME, TIME OF CHARLES II.

was heir to the throne, had become a Catholic, and
they thought that if he became King he might do
some harm to the Church of England.

2. **Danby's Ministry.**—Charles now gave his confidence to the Earl of Danby. Danby was in all
things in agreement with the House of Commons.

At home he would hear nothing of any toleration for Catholics or Dissenters. Abroad he would give no support to the King of France. After a little time peace was made with the Dutch, and not long afterwards Charles gave his consent to a marriage which produced most important consequences. The Duke of York had no sons. His two daughters, Mary and Anne, both of whom afterwards became Queens, were Protestants. Mary was now married to her first cousin, William, Prince of Orange, who, as being the son of the King's eldest sister, was the heir to the throne after the Duke of York and his daughters. William of Orange was the chief magistrate of the Dutch Republic, and was the leader of the Kings and Princes of Europe who had been struggling to free themselves from the ill-treatment which they were constantly receiving from Lewis XIV. By favouring this marriage, therefore, Danby provided that, after the death of Charles and his brother, the new Queen should have a husband who was a thorough Protestant, and would also be certain not to be on friendly terms with the King of France. It was not likely, however, that for the present England would engage in war. Charles was too dependent on the French king to wish to quarrel with him, especially as Lewis was always ready to give him money when the Commons were stingy. On the other hand, the Commons did not like to go to war even with France, because they were afraid that if Charles had a large army he would use it against them as soon as the war was over.

3. The Popish Plot.—Just at the time when men

were suspicious of the King, and knew not whom to trust, a story was told which threw the whole country into a fever of excitement. A certain Titus Oates came forward to state that he had been a Catholic, and had lately been converted to Protestantism. He asserted that some Catholics had formed a plot to kill the King. He was examined by a magistrate named Sir Edmund Bury Godfrey. Not long afterwards Godfrey was found murdered near Primrose Hill. Some people said that the Catholics had murdered him, because he had accepted Oates's story as true. At once Parliament and people became furious with excitement. There was scarcely a Protestant in England who did not believe in the reality of the Popish Plot, as it was called. What was first talked of as a plot to murder the King, was soon talked of as a plot for 'rooting out and destroying the Protestant religion,' and for massacring thousands of innocent people. Men went about armed, to protect themselves against an imaginary enemy. Oates, who was a horrible liar, profited by the credulity of the people, and swore to the truth of charges of the most dreadful kind against innocent people, especially Catholics. Judges and juries were ready to believe every word that he said, and never thought of asking whether the testimony that he gave one day agreed with the testimony that he gave another. A large number of persons who were perfectly innocent were put to death as contrivers of the plot, or as having taken a part in Godfrey's murder. So popular was Oates that his friends kept him in luxury, whilst he was swearing away the lives of men whom he was unworthy to approach. Whilst the mass of his supporters were merely credulous, there were politicians who helped him because they thought to get an advantage from this excitement in their struggle with the king. Shaftesbury, who was now the leader of the opposition, did everything in his power to encourage a belief in the reality of the Popish Plot.

4. The Exclusion Bill.—At last, in 1679, the Cavalier Parliament was dissolved, after sitting for seventeen years and a half. Danby's ministry came to an end. In three years there were three Parliaments, known as the three Short Parliaments of the reign of Charles II. In each of these Parliaments Shaftesbury's friends had a large majority. They determined that, if they could possibly contrive it, the Duke of York should never reign. They brought in an Exclusion Bill to exclude all Roman Catholics from the succession. The first Short Parliament was dissolved by the king because the Commons would not give up the Exclusion Bill. In the second Short Parliament the Commons passed the Bill. In the House of Lords, it was opposed by Halifax, a man of great ability, who was in the habit of changing sides from one party to another, always leaving his party when it was strong, and when it presumed on its strength to act harshly and tyrannically. He called himself a trimmer, because, as he said, his business was like that of a man who trims a boat by moving from one side to the other to keep it on an even keel. It was not merely to the Exclusion Bill that he objected. He knew that Shaftesbury proposed to give the Crown after Charles's death, not to the next Protestant heir Mary, the eldest daughter of James and the wife of the Prince of Orange, but to the Duke of Monmouth, an illegitimate son of Charles II., who had no claim to the Crown whatever. Halifax thought that it would be dangerous to make such a change as this. It was quite possible that after all James might die before his brother, and, even if he did not, he was not likely to outlive him long. He thought therefore that it was better to run any risk that might come from having a Catholic king for a few years, and to look forward to the peaceful succession of Mary at the end of them. He persuaded the House of Lords to agree with him, and the Lords threw out the Bill. The third Short Parliament was summoned to Oxford. The followers of Shaftesbury came with arms in their hands to defend themselves against danger. They insisted on having the Exclusion Bill, and Charles dissolved this Parliament as he had done the others.

5. Whigs and Tories.—The two parties had now the names of Whig and Tory, which remained to them for a century and a half. The two names were at first given as nicknames. Whig is a Scotch word, meaning whey or sour milk, and was first given in Scotland to some people in the West of Scotland who had lately been rebelling against the Government. When the friends of the Duke of York called Shaftesbury's followers Whigs, they meant to say that they were no better than the Scotch rebels. The word Tory came from Ireland. Irish robbers were called Tories, and the opponents of the Duke of York called his followers Tories, meaning that they were enemies of the Protestants, like the Irish robbers. After a little time these names were accepted by the parties to which they had been at first applied in contempt, and men boasted of being Whigs or Tories without thinking what the words originally meant.

6. Violence of the Tories, and the Rye House Plot.—After the dissolution of the third Short Parliament in 1681, the Tories had it all their own way. The Whigs had been strong for a time, because very few Englishmen wished to have a king who was a Catholic. But there was one thing which they liked less, and that was another Civil War. In 1681 only thirty-nine years had passed since the Civil War began, and men who were not very old could remember all the misery of that sad time. When, therefore, it was known that the Whigs had ridden armed into Oxford and had been talking about forcing the king to do as they wished, whether he liked it or not, sober men who did not usually care much about politics resolved that James should not be excluded from the throne. They would rather have a Catholic king than see another Puritan army governing England, and perhaps Shaftesbury as a new Lord Protector. People almost forgot their fright about the Popish Plot in their fright about a Whig insurrection. Whigs, who had threatened and persecuted the Catholics, found themselves threatened and persecuted in turn. Judges bullied them, and juries found verdicts against them without much regard for justice.

7. Forfeiture of the London Charter.—An accusation was then brought against Shaftesbury. The grand jury, whose business it was to say whether he was to be tried or not, would not allow him to be tried. The fact was, that the juries were chosen by the sheriffs, and that in those days a sheriff would choose a jury which was likely to condemn a man whom he disliked, and to let off a man whom he

SHERIFF OF LONDON TIME OF CHARLES II.

liked. Shaftesbury had to be tried in Middlesex, if he was tried at all, and the sheriffs chosen by the City of London were then, as they are now, sheriffs for the whole county of Middlesex. Charles was so angry when he heard that Shaftesbury had got off in this way that he ordered his lawyers to try and find out some mistake in the Charter of the City. The

Charter was the parchment on which was written the grant to it by former kings to elect magistrates and to govern itself. The lawyers managed to find out that there was something wrong in the Charter, and the judge before whom the matter was brought said so too. The king, therefore, took away the Charter, and appointed the Lord Mayor and sheriffs himself. After this Shaftesbury knew that the new sheriffs would be sure to choose a jury which would condemn him. He therefore fled to Holland, where he soon afterwards died.

8. The Rye House Plot.— About this time some Whigs, bold with anger, formed a plot to murder the king and his brother at the Rye House on their return from Newmarket. The plot was discovered, and the plotters fled or were arrested and executed.

9. The Execution of Lord Russell.— Those who had taken part in the Rye House Plot were men of no note, and the Tories wished to strike down the leaders of the Whigs. Those leaders had been concerned in a scheme for calling on all who agreed with them to form an association which was to demand the summoning of another Parliament, and some of them were of opinion that, if their demand were refused, the association should use force to compel the King to accede to it, though they do not seem to have made up their minds how the force was to be employed. Their design was discovered, and the chief Whigs were, in the King's name, brought to trial on the charge that they had taken part, not merely in a political agitation, but even in the Rye House Plot. The Earl of Essex committed suicide in prison.

Lord Russell and Algernon Sidney were condemned and executed. Russell's case excited more than usual sympathy amongst his party. He was an upright, conscientious man. He firmly believed that if a Catholic were to succeed to the throne, English liberty would no longer be secure. If he did not think that all Titus Oates' lies were true, he thought that they were founded on reality. ' As for the share I had in the prosecution of the Popish Plot,' he declared on the scaffold, ' I take God to witness that I proceeded in it in the sincerity of my heart, being then really convinced, as I am still, that there was a conspiracy against the King, the nation, and the Protestant religion.' In those days the risk run by even an innocent prisoner tried for high treason was much greater than it is now. He was not allowed to have a lawyer to argue for him, and was thus obliged to conduct his own defence. Shortly before his trial Russell received a letter from his wife. ' Your friends,' she wrote, ' believing I can do you some service at your trial, I am extremely willing to try. My resolution will hold out ; pray let yours.' When the court was opened, this true-hearted wife sat by his side taking notes of all that was said, and helping her husband whenever his memory failed him.

10. The Last Days of Charles II.—All this while Charles did not think of summoning a Parliament. There were some, however, even amongst his supporters who advised him to do it. Halifax, who had joined the Tories when the Whigs were violent, was now growing uncomfortable at the violence of his new friends. He urged the king to call Parliament.

No doubt the king would have had a majority on his side. The people were still angry with the Whigs. Charles, however, hesitated. The king of France, who knew that Charles would never make war against him, and that a Parliament might possibly do so, kept him well supplied with money. Before Charles could make up his mind what to do he was taken ill. He was soon known to be dying. Sancroft, the Archbishop of Canterbury, spoke plainly to him. 'It is time,' he said, 'to speak out; for, sir, you are about to appear before a Judge who is no respecter of persons.' The king took no notice. After a time the Duke of York came to his bedside. The bishops and the courtiers were bidden to leave the room. A priest was fetched, and Charles, on his death-bed, acknowledged the authority of the Church of Rome. He lingered yet for some little time, and begged pardon of those around him. He had been, he said, an unconscionable time in dying, but he hoped they would excuse it.

CHAPTER XXXI.

THE REIGN OF JAMES II.

(1685–1688.)

1. James II. and Monmouth's Rebellion.—The new king began his reign in 1685 under favourable circumstances. He announced that he intended to support and defend the English Church, though he clearly showed by attending the public celebration of the Mass at his chapel at Whitehall that he meant to cleave to his own religion. A new Parliament was summoned, and was thoroughly loyal. James would have had no difficulty in governing England, if he had been able to convince his subjects that, though he refused to persecute the Catholics, he would do

JAMES II.

nothing to place them in authority. It was not long before the loyalty of his subjects was put to the test. Many of the Whigs who had taken part in the schemes formed by their party in the last reign were living in exile in Holland, and they fancied that they had only to return to England to rouse the whole nation against James. Monmouth placed himself at the head of these men, and landed at

Lyme, in Dorsetshire. By the peasants and the shopkeepers he was received with the greatest enthusiasm. But the gentlemen and the clergy were all on the side of the king. For the time, however, they could do nothing against Monmouth. The common people pressed in multitudes to see him, and some of them took arms in his cause. He entered Taunton in triumph, and marched eastward as far as Philip's Norton. By this time the Royal army was hastening towards him, whilst the Tory nobles and squires gave their zealous aid to the king. Monmouth retreated to Bridgewater. He rode out with his troops in the night time in the hope that he might take his enemy by surprise. He was stopped by a deep ditch full of water. After a gallant struggle his men were slain or fled. Monmouth escaped, and wandered about till he was discovered half-starved and hiding in a ditch. He was carried to London and executed.

2. The Bloody Assizes.—The rebellion was at an end. Large numbers of the rebels were hung at once without form of trial. Then Jeffreys, a wicked and cruel judge, came down to the West to hold what will always be known as the Bloody Assizes. At Winchester he condemned to death an old lady, Alice Lisle, who was guilty of no more than of hiding in her house two poor men who were flying from vengeance. At Dorchester 74 persons were hanged. In Somersetshire no less than 233 were put to death. Jeffreys overwhelmed the prisoners with scornful mockery. One of them pleaded that he was a good Protestant. 'Protestant!' cried

Jeffreys; 'you mean Presbyterian, I'll hold you a
wager of it. I can smell a Presbyterian forty miles.'
Some one tried to move his compassion in favour of
a person who was miserable enough already. 'My
lord,' he said, 'this poor creature is on the parish.'
'Do not trouble yourselves' was the only answer
which they got, 'I will ease the parish of the burden,'

LORD CHIEF JUSTICE TIME OF JAMES II.

and ordered him to be hanged at once. The whole
number of those who perished in the Bloody Assizes
was 320, whilst 841 were transported to the West
India Islands to work hard under a broiling sun till
they died. James welcomed Jeffreys on his return,
and made him Lord Chancellor as a reward for his
deeds.

3. The Test Act violated.—To all that was being done against the rebels Parliament made no objection. But there was one thing which the king did which was called in question in the House of Commons. He had appointed some Catholic officers in the army, and had excused them from taking the test ordered by the Test Act. The Commons saw that if the king could thus dispense with the Test Act in a few cases, he might dispense with it in many. In fact, there would be nothing to prevent him from filling all the offices in the State and in the army with Catholics. They thought that in this way he might do as he liked with his Protestant subjects, just as Cromwell and his Puritan army had done as they liked. The Commons remonstrated, and asked that the king should observe the law in future. James grew very angry, and put an end to the session of Parliament.

4. The Dispensing Power.—James thought that he had a right to dispense with the laws when he saw fit. He resolved to ask the judges whether he had this right or not. But he was resolved to have his question answered in his own way. In those days a king might turn out of office a judge whenever he liked to do it. James turned out four of the judges who would have given an opinion against him, and those whom he appointed in their stead were quite ready to declare in his favour. In this way he got a declaration from the judges that he had a right to dispense with the test as required by law. If this answer was right, he could do whatever he pleased, whether it were lawful or not.

5. The Declaration of Indulgence.—James was most anxious to obtain an Act of Parliament putting an end to the Test Act altogether. He knew that he could not live many years, and that as soon as he was dead his daughter Mary would be queen, and would appoint judges to decide in a very different way from that in which his own judges had decided. He therefore sent for the principal members of both Houses, and spoke with them privately in the closet, as it was called, that is to say, in his own private room. These closetings, as they were called, had no effect. Member after member told the king that they would do anything to please His Majesty which their conscience allowed, but that their conscience did not allow them to vote for the repeal of the Test Act. James then resolved to do by his own power what he could not do by Act of Parliament. He issued a Declaration of Indulgence, announcing that all his subjects, Dissenters as well as Catholics, were free to worship as they pleased and to hold offices without taking any kind of test. The king hoped that he would gain the Dissenters to his side. Some of these, indeed, accepted his offer with thankfulness; but the greater part of them did not like even so great a boon coming in such a way. They thought that if the king could announce that certain laws were not to be obeyed, he might announce that all laws were not to be obeyed. They listened to those leaders of the Church of England who assured them that, whatever happened, they would be safe, and that the next Parliament which met would pass an Act granting them the toleration which they needed.

Members of the Church of England and Dissenters joined to resist the king. They distrusted and disliked the Catholics, and they were reasonably afraid lest the king should make a bad use of the power which he was trying to gain.

6. The Expulsion of the Fellows of Magdalen.—It was not long before James offended the greater part of his subjects even more than he had already done. The two Universities of Oxford and Cambridge were, at that time, the only places where young men could receive a good education after they had become too old to remain any longer at school. At these Universities no one could teach who was not a member of the Church of England. The consequence was that no man who was not a member of that Church could have his son well educated, unless he were rich enough to pay a private tutor. James wished that there should be a way in which Catholics at least should be educated in their own religion. In order that this might be done, he contrived that two of the colleges at Oxford should be governed by Catholics. He was not satisfied with this, and when the President of Magdalen College died James sent orders to the Fellows, who had the right of choosing a new President, to choose a Catholic. The Fellows met and chose a Protestant. They told James that they had acted according to law, and that they would not obey any one but the man whom they had lawfully chosen. James turned them out of the College, and left them to beg their bread. They were not allowed to starve. They were invited to live in the houses of country gentlemen, who were glad to have this opportunity of showing how much they respected them for resisting the king. There can be no doubt that they were right in resisting him. It would have been a good thing if everybody could have been educated in his own religion ; but it would have been a very bad thing if the king could have done as he pleased, whatever the law might say. If the king could give up three colleges at Oxford to the Catholics, he might have given up all the colleges at both Universities, and have left the Protestants without education. It was now certain that the Protestants would do all they could to prevent this.

7. The Trial of the Seven Bishops.—After this James gave orders that his Declaration of Indulgence should be read to the people by the clergymen in all the churches. Most clergymen thought that the declaration was against the law, and even wrong in itself. Seven of the bishops signed a petition to the king asking him not to force the clergymen to act against their consciences. The king was very angry, and he was more angry when the day came on which he had ordered that the declaration should be read. Scarcely a clergyman in the whole of England obeyed the king's orders, and in some places where a clergyman was found to read the declaration the congregation walked out of the church rather than listen to it. The king ordered that the seven bishops should be tried for having published a seditious libel, that is to say, a paper in which falsehood is told with the object of bringing about resistance to the Government. The trial lasted during a whole day. The lawyers who were engaged for the bishops showed that their petition was not a libel at all. The jury left the Court to determine upon the verdict. At first nine of them were for the bishops and three were for the king. Two of these latter gave way, and only one was left who was against the

A BISHOP.   LORD KEEPER OF THE GREAT
SEAL TIME OF JAMES II.

bishops. This was Arnold, who was the king's brewer. 'Whatever I do,' he had said, before the trial began, ' I am sure to be half-ruined. If I say "Not Guilty," I shall brew no more for the king ; and if I say " Guilty," I shall brew no more for anybody else.' He seems to have made up his mind that the king's custom was worth more than that of the rest of the world. Another gentleman named Austin proposed to argue with him. Arnold said that he did not want to hear arguments. ' If you come to that,' answered Austin, ' look at me. I am the largest and strongest of this twelve, and before I find such a petition as this a libel, here I will stay till I am no bigger than a tobacco pipe.' Before this threat Arnold gave way after a struggle lasting all through the night, and when the Court assembled in the morning the verdict of ' Not Guilty' was given in. Crowds in Westminster Hall and in the streets around shouted for joy. At Hounslow, where James had formed a camp, the very soldiers, with whose help James hoped to put down all resistance, shouted like the rest. James, who was there, asked what it all meant. ' Nothing,' he was told, ' the soldiers are glad that the bishops are acquitted.' ' Do you call that nothing?' he answered. ' So much the worse for them.'

8. The Invitation to the Prince of Orange.—The acquittal of the bishops took place on June 30, 1688. On the same day a message was sent to William of Orange by seven noblemen and gentlemen, some of them Whigs and some of them Tories, to request him to come to England to save the laws and liberties of the nation. There was a reason why this had not been done before. It had lately been announced that a son and heir had been born to James. Before that birth every one knew that, whenever James died, the Crown would pass to a Protestant successor, the Princess of Orange, and that everything that James had done would speedily be undone. They now knew that the heir was an infant who would certainly be brought up in his father's belief, and who would, when he became a man, act exactly in the same way that his father had acted. As people are very apt to disbelieve what it is to their interest to disbelieve, most men repeated with firm conviction a story that the infant was not the son of the king and queen, but was some one else's child who had been brought into the palace by stealth. William of Orange, whether he believed this or not, was resolved to accept the invitation. He collected a fleet and a small army, and landed at Torbay. He marched towards London. After a little time, men of rank began to join him. Very soon there were insurrections in the North and centre of England. James's own officers deserted to William, and James soon discovered that scarcely a man in England was likely to draw sword for him. Even then, if he could have given up all his plans, he might have continued to reign. But he could not make up his mind to do this. He attempted to fly to France, but was brought back. William was far too wise to wish to stop him. He did not want to keep him as an interesting prisoner like Mary Queen of Scots, or to cut off his head that people might talk of him s a royal martyr, as they had talked of Charles I. He therefore gave him every opportunity to fly. This time James got safely away. He reached France, where Lewis XIV. received him kindly. He was never again to set foot in England.

CHAPTER XXXII.

WILLIAM AND MARY.

(1689—1694.)

1. The Revolution and the Toleration Act.—Soon after James was gone, a Parliament met. After much discussion it declared that James had given up the Crown by governing badly and by leaving England. It then offered the throne which had thus become vacant to William and Mary. They were to be joint sovereigns. Mary's head was to appear on the coins, and to be named in all public announcements together with that of her husband, but as long as they both lived William alone was to govern. If either of them died the other was to continue to reign, and when they were both dead, unless they left children, the Crown was go to Mary's sister, the Princess Anne. All this was settled by Parliament, and Parliament was able to do very much as it thought right. The king and queen were on the throne because Parliament had put them there, and not because they were born to it. If Parliament declared against them they would hardly be able to keep themselves there. One of the first consequences of the change was the passing of the Toleration Act. The Dissenters at last got permission by law to worship in their own chapels. The Catholics did not get permission to do the same. People were afraid of them and angry with them, as they had

been with the Dissenters after the Restoration.
They were therefore determined to keep them down.
Yet it was not long before they found out that there
were not enough of them to be afraid of, and so after
a time the Catholics got toleration as well as the
Dissenters, and were allowed to worship in their

WILLIAM III.

own way, though it was a very long time before they
were allowed to hold offices.

2. The War in Scotland.—William knew that he
would have to fight for his Crown. He was himself
at the head of a number of States on the Continent
which were at war with the king of France, and
Lewis XIV. was sure to do all that he could do to
overthrow him in England. In Scotland the greater
part of the people took William's side. Lord Dundee,

a brave soldier, who was one of James's supporters, went into the Highlands, and got together an army of Highlanders, who were very fond of fighting, and who, being very poor in their wild mountains, were glad of an excuse to plunder the Lowlands. Dundee drew up his Highlanders at the top of a steep ascent through the pass of Killiecrankie, near Blair Athol. William's troops came panting up the hill in a hot summer day. When they drew near the top the Highlanders rushed down, slashing them with their broadswords. The soldiers turned and fled with the Highlanders after them. Dundee was shot before the flight began, and the Highlanders went back to their homes to carry off their plunder. Soon afterwards William's officers placed soldiers in forts near the places where the Highlanders were likely to come out, and gave presents to the chiefs, so that there was no more war in Scotland for a long time.

3. The Massacre of Glencoe.—The Highland chiefs were required to swear that they would live peaceably in the future. They had to take the oath by certain day. When that day came, all had sworn except one. That one was Mac Ian of Glencoe, a rocky and desolate valley in the Western Highlands. Mac Ian was an old man, the chief of a small clan. He had intended to take the oath, but he thought it would be a very grand thing to take it as late as possible, after all the great chiefs had sworn. Unluckily for him, he went to swear at a place where there was no one appointed to receive his oath. He at once went on to another place, where he took the

oath in a proper manner, but by the time he arrived
the appointed day was past. Unfortunately for
Mac Ian, the Master of Stair, who governed Scotland for William, was delighted to find an excuse

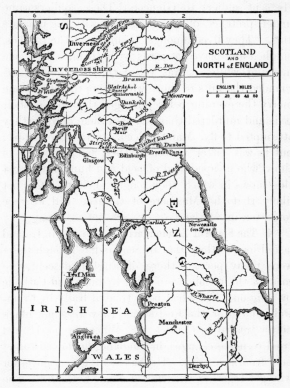

for punishing him. He knew that Highlanders
were always ready to fight, and to rob, and that
Mac Ian's clan was rather more ready to carry off
cattle from the Lowlands than other Highlanders.

He determined to make an example of them. He got permission from William 'to extirpate that set of thieves.' He proceeded to do his cruel work in a particularly cruel and treacherous manner. He sent soldiers to Glencoe. These soldiers came under pretence of being friendly with the inhabitants. They lived amongst them, ate at their tables, laughed and played at cards with them. Early one morning, whilst it was yet dark, the soldiers surrounded the huts of those with whom they had made merry the evening before, dragged them out of their beds and murdered them, or shot them down as they attempted to fly. Many, indeed, contrived to escape ; but it was bitter winter weather, and not a few of those who escaped died of cold and hunger amongst the snows in which they sought shelter. It is not likely that the Massacre of Glencoe will ever be forgotten in Scotland.

4. The Siege of Londonderry.—The war in Ireland lasted longer than that in Scotland. Though there were many persons there of English descent, the mass of the people were Irish by birth and Catholic by religion. They had been treated badly by Cromwell, and after the Restoration they were not much better treated by Charles II. When James II. had tried to make changes in England, he hoped to get help from the Irish. He had sent over a governor who got together an army of Irish Catholics. The Irish, for once, had everything their own way. They chased out the English Protestants from their homes and robbed them and ill-treated them as they had done in 1641. The English had only a few towns left where they were still safe. One of these was Londonderry. James himself came to Ireland, and hoped that Londonderry would soon surrender, and then all Ireland would be his. Lundy, the governor, made up his mind to surrender the place, and gave orders that when the Irish army arrived there should be no resistance. Two brave soldiers refused to obey such orders as these. A clergyman named Walker called on the men of Londonderry to resist. Shouting ' No surrender,' the people rushed to the open gates and closed them in James's face. The Irish then surrounded the town, so that no food could enter in, and threw across the river on which it stands a boom, that is to say, a barrier formed of pieces of timber fastened together, which might prevent any ships coming up to bring in food. The defenders of the town were almost starved. After some time they had no meat except horseflesh to eat, and they had not much of that. From the top of the cathedral they could see far off the vessels which William had sent to help them, but for weeks the vessels did not venture to come up the river to try to break the boom. During this time a large number of the inhabitants died from famine and sickness. Men who had once been well off were glad if they could buy a piece of dog's flesh. If a little fish was caught on the river it was looked on as a splendid prize, which the fisherman who had secured it would not sell for any money. Even hides were gnawed, in the hope of getting some nourishment out of them. Still, though many perished, those who remained alive refused to think of surrender.

Walker's voice was always raised to encourage the sufferers to bear anything rather than give up the town. At last three of the ships which had waited so long began to move up the river. One of them dashed at the boom and broke it, though it was itself driven on shore. The others passed through and carried the store of food which they bore to the stout defenders of the city. The besiegers gave up in despair the task of forcing their way into Londonderry.

5. The End of the War in Ireland.— The siege of Londonderry took place in the year after William arrived in England. The next year after that William crossed to Ireland, and defeated James thoroughly at the battle of the Boyne. James gave up hope, and fled to France once more. The Irish, however, struggled on, and it was not till the next summer that their resistance was finally overcome. They were defeated in another great battle at Aghrim, and those who fought longest took refuge at Limerick. When Limerick was taken they had no hope left. For many years the Protestants, who were almost all of English birth, ruled in Ireland. There was a Parliament at Dublin in which only Protestants could sit, and from time to time they made hard laws against the Catholics.

6. The Battle of Beachy Head.—William was now not popular in England. He did not understand English ways, and he did not know how to make himself agreeable to Englishmen. He did not even talk English very well, and the people never quite liked having a Dutchman on the throne. But they preferred having a Dutchman on the throne to having a French army in England, and, as Lewis wanted to invade England to set James up again, almost all Englishmen were ready to fight for William at such times of danger. When William was in Ireland, a French fleet appeared in the Channel. It was met off Beachy Head by a fleet composed partly of English and partly of Dutch vessels. The English Admiral, Lord Torrington, was in a bad temper. He

LIMERICK.

let the Dutch fight, but would not fight himself. He had consequently to sail away to seek shelter in the Thames. The French Admiral sailed down the Channel, landed some men at Teignmouth, and burnt the few cottages of which the place was then composed. It was not much to do, but it was enough to rouse the spirit of the nation. There were many people in England who would have been glad to see

James on the throne again. But there was scarcely one who was not ready to shed his blood to prevent a French invasion of England.

7. The Battle of La Hogue.—Two years later the same feeling was again roused. Another French fleet, more powerful than that which had fought at Beachy Head, and a great French army, were prepared for the invasion of England. Frenchmen thought that, because Englishmen grumbled against William, they would welcome the French who were to come to restore James. The English fleet which was to resist them was placed under the command of one of the grumblers, Admiral Russell, a brother of the Lord Russell who had been beheaded in the reign of Charles II. He was an ill-tempered man, always fancying that he was not sufficiently respected, and though he was in William's service he had even told some friends of James that he would be ready to help his old master back. One of these men now came to ask him to help James. 'Do not think,' answered the Admiral, 'that I will let the French triumph over us in our own sea. Understand this, that if I meet them I fight them, ay, though His Majesty himself should be on board.' Russell kept his word. He met the French fleet near Cape La Hogue and utterly defeated it. The English sailors followed up their victory, and set the greater part of the French fleet on fire as it lay under the batteries from which they had hoped to find shelter. No such victory had been won by an English fleet since the day when Essex and Raleigh sailed triumphantly into Cadiz Bay. No such victory was won again till

Nelson struck down the French navy at the Nile and at Trafalgar.

8. The War in the Netherlands and the Death of Mary.— Year after year William passed over to the Netherlands to resist the armies of Lewis. In the battles which were fought the French were always

successful, but William never allowed them to gain much by their success. Whilst he was absent his faithful wife, who loved him dearly and whom he loved dearly in return, occupied his place at home. In 1694 she was attacked by the small-pox. In those days vaccination had not been discovered, and a large number of people died of the small-pox every year. When the physicians told William that there was no hope, his grief was heartrending. 'There is no hope,' he said to one of the bishops. 'I was the happiest man on earth, and I am the most miserable. She had no fault; none, you knew her well: but you could not know, nobody but myself could know her goodness.' The queen died, but she left her memorial behind her. Charles II. had begun to build on the banks of the Thames at Greenwich a magnificent palace on the site of an old one which had sometimes been occupied by his predecessors. When the Battle of La Hogue was fought, and hundreds of sailors came home wounded, Mary announced her intention of completing that palace, not as a residence for herself or her husband, but as a place of refuge for sailors who had been disabled in the service of their country. Greenwich Hospital is the lasting monument of the gentle queen.

9. The Liberty of the Press.—About this time a most important change was made. No one had been allowed to publish a book till it had been shown to an officer called a licenser, who might, if he thought right, stop the sale of the book altogether. In this way those who thought that the Government was doing wrong were prevented from writing books to say so. Now an end was put to the law which forced authors to get leave from the licenser to publish their books. The result was that men became more peaceable than they had been before, because a man who thought things were being done wrong wrote books or newspapers to persuade others to join in setting them straight instead of secretly forming plots to overthrow the Government.

CHAPTER XXXIII.

WILLIAM III.

(1694—1702.)

1. The Siege of Namur.—Till the year 1695 Lewis XIV. had always been victorious. His victories had cost thousands of lives and immense sums of money, and the French people were growing poor, and were not able to find so much money to pay the soldiers as they had once done. Lewis, too, was spoiled by his good fortune. In the early part of his reign he had taken care to appoint good generals to command his armies, and good ministers to manage his affairs at home. Now he behaved very differently. He gave power to men who flattered him and were agreeable at Court, whether they were fit for their work or not. On the other hand England and Holland were both trading countries, and merchandise made them wealthy. William, too, took good care to employ men who were able and willing to work. In 1695 he laid siege to Namur. He managed the siege so skilfully that the French armies were not able to drive him off. At last the place surrendered. It was like the turn of the tide. It was the first time in this war that Lewis had lost a town.

2. The Assassination Plot.—James had not given

U

up all hope. He had still some followers in England, who were called Jacobites, because his name James was Jacobus in Latin. Lewis had promised to send French soldiers into England, if the English Jacobites would first rise in insurrection against William. The English Jacobites, however, said that they would not rise unless the French soldiers were actually in England to protect them, and Lewis did not think it prudent to send his men across the sea without being quite sure that they would be helped by the Jacobites. Whilst this plan was being discussed, about forty Jacobites resolved to murder William. They knew that when he came back to Hampton Court from hunting he passed through a narrow lane, and that he was accustomed to have only twenty-five guards with him. The Jacobites resolved suddenly to spring into the lane, to shoot the guards, and then to shoot the king. Fortunately there were some amongst the plotters who did not like having anything to do with assassination, and they let the king know what had been proposed. The plotters were seized, and some of them were executed. The knowledge that there were Jacobites who intended to murder William had much the same effect as the knowledge that there were Catholics who intended to murder Elizabeth had had a century before. For a long time William had not been popular. He was not only a foreigner, but he was not cheerful or friendly in his conversation. Now all this was forgotten. He became for a time popular, because there had been an attempt to assassinate him. The greater part of the

Lords and Commons eagerly signed a paper which bound them to join in an association in defence of William's Government, and which engaged them to avenge his death upon his murderers, and to support the law which gave the throne to the Princess Anne after William's death. This paper was circulated in the country, and was eagerly signed by thousands of persons, many of whom probably would not have been very ready to help William, if no one had attempted to murder him.

3. The Restoration of the Currency.—About this time the Government had to turn its attention to a very different subject. A great part of the silver money in use had been made with smooth edges, unlike the shillings and sixpences with the milled edges which we now have. The consequence was that rogues used to clip the money, that is to say, shave off small strips of silver from the edges of the coins, and then pass them on a little smaller than they were before. If this trick were attempted now, it would be found out at once, because the milled edge would be cut away. It could not be so easily found out then, but it was quite evident that the money in use was getting smaller. A man who received a shilling in payment might be pretty sure that it would not be worth more than ninepence, and it was very likely that it would not be worth more than sixpence. The result was that scarcely any one paid or received money without quarrelling about it. Those who had to pay a shilling wanted merely to give a coin called a shilling. Those who had to receive a shilling wanted to have as much as would really be worth a shilling. Persons who sold goods hardly knew what they ought to charge, and, as usually happens in such cases, they often ended by charging more than they ought. At last the Government and Parliament interfered. New milled money was coined, and given in exchange for the old clipped money. The loss was borne by the public.

4. The Peace of Ryswick.—For two years there had been no more fighting. Lewis did not venture to attack William, and William was content to keep what he had gained. At last, in 1697, a peace was signed at Ryswick, where Lewis acknowledged William to be King of England, and gave up the cause of James. When William went in state to return thanks for the blessing of peace, he went to the new St. Paul's, which still lifts its lofty dome above the City of London, and which was then used for the first time for public worship. It had been slowly rising, after the plan of the great architect Sir Christopher Wren, on the site where the old cathedral had been burnt down thirty-one years before.

5. The Dismissal of the Dutch Guards.—William thought that though the war was over it would be well to keep a large part of the army together. He knew that Lewis was still ambitious, and that the French king was much more likely to keep the peace if he saw that there were many of those English soldiers who had fought at Namur ready to fight him again. The Commons did not think much of this danger. They wanted to have as little expense as possible, and they remembered too well how Cromwell had ruled England with his soldiers to like to see a larger army than was absolutely necessary. They insisted not merely that the army should be diminished, but that the Dutch Guards which William had brought over with him should be sent back to their native country. William was bitterly displeased, but he gave way, and allowed the Commons to do as they pleased.

6. The Spanish Succession and the Partition Treaty.—William was thinking more of the Continent of Europe than of England. The king of Spain, Charles II., was an invalid and almost an idiot, and was not likely to live long. Lewis had married his eldest sister, and claimed the Crown of Spain for his descendants. Other princes had claims in other ways. William did not care much what their claims were, but he did not want a son or grandson of a king of France who was so powerful already to rule over the Spanish dominions, which reached over a great part of Italy and the Southern Netherlands, as well as over enormous tracts of country in America. Lewis was not anxious at first to go to war again, and a treaty was made, known as the First Partition Treaty, which gave most of the Spanish lands to a young Bavarian prince whom nobody was afraid of. Unfortunately the youth died, and the arrangement had to be made all over again. This time it was settled by the Second Partition Treaty that some parts of the Spanish dominions should go to Lewis's grandson Philip, and other parts, including Spain itself, to the Archduke Charles, a younger son of the Emperor who, under other titles, ruled in Austria and the neighbouring countries. At last, in 1700, the poor king of Spain died, leaving a will directing that the whole of his dominions should go to Philip. Lewis accepted the great inheritance for his grandson, and refused to carry out the Partition Treaty.

7. Rise of a War-feeling in England.—In England very few people wanted to have James back. In 1701 the Act of Settlement was passed, which directed that if William died without children the Crown should go to Anne, the sister of his wife Mary and the daughter of James. After that it was to go to the Electress Sophia, the next heir who was a Protestant. She was the daughter of Elizabeth, the Electress Palatine, and through her the granddaughter of James I. At this time the Tories had a majority in the House of Commons, and the Tories were more anxious than the Whigs to keep out of war. They therefore refused to assist William in compelling Lewis to carry out the Partition Treaty. Lewis did a great deal to provoke England, and even sent French soldiers to occupy fortresses in the Spanish Netherlands, just as if he were the master of his grandson's dominions. But Englishmen seemed determined to keep the peace whatever Lewis might do. At last news arrived which entirely changed their temper. James II. died in France. Lewis at once sent to his son, the boy who had been supposed by so many in England not to be in reality the child of his father and mother, and acknowledged him as James III. of England. At once all England was filled with anger at the insolence of a king of France who imagined that he could give even the name of an English king to a boy whose title had been rejected by the English

Parliament and nation. William found no difficulty now in providing for war. He summoned a new Parliament, which voted money and soldiers. At the time when William was expecting to lead an army on the Continent, his end was near. His horse stumbled over a mole-hill in the park of Hampton Court. William broke his collar-bone, and after lingering a few days he died. He had done great things for England, and he had done more than any one else could have done to stop the civil wars and executions of the reigns before him. He ruled according to law, and he was able to guide his Parliaments, because he was always able to keep his temper, and never insisted on having his own way, even when the nation was determined to do things which he thought to be wrong.

CHAPTER XXXIV.

QUEEN ANNE.

(1702–1714.)

1. **The Occasional Conformity Bill.**—Anne was popular from the beginning of her reign. She was dull and uninteresting to those who saw her every day, but the mass of people who scarcely ever saw her, or did not see her at all, did not care about that. They were pleased that she was an English-woman and not a foreigner as William had been. Besides this, it was well known that Anne did not like the Dissenters, and most people in England did

not like the Dissenters either. They had become accustomed by this time to see them using their own chapels, but they did not like to see them holding offices. The Test Act had excluded them from office, as well as the Catholics, because it required that every one who was appointed to office should receive the communion in a church. Lately some of the Dissenters had got into offices in spite of this rule, because they did not mind coming to church and receiving the communion there once, though they afterwards went back to their own chapels. This was called Occasional Conformity. The Whigs, who were always friendly to the Dissenters, did not object to this, but the Tories did not like it, and they proposed a Bill against Occasional Conformity, to punish any Dissenter who went to chapel after obtaining office. The House of Commons, where the greater number were Tories, adopted this plan. But it could not become law unless the House of Lords adopted it too, and as the Whigs were stronger than the Tories in the House of Lords, the proposal was for some years always rejected there.

2. Blenheim and Ramilies.—The chief command over the army on the Continent, which was to make war against Lewis, was given to the Duke of Marlborough. His wife the Duchess was a great favourite of Anne, and he was himself the greatest general who was born in England before the Duke of Wellington. He had to command not only English soldiers, but Dutch and German soldiers as well, and the kings and princes who sent the German troops were full of their own

ideas, and were seldom ready to do what Marlborough wanted them to do. He had to be civil to
everybody, and to coax them all to do what was for
their own good. During the first two years of the
war he had enough to do to defend the Dutch
Netherlands. In 1704 he did more than that. The
king of France had Bavaria on his side, and a
French army was in Bavaria. Marlborough suddenly
marched up the Rhine and across the wooded hills
of the Black Forest. He found the French army at
Blenheim on the Danube, and utterly defeated it.
It was the first time that a French army had been
defeated during the whole reign of Lewis XIV. The
result of the battle was that the French were turned
out of Germany. Parliament gave to the Duke a
large estate near Woodstock, where he built a splendid mansion, which is known to this day as Blenheim
House. Afterwards Marlborough won another great
battle at Ramilies, after which the French were
turned out of nearly the whole of the Netherlands.

3. The War in Spain.— There had also been
fighting going on in Spain. In the year in which
the Battle of Blenheim was fought, Admiral Sir
George Rooke found himself at Gibraltar, with a
large fleet and nearly 5,000 soldiers. There were
only about 150 Spanish soldiers inside the fortress,
and on a saint's day they all went to church. Whilst
they were at prayers the English sailors landed, and
took the place without difficulty. It has never
been lost again, as the rock which rises above the
town has a cliff towards the land side which no
enemy can climb, and on the only occasion on which

an enemy has been strong enough at sea to attack it from the water, the attempt was defeated. Besides this there were other victories in Spain, and the English and their friends hoped to be able to conquer the country for the Archduke Charles. The Spaniards were determined not to submit to him. They clung to Philip V., for much the same reason that the English had clung to William. They did not like having a foreign king, but they preferred a king who lived among them to one who tried to force them to obey him by using the help of foreign armies.

4. The Union with Scotland.—In the midst of all these victories a question was raised which was of much greater importance to Englishmen than the question whether the king of Spain was to be Philip or Charles. The Act of Settlement had provided that after Anne's death the throne of England should be occupied by the Electress Sophia or her son. But the Scottish Parliament had not done the same thing. As Scotland was a separate kingdom, with a Parliament and laws of its own, it might make arrangements for having a king after Anne's death who might be a different person from the king of England. Of course the English did not like this. They did not want to have Scotland again unconnected with England, and perhaps ready to make war upon it as it used to do before James I. had come to rule in England. The Scotch did not in reality want this any more than the English did, but they had hitherto been forced to pay heavy duties whenever they brought goods to England to sell, as if they had been foreigners, and they were determined that they would not do as the English asked them to do about the throne, unless they could have freedom of trade with England. The English fancied that if they allowed the Scots to buy and sell in England without paying duties, they would be able to sell goods much more cheaply than the English did, because Scotchmen lived so much more economically than Englishmen, who fed upon bread and beef instead of feeding on oatmeal porridge. The English were therefore very much frightened lest they should all be ruined, because every one would buy goods from the Scots. At last, however, the English gave way, and in 1707 the Act of Union was passed, by which England and Scotland became one people with one Parliament, and with free trade between the two countries, though Scotland kept its own laws and its own Presbyterian Church. After all, the English did not find that they were ruined.

5. The Whig Ministry.—The war was still going on. Marlborough won two more great battles, one at Oudenarde, and another at Malplaquet. In both the French fought desperately, and there was less advantage gained by the conquerors after these battles than had been gained after those of Blenheim and Ramilies. As the war went on the Tories began to get tired of it. They thought that it would be quite enough if the French could be driven out of the Netherlands, and that it did not matter to England whether a French prince were king of Spain or not. Ever since the great war in William's time a practice had been growing up of giving the chief offices in the State to men who agreed together in their political opinions. These officers—a Lord Chancellor, who was at the head of the law ; the First Lord of the Treasury, who looked after the payment of the public money ; the Chancellor of the Exchequer, who looked after the raising of taxes ; the First Lord of the Admiralty, who looked after the Navy ; the Secretaries of State who gave orders on behalf of the Government in various matters at home and abroad—met together with one or two other officials to consult about affairs of State. They were themselves called Ministers, and their meetings were called the meetings of the Cabinet. The Cabinet in reality governed England. As the Whigs were in favour of the war, and as for some time the war was popular, the Whigs gained a majority in the House of Commons after the Battle of Blenheim ; and Marlborough, who wanted the war to go on, persuaded the queen to appoint a Whig Cabinet. Before long, however, there came a change in the feelings of the people. Many thought that the time had come to make peace, and this made the Whigs as unpopular in 1709 as they had been popular in 1704, the year of the battle of Blenheim.

6. The Sacheverell Trial.—At the end of 1709, when people were getting tired of the war, a certain Dr. Sacheverell preached a sermon against the Dissenters and the Whigs who favoured them. In the course of the sermon, he declared his belief that all resistance to a king was unchristian as well as unlawful. The Whig ministers considered this to be an attack on the resistance which had brought about the Revolution at the end of the reign of James II.

They had not yet learned that liberty of speech was a good thing when things were said against themselves, and they were unwise enough to impeach Sacheverell. The preacher became at once popular with the London mob. Crowds ran about the streets, pulling down the Dissenters' chapels and shouting for the Church and Dr. Sacheverell. The House of Lords condemned Sacheverell's sermon to be burnt, and forbade him to preach for the next three years. It was not a very hard punishment, and Dr. Sacheverell did not lose much by it. As he went about the country he found himself received as if he had been a king making a progress amongst a loyal people. The church bells were rung, healths were drunk, and bonfires lighted up in his honour. It was quite plain that the people had grown tired of the Whigs.

7. The Tory Ministry.—The queen, too, had never really liked the Whigs, and had only been persuaded by Marlborough to favour them. Just at this time she quarrelled with the Duchess, who had been her great friend ever since she was a child. The Duchess was proud and violent in temper, and treated the queen so haughtily that Anne could bear it no longer. The queen sent away the Duchess and dismissed the ministers. A new Tory ministry was formed, of which the principal members were Harley, a diligent, plodding man of no great powers of mind, and St. John, a man of very great ability, who could make better speeches than any one in the House of Commons, and who looked on politics as a very amusing game, which was particularly amusing if it brought riches and power to himself.

8. The Peace of Utrecht.—The first thought of the new ministers was to make peace with France. It was quite right that they should do this, for France had become so weak by its many defeats that nothing more was to be gained by war. In 1713 the Treaty of Utrecht was signed. The Archduke Charles, who had failed to conquer Spain, was now Emperor and ruler of the Austrian dominions, and

UTRECHT.

he was allowed to add to his other territories the Spanish lands in Italy and the Netherlands   Philip V., the grandson of Lewis XIV., kept Spain itself and the Spanish colonies in America and elsewhere.

9. The Last Days of Queen Anne.—Besides making peace, the new ministers had been doing all they could against the Dissenters. Parliament had at last made a law against Occasional Conformity, and a little later it made another law called the Schism Act, by which no one was allowed to keep a school without license from the bishop, the object of which was to prevent the Dissenters from having schools of their own. The Tories, however, were in the same difficulty which James II. had been in. Just as James had known that whatever he did would be undone, as soon as he died, by his daughter Mary, so the Tories knew that whatever they did would be undone whenever Anne died. By law Anne's heir was the Electress Sophia, and when she died, in 1714, her son George, Elector of Hanover, succeeded to her right. The Tories knew that George would favour the Whigs, and some of them would have been glad to change the law, and bring the son of James II.— the Pretender as he was usually called—to reign after Anne. If the Pretender had been a Protestant, this would perhaps have been done ; but as he was not, the Tories could not make up their minds to have a Catholic king. Before they could resolve what to do, the queen died.

CHAPTER XXXV.

THE REIGNS OF THE FIRST TWO GEORGES TO THE DEATH OF HENRY PELHAM.

(GEORGE I., 1714—GEORGE II., 1727—DEATH OF HENRY PELHAM, 1754.)

1. The First Years of George I.—The new king sent away the Tory ministers and put Whig ministers in their places. In 1715 the Jacobites rose against the Government in the North of England and in Scotland. The Pretender himself landed in Scotland. He was a slow and inactive man, and made a very bad soldier, so that no one felt much interest in him. The insurrection was put down, and the Pretender had to go back again to the Continent.

GEORGE I.

The Whig Government had everything its own way. It took away the laws which had been made in Anne's reign against the Dissenters, and some of the Whigs talked of putting an end to the Test Act, as far as the Dissenters were concerned, and allowing them to hold offices. The Whigs who proposed this soon found that it would make them very unpopular. The greater part of the English people did not know much, or care much about politics, but they had strong prejudices, and they fancied that if the Dissenters had power they would behave in the way in which the Puritans had behaved in the time of Cromwell. Just at the time, however, when this matter was talked of, the Whig ministers, who were then in office, were driven out of it by an affair which had nothing to do with politics.

2. The South Sea Bubble.—In consequence of the peace which had followed the Treaty of Utrecht, there was more trade than there had been before, and many people who had a little money began to think that they had only to spend it on trade to make themselves rich. They began to form companies for trade, and some of these companies did good work, and brought profits to the shareholders. Others were only invented by ignorant or knavish men, in order to get money for themselves out of the pockets of people who were foolish enough to believe them. One of the companies which was most popular was the South Sea Company. It had been formed to carry on trade in South America, and it might have gained a profit there. But people fancied that its profit would be enormous, and large numbers paid for the right of joining in the company a great deal more than it was worth. At one time they were ready to give 1,000*l.* for such a share in the company as had at first been worth only 100*l.*, and which was probably never worth more than that. By-and-by these people found out that they had been deluded, and had to sell for less than it was worth what they had bought for more than it was worth. Of course they were very angry, and as some of the ministers had been bribed by the people who managed the company to give them support in Parliament, there was a great outcry against them. One of the ministers was sent to the Tower. Another poisoned himself from shame and grief.

3. Sir Robert Walpole, Prime Minister.—A new ministry was formed, of which the chief member was Sir Robert Walpole. He was a Whig like the last ministers, but he was careful not to do anything which would rouse opposition. He was the first man who was called a Prime Minister in England. In the time of William III. and Anne the king or queen had been in the habit of being present at the meetings of the Cabinet and of listening to the advice of the ministers there. George I., however, could not talk English well enough to take an interest in the discussions of his ministers, and none of his ministers could talk German. He therefore stayed away, and none of the kings since have ever been present at a meeting of the Cabinet. When the king ceased to come, it was necessary that some one should take the first place, and in this way grew up the practice of having one minister, called a Prime Minister, who is superior to the rest.

4. Parliamentary Corruption.—Walpole understood business very well, and he understood how to manage the members of the House of Commons. Many of them would not vote as the ministers wished unless they were bribed, and Walpole was quite ready to bribe them. At that time no one, unless he were a member of the House, knew how a member spoke or voted. Newspapers were not allowed to publish the speeches in Parliament or to tell how any vote had been given. The consequence was that a member could sell his vote, because none of those who had elected him would know anything of what he had done. Very few of them would have cared much about the matter if they had known. When election time came they knew that the candidates gave them money for their votes and plenty of beer without asking them to pay for it, and that was all that most of them thought of.

5. **Walpole and the Excise Bill.**—In 1727 George I. died, and was succeeded by his son George II. Walpole remained Prime Minister. There was beginning to be an opposition against him in the House of Commons. Some members opposed him because he had turned them out of office, or because he would not bribe them enough. There were others, too, who opposed him because they did not like seeing bribes given. He had the advantage over his opponents for a long time, not only because he had the money of the nation to give away, but because he never did anything imprudent. Once he proposed an Excise Bill to enable the Government to get money by an excise levied upon goods when they are ready to be sold, instead of getting it by customs, levied on goods when they are brought into the country. In this way he hoped to put an end to smuggling. Every one now thinks that this would have been a great improvement. But the people took it into their heads that it would be very

tyrannical if officers came into their shops and houses to see what was there for sale, and they fancied that they would have to pay more for what they bought than they had paid before. Walpole knew that this would not really be so, but when he saw how excited the people were he preferred to give up his proposal rather than take the chance of open resistance. He thought that no improvement was worth the risk of an insurrection.

6. Walpole and the War with Spain.—Some time after this the people again became excited. This time it was about a quarrel with Spain. In those days no country liked to allow freedom of trade, and colonies were not permitted to buy or sell unless when they traded with persons coming from the mother-country to which they belonged. In the Treaty of Utrecht, however, Spain had been obliged to promise that one English ship only in the year might sell goods to the Spanish colonies in South America. The English had not kept strictly to their part of the bargain. One great English ship came near the shore, and the goods on board were unloaded in the day-time. But she was accompanied by several smaller vessels which remained out of sight of land, and which came up in the night-time and filled up with fresh goods the space in the large ship which had been emptied the day before. Besides this trickery there was a great deal of smuggling going on. English vessels sailed to the West Indies to put their goods on shore whenever they could escape the notice of the Spanish coastguards. Of course, the coastguards were very angry, and did not treat the

English smugglers very well when they caught them. One day a man named Jenkins appeared before the House of Commons, and produced one of his ears out of a box where it was wrapped up in cotton. He said that it had been cut off by the Spaniards in the West Indies, and that they had bidden him to carry it to his king. Many people believe that this story was untrue, and that he had lost his ear in the pillory. Whether it were true or not, England was enraged. Parliament and people called on Walpole to go to war with Spain. Walpole believed that this was unjust, but he weakly consented to do what he was asked to do. When war was declared, the bells rang loudly for joy. 'They are ringing the bells now,' said the Prime Minister. 'They will be wringing their hands soon.'

7. **Fall of Walpole.**- To make war when he knew that it was unjust was the worst thing that Walpole ever did. It was also the most unfortunate thing for himself. It would have been better for him if he had been honest; and if he had resigned, rather than do what he thought wrong, he would probably have been asked before long to take office again. As it happened, the war did not go on as well as people thought that it ought, and they threw the blame on Walpole. They said that he did not take any trouble about it because he did not like it. At last the opposition grew so strong that he was obliged to resign, and in 1742 his long Ministry came to an end.

8. **The Ministry of the Pelhams.**---After Walpole had been turned out there was a new set of ministers,

but they bribed the members of Parliament just as much as Walpole had done. After a short time the leading ministers were two brothers. The younger, Henry Pelham, was Prime Minister. He was a very good man of business, and managed to keep the House of Commons quiet by giving office to everybody who could speak well, without caring what his principles were. For this reason his ministry was known as the Broad-bottomed Administration. The elder brother, the Duke of Newcastle, was very ignorant, but he knew how to keep people who had votes in Parliament in a good humour. Every day his rooms were filled with men who wanted something. One wished his brother or son to be made a bishop or a general. Another had some poor friend for whom he wanted a clerkship or some lower office. Newcastle gave offices to some and civil speeches to every one. By obliging people in this way he got many votes for the Government, though he was himself very ridiculous. He was always in a bustle, and it was said of him that he seemed to have got up half an hour too late every morning, and to be running about all day to try to catch it.

9. **The Young Pretender in Scotland.**—In 1745, after Henry Pelham had been in office for a short time, Charles Edward, the Young Pretender, as he was called in England, landed in the Highlands of Scotland. He was the son of the Old Pretender, who called himself James III. of England and James VIII. of Scotland, and, as his father was still alive, he called himself Prince of Wales. The Highlanders were quite ready to join him, and he soon found himself

able to march at their head to Edinburgh. Many of
the people of Edinburgh were much pleased to see
him. Scotland had prospered since the union with
England, but the people of Edinburgh did not forget
that there was no Parliament meeting in their city
any longer, and that the members went up to London

PRESTON TOWER, NEAR THE SITE OF THE BATTLE.

to spend their money instead of spending it in the
Scottish capital. Charles Edward, too, was a brisk and
handsome young man, and that always counts for
something. The Prince, however, could not stay
long in Edinburgh, as an English army was coming
against him, and was at Preston Pans, a few miles east
of Edinburgh. He therefore marched to attack

them there. The Highlanders fought as they had
fought at Killiecrankie. They rushed upon the
English soldiers with their broadswords flashing, and
swept them away. The victory of the Highlanders
was complete in a few minutes. The conquerors
plundered the slain, and often did not know the value
of the things which they found in the pockets of the
Englishmen. One Highlander took a watch, and
when he heard it ticking he fancied that it was alive.
As he did not wind it up, it soon ceased to tick. He
then sold it for very little, and thought that he had
made a good bargain. ‘I was glad,’ he said, ‘to be
rid of the creature, for she lived no time after I
caught her.’

10. The Young Pretender in England.—The Pre-
tender resolved to try whether he could not win
England as he had won Scotland. He crossed the
Border and marched steadily southwards, hoping that
his father’s old friends would rise to support him.
But there were few of his father’s friends left.
England was well off, and did not want a change.
Men could not be very enthusiastic on behalf of
George II., and still less about Newcastle, but even
those who did not care anything about politics knew
that the country was much better off under the
kings of the House of Hanover than it had been
under James II. As soon as it appeared that Englishmen would not rise for Charles Edward, it became
quite certain that he would have to go back. He
and his Highlanders could not conquer England. He
reached Derby, and found that if he went on further
he would soon be surrounded by George’s armies

Sadly he turned his face northwards, and reached Scotland again in a miserable plight.

11. Falkirk and Culloden.—Charles Edward had one more success. He fought a battle at Falkirk. The English general Hawley despised his enemy, because the Highlanders did not understand the drill of the regular soldiers, and so he got well beaten. The king's son, the Duke of Cumberland, was sent to Scotland to see whether he could not do better than Hawley. Charles Edward wanted to remain to fight him, but his chief officers told him that his army was not large enough, and that he had better retreat northwards. Cumberland followed him. When the English army reached Nairn, the prince was at Culloden about twelve miles off. The Highlanders determined to try to surprise Cumberland's army in its sleep. They started in the evening and marched all night. They had to pass over a rough and boggy moor, and the wearied men found it impossible to push on fast enough in the dark to reach the enemy's camp before daylight. They struggled back to Culloden. The next day Cumberland was upon them. Charles Edward ordered his Highlanders to charge. They dashed upon the soldiers, and drove back the first line. The second line stood firm, and received them with a steady fire. The bold warriors in the tartan kilts wavered. Then they broke and fled. Discipline had at last shown, as it has often shown, that it is too strong for undisciplined valour. Cumberland had won a victory. But he disgraced the English name by the use which he made of it. The Highlanders were treated worse than vermin are treated by the farmer. After the battle the soldiers knocked the wounded on the head. Several of the wounded men had taken refuge in a cottage. The soldiers shut the door fast, set the house on fire, and burnt the wretched men alive. Prisoners taken were sent in great numbers to execution. Three Scotch noblemen were beheaded on Tower Hill. It was the last time that the axe and block were used in England. To the day of his death the general who had won the day was known as The Butcher Cumberland.

12. The Escape of Charles Edward.—The Prince himself escaped. He wandered about for five months amongst the hills and islands of the Western Highlands. A lady, Flora Macdonald, took him under her special care, concealed him when danger was near, and aided his flight. Sometimes he was disguised as a servant, sometimes as a woman. Of the many who knew him not one would betray him to his enemies. At last he escaped in a French vessel. He lived for many years on the Continent a broken-hearted man, without hope and without employment for his energy. He sunk into dissipation and vice. In Scotland he has never been forgotten. To this day songs in honour of Prince Charlie are sung there, which were composed by a lady many years later, but which tell the thoughts which were once in so many Scottish hearts. Now that Scotchmen are all loyal to their queen and country, they can still sing that,

> Charlie is my darling,
> My darling, my darling,
> Charlie is my darling,
> The young chevalier.

13. The Death of Henry Pelham.—Henry Pelham lived for eight years after the Battle of Culloden, doing his business quietly and offending nobody. He died in 1754. ‘ Now,’ said the old king, ‘ I shall have no more peace.’ The old king spoke truly.

CHAPTER XXXVI.

THE LAST SIX YEARS OF GEORGE II.

(1754–1760.)

1. Englishmen Spread over the World.—The wars which England had hitherto waged had been waged for power on the Continent of Europe. The nation had striven to conquer France in the days of Edward III. and Henry V., to resist the enormous strength of Spain in the reign of Elizabeth, and the enormous strength of France in the reigns of William III and Anne. For some time, however, Englishmen had been spreading over the world. They had gone forth to trade and to colonise, and before the end of the reign of George II. England was at war with France, not on account of anything that had happened in Europe, but on account of things which had happened in America and Asia.

2. English and French in America.—In the time of James I. and Charles I. Englishmen had gone to live in that part of the American Continent which is now known as the United States. Some of them who had gone to the southern part went, just as people now go to Australia or Canada, because they wanted to have land of their own to cultivate. Those who went to New England in the North went because they were Puritans, and wanted to be allowed to live and to worship God in their own way without interference. The descendants of these men had increased and multiplied, and there were in the middle of the reign of George II. thirteen colonies, full of prosperous people, managing their own affairs, but each having at its head a Governor appointed by the king of England. They all lived along the Atlantic coast, and it was only very occasionally that any one of them crossed the Alleghany mountains. Those who did found a vast plain, the northern part of which is watered by the River Ohio, and the streams which fall into it. The country was covered with forests, in which were Indians who hunted the fur-covered animals which abounded there, and sold the furs to Europeans. Most of these Indians were not friendly to the English, who would cut down their woods, and ploughed up their lands if they could come into possession of them. At that time Lower Canada belonged to the French, and as the French did not want to cultivate the land on the Ohio the Indians were on very good terms with them and sold their furs to them. Even before the death of Pelham there had been some fighting going on between the English and French, and General Braddock had been sent to protect the English. He was a brave but stupid man.

Officers in those days were appointed not because they understood how to lead an army, but because they were the friends of Newcastle, or of some one whose vote Newcastle wanted to gain. Braddock marched on till he came to a place where the French and Indians surrounded him in the forest, and he and most of his men were shot down from behind the trees.

3. Beginning of the Seven Years' War.—After that there could be no continuance of peace with France. The two nations were in reality contending for all that vast country which stretches from the Alleghany mountains to the Pacific. Whichever of the two gained its object would some day occupy almost all the territory which now belongs to the United States. The war would decide whether French or English was to be spoken on the banks of the Mississippi and the shores of California. But England and France did not know this; they only knew that they were fighting for the possession of the forests at the head of the Ohio. The war, which began in 1756 and lasted till 1763, is known as the Seven Years' War.

4. Newcastle driven from Office.—Newcastle was now Prime Minister. He was quite ignorant how to manage a war. At that time Minorca in the Mediterranean belonged to England. It was attacked by a French fleet and army. Admiral Byng went to take help to it, but he thought that the French were too strong, and came back without fighting. Minorca was taken by the enemy. People in England were enraged. They thought that Byng was a coward, and cried out to have him punished. Newcastle was horribly frightened. He thought that the people would ask to have himself punished next. 'Oh,' he cried out to some persons who came to ask him to have the Admiral tried; 'indeed, he shall be tried immediately—he shall be hanged directly.' Byng was tried, and shot. A witty Frenchman said that it was the custom in England to shoot an admiral to encourage the others. Before Byng was condemned Newcastle resigned his office. He loved it dearly, but he was too frightened to keep it any longer.

5. Pitt in Office.—There was a man in the House of Commons who had more confidence in himself. William Pitt had kept himself pure when every one around him had been giving or taking bribes. He had confidence in his countrymen as well. He knew how brave they were, and he thought that if they had good leaders they would be sure to beat the French. 'I know,' he once said, 'that I can save this country and that nobody else can.' He became immediately the most popular minister who had ever held office. He was known as the Great Commoner. But the corrupt members of Parliament, who wanted a minister who would buy their votes, did not like him at all, and they voted against him. He was obliged to resign. Then many weeks passed during which there was no ministry at all. Newcastle could not bear to let Pitt be minister, and he was too much afraid of the people to try to manage the war himself. At last it was arranged that Newcastle and Pitt should be ministers together. Pitt was to manage the war, and Newcastle was to manage the bribery.

6. Wolfe's Expedition to Canada.—Pitt succeeded in managing the war, because he appointed men who had done well in command of small forces

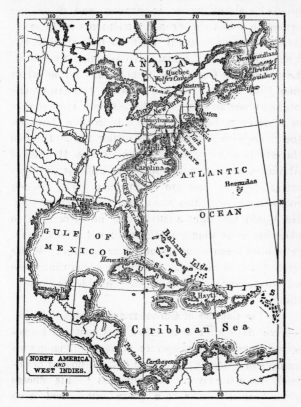

NORTH AMERICA
AND
WEST INDIES.

to command great ones, because he made every one understand that the surest way to his favour was to succeed, and because he never favoured any one only because he was rich, or related to some great man. He sent money to Frederick the Great, king of Prussia, who was at war with France and many other countries besides. He sent out regiments to attack places in France, and fleets and armies to attack the French settlements in America. At last he sent General Wolfe to take Quebec, the French capital of Canada. Wolfe sailed up the St. Lawrence, and found that Quebec was not at all an easy place to take. It lies between two rivers, the St. Lawrence and the St. Charles, and a great part of it is on a high ridge of hill looking down on the rivers with steep cliffs on either side. Outside the city is a lofty place known as the Heights of Abraham, and for some miles the cliffs at its edges are as steep as they are at the city. The French commander Montcalm was a brave and skilful man. He would not fight a battle, but he took care to place his men where Wolfe could not attack them, or pass by them so as to get near Quebec. Wolfe wrote home in despair. He did not think that there was any chance that he would be able to do anything.

7. **The Capture of Quebec and the Death of Wolfe.** —Five days after this letter was written, he resolved to make one desperate attempt. Placing his soldiers in boats in the dark night, he floated noiselessly down the river. He repeated to his officers some beautiful lines of a poem which had been published by Gray some years before. One of these lines was,

'The paths of glory lead but to the grave.'

' Now, gentlemen,' he said, ' I would rather be the

author of that poem than take Quebec!' At last the boats reached the point at the foot of the cliffs for which they had been steering. The men leapt on shore. Above them was a narrow zig-zag path winding up in the darkness amongst the precipitous rocks, so narrow that in some places two men could not stand on it side by side. The soldiers clambered up. When they reached the top, the Frenchmen were so astonished to see them coming up the cliff that they ran off. Before more had time to arrive, the British army was drawn up on the plain. Montcalm came out of the city with the French army. In the battle both Wolfe and Montcalm were killed. As Wolfe lay dying, he heard an officer cry ' See how they run !' Wolfe roused himself to ask, 'Who run ?' When he heard it was the enemy he was satisfied. ' God be praised,' he said ; ' I shall die happy.' These were his last words. Quebec gave itself up, and before long all Canada was conquered. French and English are happily good friends now, and a monument has been erected on the Heights of Abraham which bears the names of both the commanders who died there, each fighting for his own country.

8. Victory at Quiberon Bay.—Englishmen in Pitt's days fought as well by sea as they fought by land. Admiral Hawke sailed to attack a French fleet in Quiberon Bay. The French ships had been placed for safety amidst rocks and shoals. The wind was blowing hard. Hawke's pilot told him it was not safe to venture into such a dangerous place. ' Lay me alongside the French Admiral,' answered

Hawke.   You have done your duty, but now obey my orders. Hawke dashed in amongst the rocks,

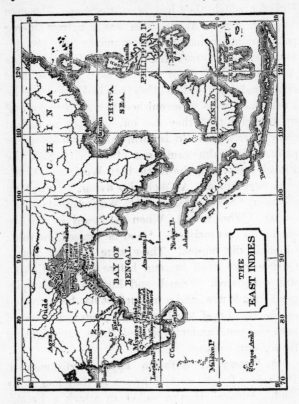

Four of the French fleet were sunk, two surrendered, and the rest fled up a river.

9. Struggle between the English and French.— There were victories in India as well as in America. At the end of the reign of Elizabeth, the East India

Company had been formed to trade with India. In the reign of Charles I. the Company bought some land at Madras, and built a fort on it. In the reign of Charles II. it obtained Bombay from the king, who had received it from the king of Portugal on his marriage with Catharine of Braganza. In the reign of William III. an English fort was built on the Hooghly, round which sprang up the town of Calcutta. Only these three towns belonged to the English, who wanted to trade, not to conquer. The rest of India was governed by native princes. About the time when the Young Pretender was fighting in Scotland, there began a contest between the English and French in the part of India near Madras. The French for some time got the better. The French governor Dupleix was a skilful man, and managed to secure the friendship of some of the natives, and to defeat those who opposed him. He was the first to drill native soldiers, or Sepoys as they were called, in the European fashion. He was so proud of his success that he built a town and called it by an Indian name, which meant 'The City of the Victory of Dupleix.'

10. Clive at Arcot.—In Madras there was a young English clerk, named Robert Clive. He was not a man to be easily frightened. One day he accused an officer with whom he was playing at cards with cheating. A duel was fought, and Clive missed the man at whom he fired. His antagonist came up to him and held his pistol at his head, bidding him acknowledge that his accusation had been false. 'Fire,' said Clive, without shrinking; 'I said you cheated, I say

so still, and I will never pay you.' The officer threw
down his pistol, saying that Clive was mad. Clive
was not mad. Not long afterwards there was a
call for soldiers, and Clive offered to serve as one.
He was sent to seize Arcot, a fortified town not far
off, which belonged to a native prince, who was
friendly to the French. When Clive approached the
place a thunderstorm came on. The garrison of
Arcot expected that Clive would stop to take shelter.
When they saw that he marched on in spite of the
weather, they were so astonished that they all ran
away, and left Arcot to him. Before long a great
army was sent to besiege him there. He fought
desperately, but he was all but starved out. Nothing
but rice was left to feed on, and there was not much
of that. Clive, like Dupleix, had sepoys with him.
Some of these faithful men came to him and begged
that all the rice might be given to his English
soldiers. The natives, they said, did not need so
much nourishment as Europeans did, and the water
in which the rice had been boiled would be enough
for them. Clive's brave resistance saved him in the
end. A native chief who had been paid to help the
English had for some time kept away. When he
heard how Arcot was being defended, he ordered his
men to march. 'I never thought till now,' he said,
'that the English could fight. Since they can, I
will help them.' With this help Clive was successful. The besiegers gave up trying to take Arcot.
The English troops got the better of the French.
Not long afterwards Clive returned to England.

11. The Black Hole of Calcutta.—For some little

time there was peace between the French and English. When the Seven Years' War began Clive was sent out again. The first news which reached him on his arrival was sad enough. A native prince named Surajah Dowlah ruled in Bengal. He knew that the English merchants at Calcutta were rich, and he seized Calcutta and all the English in it. He ordered them to be thrust into a very small room measuring only eighteen feet one way and fifteen the other. Into this place, known afterwards as 'The Black Hole of Calcutta,' a hundred and forty-five Englishmen and one Englishwoman were driven. It was in the heat of the day, and the day is far hotter in India than it ever is in the hottest summer in England. So hot and close was it that those who were within soon knew that but few of them would come out alive. They called for water, and, when some was brought in skins, these skins were too large to be thrust in through the bars of the window. The prisoners struggled madly for the smallest drop, trampling one another down to reach it. The guards outside laughed cruelly at the sight. All through that day and the night which followed men were dying in agony. When the morning came, and the door was opened, of the hundred and forty-six who had entered only twenty-three, almost as pale as corpses, staggered out alive.

12. The Battle of Plassey.—Clive soon arrived to avenge his countrymen. He had with him three thousand soldiers. Surajah Dowlah had fifty thousand. In spite of these enormous odds, Clive attacked him at Plassey. Part of the army of the enemy deserted in the middle of the battle. The rest fled with very little resistance. From the example of that day English armies have learned to face any odds in India. Step by step they have overcome all resistance. India has been brought in the course of years under English rule. India has had peace given to it. The native princes who remain in some parts are not allowed to plunder and slaughter their neighbours. The English governors of India have still a hard task before them, to rule justly and wisely for the benefit of the natives, and to teach them, if it be possible, to govern themselves.

CHAPTER XXXVII.

FROM THE ACCESSION OF GEORGE III. TO THE END OF THE AMERICAN WAR.

(1760–1783.)

1. Peace with France.—George II. died suddenly, and was succeeded by his grandson, George III. The young king was anxious to make peace with France. Pitt discovered that the Spaniards wanted to join the French, and proposed to declare war against Spain. The king and the other ministers refused to do so, and Pitt resigned. After all, Spain did join France, and in the war that followed the Spaniards were beaten as much as the French had been. Before long, however, peace was made in 1763, seven years after the war had begun. England kept Canada.

2. The Stamp Act.—Even before the peace was made George III. tried to get rid of the Whigs. He had set his heart on naming the ministers whom he liked to name, and not the ministers whom the great Whig noblemen asked him to name. He found out that he could gain votes by giving offices away, especially if the offices were well paid, and if, as often happened, the officers had nothing to do. Still it was a long time before he got his way. After a little time he was obliged to accept George Grenville, who was a Whig, as Prime Minister, whom he very much disliked. Grenville was a conscientious man, but not a wise one. The last war had been very expensive, and Grenville thought that he could make the Americans pay some of the expense. He therefore persuaded the English Parliament to pass a Stamp Act, ordering the Americans to pay money for stamps to be put on all their law papers as they are now in England. The Americans grew very angry, and declared that the English Parliament had no right to tax them. Before it was known in England how angry they were, the king had turned Grenville out of office. Grenville was succeeded by Lord Rockingham, who was now leader of one portion of the Whigs. The Whigs who were led by Rockingham were never very popular. They would not bribe, so that all who wanted to be bribed turned against them. They offended others because they did not mix with the people, and did not like to have anything to do with any great changes. Rockingham himself was a well-meaning, timid man, who listened respectfully to Edmund Burke, who was

the wisest man in England. When the news came
of the ill-feeling in America, the Rockingham ministry advised that the Stamp Act should be repealed.
As soon as the English Parliament left off taxing
the Americans, the Americans again became quiet
and loyal.

3. The Tea Duties.—The king did not like Rockingham any better than he had liked Grenville, and
turned him out. He made Pitt Prime Minister, and
created him Earl of Chatham. Chatham's ministry
might have been a splendid one if he had remained
in health, but he soon became so ill that he was
unable to attend to business. The other ministers
did as they pleased, and were foolish enough to try
to tax America again. This time they persuaded
Parliament to place duties on tea and other articles
going into America. Parliament did not need much
persuasion. Most English people thought that the
Americans ought to pay more taxes than they did, and
were glad to make them pay whether they liked it
or not. The Americans again grew angry. But
this time there was no Rockingham ministry to be
wise enough to take away the duties.

4. Wilkes and the Middlesex Election.—The fact
was that the House of Commons only thought of
making people do as it pleased, just as Charles I. had
only thought of making people do as he pleased.
Just then the Middlesex electors chose a man named
Wilkes as their member of Parliament. His character
was not good, and some years before he had made
the king very angry by finding fault with the king's
speech at the opening of Parliament. As soon as he

was elected the House of Commons expelled him.
The Middlesex electors chose him a second time,
and the House of Commons expelled him again.
The Middlesex electors chose him a third time, and
then the House of Commons declared that another
candidate, who had received very few votes, was
properly chosen, and allowed him to sit in the House

LORD NORTH.

instead of Wilkes. Soon after this Chatham got
well again.   He declared in the House of Lords that
the House of Commons had no right to do what it
had done, and he also declared that an English
Parliament had no right to tax America.

5. Throwing of Tea into Boston Harbour. -- The
king would not listen to Chatham's good advice. He
made Lord North Prime Minister.   Lord North was

one of those men who were now called Tories. They were different in many ways from the Tories of the reign of Anne. They thought that the king and not the great Whig noblemen ought to choose the ministers. Lord North was a sensible man, but he allowed himself to be persuaded to do whatever the king told him to do. He was very fat, and used to go to sleep in the House of Commons when the members were abusing him in their speeches. When he was awake he was fond of making jokes, and he never lost his temper. Some time afterwards a large quantity of tea was sent to Boston. The inhabitants determined that it should not be landed, because they were afraid lest if it were allowed to come on shore some people might be tempted to buy it, and so to pay the duty to the British Government. They asked the governor to allow the ship which brought the tea to go back to England. As soon as it was known that he had refused, about forty or fifty men disguised as Red Indians rushed down to the quay. They leapt on board the ship, split open the tea-chests, and emptied their contents into the harbour. When the news of what had been done reached England, the king and the ministers were extremely angry. They got Parliament to pass a law forbidding any ships to take in cargo, or to unload cargo at Boston, and another law providing that the colony of Massachusetts, in which Boston was, should be governed by persons appointed by the king. Chatham and Burke did all they could to stop the making of these laws, but it was all in vain. Soldiers were sent out to force the colonists to obey the orders of the British Parliament.

6. The Beginning of the American War.—The Americans prepared to resist. They elected a Congress, in which persons chosen by the different colonies might meet to decide what was to be done. In 1775 fighting began. A British force marching

BUNKER'S HILL.

to seize some arms was attacked, and many of the soldiers were killed. The first serious fighting was on a hill near Boston called Breed's Hill, though the battle is usually known as that of Bunker's Hill, which is a height in the same range. The British troops attempted twice to ascend the hill. Twice they were driven back with great slaughter. The

third time they were successful, as the Americans
had used nearly all their powder and shot, and were

obliged to retreat. The British general wrote home
saying that he had now found out that the rebels

were not 'the despicable rabble too many have
supposed them to be.' In spite of this the English
people thought that the war would soon be over.
They were many and the Americans were few.
Their soldiers were well disciplined, and the Americans had no regular soldiers at all. But the Americans were fighting for their own land, and for their
liberty. Before long they issued their Declaration
of Independence, declaring that they were a free

NEW YORK.

nation, and would submit to King George no longer.
The Americans had a difficult battle to fight. They
were sometimes victorious, and sometimes beaten.
The British forces seized on New York, and kept it
to the end of the war. After that the Americans
surrounded a British army under General Burgoyne
at Saratoga, and forced it to surrender. They had a
great man to lead them, George Washington. He
was not merely a good general, but he was patient

and modest, utterly regardless of himself and ready
to suffer anything rather than injure his country.
Yet, after two years of war, in spite of all Washington's heroism, the American army was almost starved
to death. The horses died for want of forage, and
for six days the men had no meat. There was
scarcely a pair of shoes to be found in the whole
camp.

7. **The Alliance between America and France.**—
Help came to the Americans from France. The
French had not forgotten how the English had
treated them in the last war, and they were glad to
find an opportunity of taking their revenge. They
engaged to make war with England till America was
acknowledged to be independent. Lord North was
frightened, and offered to do anything that the
Americans wished if they would not ask for independence. Chatham himself could not make up his
mind to agree to that. He was old and ill, and he
went to the House of Lords to call on Englishmen
not to give way before France. 'As long,' he said,
'as I can crawl down to this House, and have
strength to raise myself on my crutches, or lift my
hand, I will vote against giving up the dependency
of America on the sovereignty of Great Britain.'
The Peers listened respectfully, but they could
hardly hear his words. He was not what he once
had been. He repeated the same sentences and
could not recollect what he had intended to say.
After an answer had been given him, he rose to
speak again. He staggered and fell, struck down by
apoplexy. His son and son-in-law—the son the

young William Pitt who was one day to be Prime
Minister—hastened to carry him away. In a few
days he died.

8. The End of the War.—If Chatham had been
living, and had been ruling England, he could not
have stopped the Independence of America. Fighting went on, and Spain joined France and America.
At last an English army, under Lord Cornwallis, was

GIBRALTAR.

shut up in Yorktown. The Americans hemmed it
in on the land side, and a French fleet blocked it up
by sea. Cornwallis was forced to surrender. When
the news reached England in 1782, every one knew
that it was no use to struggle longer. Lord North
gave up his office, and Rockingham again became
Prime Minister. Besides giving offices to his own
followers, he gave some to the chief men amongst

Chatham's followers, of whom the principal was Lord Shelburne. Before peace was made Admiral Rodney gained a great victory over the French by sea, and a large French and Spanish fleet, which was trying to take Gibraltar, had to give up the attempt in despair. Before Gibraltar was freed Rockingham died, and the king named Shelburne to succeed him. Shelburne made arrangements for peace, though the actual treaty was not signed till after he had left office. In 1783 the Independence of America was acknowledged in the treaty.

CHAPTER XXXVIII.

FROM THE END OF THE AMERICAN WAR TO THE FRENCH REVOLUTION.

(1783–1789.)

1. Shelburne turned out of Office.—Lord Shelburne did not remain Prime Minister long. The friends of Rockingham in the ministry did not like him, and they thought that the king had no right to choose the Prime Minister. Their leader, now that Rockingham was dead, was Charles James Fox, who was one of the ministers under Lord Shelburne. Fox was a great orator, and the most amiable of men. He had, however, quarrelled with Shelburne, and he and his friends resigned their posts rather than hold office under him. They were no sooner out of office than they wanted to get back again, and though they were Whigs they actually went so far as to make an agreement with the Tory North and his friends to attack Shelburne. All through the American War Fox had been speaking all kinds of evil of North, so that the friendship which was thus suddenly made was not likely to be respected. The two parties, however, which were led by Fox and North had together more votes in the House of Commons than the party led by Shelburne. They therefore succeeded in turning him out, and a new ministry was formed which is known as the Coalition Ministry, because Fox's friends coalesced, or joined together, with those of North.

2. **The Contest between Pitt and the Coalition Ministry.**—The Coalition Ministry did not last long. It proposed a law about the government of India which offended a great many people, and the king turned it out of office. The king appointed young William Pitt, the son of Chatham, to be Prime Minister. No one so young as he was had ever been Prime Minister before. He was only twenty-four. Fox and North had many more votes in the House of Commons than he had, and the House voted that he ought to resign. He told them that he would not, unless they could show that he had done something wrong. Week after week the numbers who voted for him grew more, and the numbers who voted against him grew less. There were at that time a large number of members of Parliament who would vote for anybody who was likely to remain in office, because they expected to get offices for themselves and their friends, which would bring them money, and they did not care the least whether the

thing for which they voted was right or wrong.
These men began to think that Pitt was likely to
win ; and one reason why they thought this was because people who were not members of Parliament
had begun to take an interest in him. Quiet people,
who did not care much about politics, thought that
the friendship between men who had not long ago
been quarrelling, as Fox and North had quarrelled,
could not possibly have been formed in order to do
good to any one but themselves. At last Pitt advised
the king to dissolve Parliament. A new Parliament
was elected, in which Pitt had the greater number
of the members on his side.

3. Pitt and Public Opinion.—This support, given
by the voters to the young minister, was a thing
which could not have happened thirty years before.
The feeling of those people who cared about politics
had been just as strong in favour of Chatham at the
beginning of the Seven Years' War as it was now in
favour of Chatham's son. But Chatham had found
that he could not keep office unless he made friends
with Newcastle, and got the votes for which Newcastle paid. The reason was because a great many
more people cared about politics in Pitt's time than
had cared about them in Chatham's time. One cause
of this was, that just before the American War broke
out the House of Commons allowed the speeches
made by its members to be printed in newspapers,
and in this way many people began to take an interest in politics who had taken no interest before.
There were also more people who were well off from
taking part in trade, and who did not like to see the

Government of England managed by a few great noblemen and their friends. A great many of the country gentlemen, too, took the side of Pitt and the king. The country gentlemen were much better fitted to take part in politics than they had been in the days of Walpole. Those who remained at home then had been very ignorant, and those who became members of Parliament usually only thought of what they could get for their votes. Now they were better educated, read more, thought more, and were more anxious to do their duty. The party which Pitt led was called the Tory party, because it was the party which thought that the Prime Minister ought to be chosen by the king.

4. The Proposed Reform Bill and the Commercial Treaty with France.—Pitt wished to make a good many wise reforms, some of which became law, though some were rejected by the House of Commons. He proposed a Reform Bill, that is to say, a Bill for allowing many more persons to vote at the election of members of Parliament than before, but the House of Commons would not allow this Bill to pass. He was more successful in making a treaty with France, by which goods were to be allowed to come from one country to the other without being subjected to very high duties. Up to that time nations had been in the habit of thinking that they were hurt if they bought goods made by another nation more cheaply than they could make them themselves. A great man, Adam Smith, had written a book called the 'Wealth of Nations,' to show that this was a mistake. Pitt had learned the lesson from him, and he now persuaded the English Parliament that Adam Smith's lesson was true. Nations, like men, are better off when their neighbours are better off. Pitt had a difficult task to perform in convincing Parliament that this was true. England and France had been fighting with one another for centuries, and many people thought that they never could do anything else. Pitt told his hearers that it was weak and childish to suppose that one nation could be for ever the enemy of another. He asked that Englishmen and Frenchmen should trade together, not merely because they would both make money, but because they would become more friendly to one another.

5. The Slave Trade.—Pitt had room in his large mind for things of even more importance than a treaty of commerce. Ever since the days of Queen Elizabeth Englishmen, like men of other nations, had been in the habit of carrying off negroes from Africa to work as slaves in the West Indies and in other parts of America. It was calculated that at the beginning of the reign of George III. no less than 50,000 unhappy black men were thus carried off every year in ships belonging to the merchants of Bristol and Liverpool. About the time when Pitt became minister, a young man named Thomas Clarkson gained a prize at the University of Cambridge for writing on the question whether it was right to make slaves of others against their will. Many young men would have forgotten all about the matter as soon as they had got their prize. As Clarkson was riding home he got off his horse, and sat down on the grass by the side of the road, asking

himself what he could do to put an end to the great
evil about which he had been writing. He concluded
in the end that the best thing would be to find out
facts about slavery and the slave trade, and let the
English people know what horrible things were being
done. For some years he used to go about among
the sailors at Liverpool, asking them to tell him
what they knew. It was not at all a pleasant thing
to do, for the sailors were often rude to him, and
treated him very badly. But he learned a good deal
that he wanted to know, and when he knew it he
published it. By-and-by others began to inquire,
and horrible tales were told. The wretched negroes
who were seized in Africa were packed on shelves
so closely that they had hardly room to breathe,
especially as they passed across the hottest part of
the Atlantic. They had not nearly enough given
them to eat. In order to keep them in exercise
they were brought up on deck and flogged to make
them jump about. Whenever, as was often the
case, the voyage was longer than was expected, and
there was not food enough on board, the captain
picked out those who looked least strong, and threw
them into the sea, to be drowned or eaten by the
sharks. In the House of Commons a friend of Pitt
named Wilberforce did all he could to persuade
Parliament to prevent this wicked trade in slaves.
Pitt himself spoke strongly against the trade, but he
was unable to persuade the members to stop it.

6. The King's Illness and Recovery.—After Pitt
had been Prime Minister for nearly five years, the
king went out of his mind. It was agreed that

there should be a Regent to act for him, and
that the king's eldest son, who was afterwards
George IV., was to be the Regent. The Prince's
character was so bad that almost every one was glad
to hear that the old king was well again, and that
the Prince was not to be Regent. George III. went
in state to St. Paul's to return thanks for his recovery.
The streets were crowded as he passed. At night all
London was illuminated. George III. was popular
now. He had got a minister who knew how to rule
well, and who did not insult the people as some of
the ministers had done in the beginning of the reign.
People were pleased to hear of the simple ways of
the old king, and to be told that he liked to dine on a
plain leg of mutton better than on more luxurious
food. They did not think the worse of him when
they laughed over a story which had been invented
against him, that he had been puzzled to know how
the apple got inside a dumpling. They liked him,
too, because he was fond of farming.

7. **Agricultural Improvements.**—Other things
besides good government were making the country
prosperous. Men were learning how to farm, and how
to manure and drain the ground, so that corn was
growing where there had been nothing but furze and
heath not many years before. One plain farmer
named Bakewell taught how it was possible to
improve the breed of sheep, so that twice as many
pounds of good mutton might be had from one sheep
as had been had before. When the soil produced
more food, more people could be fed, and the number
of the population began to increase.

8. The Bridgewater Canal.—A people may become better off not merely from the increase of food, but from the increase of trade. English trade had grown very much before the reign of George III., but there were still difficulties in its way. Those who lived at a distance from the sea might be able to make articles which might be sold for a good price in foreign countries, but if they were at all heavy the expense of carrying them to the sea-ports to put them in vessels was so great that it would cost more to send them to the coast than would be repaid by even a good price. They would have to be carried on the backs of horses, or in carriers' carts. Unless some one invented a way of carrying heavy goods cheaply, many men would be without employment, who might have earned good wages by their work. The man who helped these men to work was James Brindley, a millwright. It happened that the Duke of Bridgewater had some land at Worsley, about six miles from Manchester. On that land there was a coal mine, and the inhabitants of Manchester were very much in want of coal, which was very dear. Yet high as the price was, the expense of carrying the heavy coal in carts was so great that it was not worth while to send it from Worsley to Manchester. The Duke consulted Brindley, and Brindley planned a canal which should go through tunnels under the hills and cross rivers on high bridges. As is usually the case when anything new is proposed, many people laughed at it. One famous engineer was taken to the place where the canal was to be carried across a valley. When he was shown the place, far above

his head, where the water was to flow, he said that
he had often heard of castles in the air, but he had
never before been shown where one was to be built.
Brindley persevered, and at last the canal was
finished. The Manchester people got their coals
cheap, and the Duke got the money for which he was
now able to sell them. By-and-by his example was
followed. Canals were made from one part of England
to the other, and heavy goods were carried easily and
cheaply along them in barges.

9. **Improvements in Spinning Machines.**—Another
improvement was the introduction of machinery for
spinning cotton into thread. Soon after the beginning
of the reign of George III. Hargreaves invented a
machine which was called the spinning-jenny. It
was more dangerous then to invent machinery than
it is now. Workmen thought that if a machine
could do more work than several men, several men
would be thrown out of work. They forgot that
the machine would produce the article so cheaply
that a great many more people than before would be
able to afford to buy it, and that therefore so much
more would be wanted that more men would be
employed with the machines than had been employed
without them. Hargreaves' neighbours attacked his
house, broke his machine, and forced him to fly for
his life. A little later, further improvements in
spinning were made by Arkwright. He, too, had
trouble enough. A mob broke into his mill and
burnt it down. But he was determined to succeed
at all risks, and at last he was allowed to live in
peace. A further improvement was made by

Crompton, who invented what is known as the mule. He was a poor weaver; when his machine was finished, he heard that mobs were gathering to break all machines. He pulled his to pieces and hid it away. When quiet was restored be began to spin. The yarn which he sold was better than any that had been known before. Manufacturers came round him to find out how he did it. The manufacturers were as bad as the workmen had been. They peeped in through the windows to see what his secret was. Poor Crompton had not money enough to pay for obtaining a patent, which would have prevented any one from copying his mule. He therefore told his secret, on the promise that the manufacturers would make a subscription to reward him for his improvement. The whole of the money subscribed by them was less than 68*l*. The manufacturers gained thousands of pounds by the poor man's invention, which they had thus taken from him.

10. The Steam-Engine. —The invention of machinery for spinning was accompanied by many other inventions in different manufactures. The most important of all was the invention of the steam-engine. For some time an attempt had been made to use steam-engines to turn wheels and for other purposes. But they consumed so much fuel in heating the steam that they cost too much to be of use. James Watt, of Glasgow, with patient study discovered a way of getting over the difficulty. Watt's engines, after a little time, came into general use, and manufacturers found that they could not do without them. The invention of the steam-engine brought about one great change which Watt had not thought of. Down to this time the North of England had been the poorest part of the country. It was more covered with wild heaths and moors than the South. The population was small, and the people were usually found on a different side from those of the South. The new ideas which came into men's minds were always to be found first in the South before they reached the North. In the reign of Henry VI. the North fought against the Yorkists. In the reign of Henry VIII. it fought to stop the dissolution of the monasteries, and in the reign of Elizabeth it fought against Protestantism. In the reign of George I. it fought for the Pretender. All this is changed now. Steam-engines were put up and factories built where coal was cheap, and coal is cheaper in the North because it is dug out of the ground there. These factories drew to them a large population to work in them, or to provide whatever was needed by those who worked in them. This work demanded men who were quick-witted, and the consequence is that the people in the North are far more numerous than they used to be, and that they are very intelligent and thoughtful. Some one has said that what Lancashire thinks to-day England will think to-morrow; and though this may not always be the case, it is quite certain that no one would have thought of saying so two or three hundred years ago.

CHAPTER XXXIX.

FROM THE BEGINNING OF THE FRENCH REVOLUTION TO THE PEACE OF AMIENS.

(1789–1802.)

1. **Beginning of the French Revolution.**— In 1789, a few days after the king had returned thanks at St. Paul's for his recovery, the French Revolution began. For a great many years the French had been governed almost as badly as was possible. Not only had the people to pay very heavy taxes, but the taxes were not fairly laid on. Poor people had to pay whilst rich people were let off. The rich people were favoured in all sorts of ways. Besides the taxes paid to the king, the peasants in the country had a great deal to pay to the nobles and gentlemen who lived in their country houses, and who very seldom did any good to those amongst whom they lived, in the way in which English country gentlemen often did. The king of France, Lewis XVI., was a well-meaning man, but he was not wise enough to know how to set things straight. He was so much in debt, and spent so much more than he received, that he was now obliged to call together an assembly elected by different classes of his subjects, which called itself the National Assembly soon after it had met. It was not long before the National Assembly began to do things that the king did not like, and the king then wanted to force it to do what he thought right. When this was known there

was an insurrection in Paris. The people took a great fortress called the Bastille, and the king was so frightened that he let the National Assembly do as it pleased. A few months later the mob of Paris went to the place where he lived and brought him into Paris. After that, though he was called king still, he was really more like a prisoner than a king. The National Assembly made a great many new laws, and abolished all the payments which had been made by the peasants to the gentlemen. Some of the gentlemen were very badly treated, and of these several left the country. The king, too, tried to escape and leave the country, but he was stopped and brought back to Paris, and was treated more like a prisoner than before. In 1792, three years after the Revolution began, the Prussians and the Austrians seemed likely to help the king and the gentlemen. The French declared war against them, and they invaded France. The people of Paris thought that the king wished the enemies to succeed, and there can be very little doubt that he did. They rose in insurrection, and drove him out of his palace. A new Parliament, as we should call it, named the National Convention, met, declared the king to be deposed, and established a Republic. They sent the king to prison, and in the beginning of 1793 they tried him on the charge of favouring the enemies of France, and condemned him to death. He was executed on the guillotine, an instrument made to cut off heads quickly.

2. War between England and France.—When the French Revolution began, people in England

were much pleased. They thought that the French were going to have a quiet parliamentary government like their own, and they did not think how angry different classes of people in France were with one another, and how little likely it was that a nation which had never had a parliamentary government before should know at once exactly how to behave when they had it. When news came of disturbances and insurrections, and murders, most people in England began to think that the French Revolution was altogether bad, and when a great many of the French gentlemen took refuge in England after losing all, or nearly all their property, the English gentlemen were so very sorry for them that most of them were ready to go to war with France for their sake. For a long time Pitt did all he could to keep peace. He said that England ought not to go to war because it did not like the way in which another nation managed its own affairs. After the invasion of France, however, by Austria and Prussia, the French got the better of their enemies, and invaded the country which was then known as the Austrian Netherlands, and which was very much the same as that which is now known as Belgium. Pitt thought that it would be dangerous to allow France to join to itself a country so near England, and just as he was making up his mind that he must try to stop the French from doing this, the news came that the king of France had been executed. A feeling of horror and anger passed over almost the whole country, and within a few days England and France were at war with one another.

3. English Feeling against the Revolutionists.—
The mass of the English people, both rich and poor,
had no wish to see the violence of the French Revolutionists copied in England. People in general
were far better off than they were in France, and
when people are well off they do not usually rise in
insurrection. But there were people, especially in
the towns, who thought that there ought to be a
great many changes made in the Government here,
and that a much larger number of people ought to
have votes to elect Members of Parliament. Some,
no doubt, used very violent language, and even
spoke of imitating the French Revolutionists in
almost everything that they did. This language
frightened the upper and the middle classes, and
the House of Commons, supported by the great bulk
of the nation, resolved to have nothing more to do
with any changes, and to put down with violence
all who joined together in asking for them. This
feeling soon turned into a thorough alarm. Almost
every European nation joined in the war against
France. France was again invaded, and the French
people grew suspicious of every one whom they suspected of wishing to help the enemy, or even of not
caring much about keeping him off. Hundreds of
persons were hurried off to the guillotine and beheaded without any fair trial. This was called the
Reign of Terror, and lasted for more than a year. In
England and Scotland juries were ready to give
verdicts, and judges were ready to pass the heaviest
sentences on all who were trying to urge others to
ask for Parliamentary Reform, as if they could not

ask for this without wanting to bring in all the horrors which were heard of in France. Pitt persuaded Parliament to pass a law allowing the king to imprison without trial those whom he suspected to be conspiring against him. Several persons were accused of high treason for very doubtful reasons. Fortunately for them their trials were delayed till after the Reign of Terror was at an end in France. The juries were not so excited then as they had been some months before, and they gave verdicts of not guilty. After this the excitement died away.

4. Progress of the War.—On land the war against France did not prosper. The French reconquered the Austrian Netherlands and conquered Holland. At sea, Lord Howe defeated the French, near the mouth of the Channel, in a battle known as the Battle of the First of June. Then Prussia made peace with France. After a time a young French General, Napoleon Bonaparte, was sent to Italy. He won a number of victories, and drove the Austrians out of Italy. So useless did it seem to attempt to stop the French conquests that Pitt offered to make peace. He and the French, however, were unable to agree, and the war went on as before.

5. The Battle of St. Vincent.—The year 1797 was one of great danger for England. The Dutch and the Spanish had joined the French, and it was expected that their fleets would attempt to combine with the French fleet against England. The English Admirals were ordered to keep them separate. Admiral Jarvis came up with the Spanish fleet off Cape St. Vincent. There were twenty-five Spanish

ships and only fifteen English. Some of the Spanish
ships were of huge size, as they had been in the days
of the Armada, and one of them had four decks, and
guns on each deck. The English ships were not so
large, but they were better fitted out, and the sailors
on board them thoroughly understood their work,
whilst many of the Spanish sailors had never been at

BATTLE OF CAPE ST. VINCENT.

sea before. Yet they were brave men, and the fight
was a hard one. All the English captains fought well,
but he who fought the best was Captain Nelson.
His ship had been terribly knocked about, but he
ran it close up to a Spanish vessel, leapt on board with
his men, and took it. He had scarcely got possession when the ship of the Spanish Admiral fired
upon the one which Nelson had just taken. With-

out a moment's delay he leapt on board the Admiral's ship too. The Spanish officers at once surrendered to him, and brought him their swords. They were so many that Nelson gave them to one of his bargemen to hold. The man coolly tucked them under his arm in a bundle, as if they had been so many sticks.

6. The Mutiny at Spithead.—There was a worse danger at home than any that could come from a Spanish fleet. The sailors who fought the battles of England were discontented, and not without cause. They were paid at the rate which had been settled in the time of Charles II., though the price of provisions which they had to buy had risen a great deal since those days. The provisions given them were very bad. When they were ill, and even when they had been wounded in battle, their pay was stopped till they were well again. Order was kept by constant flogging, and floggings were given for very small offences indeed, and sometimes where no offence at all had been committed. The sailors on board the fleet at Spithead sent a petition to the Admiralty asking for better treatment. As no notice was taken of their petition, they mutinied. They refused to go to sea when ordered. They would obey their officers no longer, till their requests were granted. But they did no harm to the officers, and contented themselves with sending on shore those who had treated them most brutally. The Lords of the Admiralty acted wisely. They saw that the sailors asked nothing but that which ought to have been granted before, and they sent Lord Howe on board to tell the men that they should be pardoned, and that their requests should be granted if they would return to their duty. Lord Howe, who had commanded in the Battle of the First of June, was a great favourite with the sailors, and they agreed to submit. Their grievances were redressed, and though a short time afterwards, when they suspected that they were not to be treated fairly, they began once more to mutiny, the disturbance came to an end as soon as they found out that the Admiralty intended to deal honestly with them, and after this they never thought of mutinying again.

7. The Mutiny at the Nore.—The mutiny at Spithead was scarcely over when another mutiny broke out in the fleet at the Nore, near the mouth of the Thames. The sailors at the Nore asked not merely that the complaints made at Spithead should be attended to, just as if they had not been attended to already, but they asked to command their own ships instead of the officers. If the proposal had been accepted, the ships would have been of no use at all. The mutiny spread to Admiral Duncan's fleet, which was keeping watch over the Dutch ships in the Texel, to prevent them from coming out to help the French. Most of his ships sailed away to join the others at the Nore. At one time he was left with only his own ship to guard the sea. He boldly remained in sight of the port in which the whole Dutch fleet was, and ran up flags every now and then, as if he were making signals to his other ships. By this means he deceived the Dutch, who thought that he had a fleet out of sight, and they kept quietly in port till he received help and became strong enough to fight them if they came out. In the meanwhile the Government at home got the better of the mutineers. Some of their own ships deserted them, and after a time the others surrendered. The chief leader of the mutiny was hanged, and the rest of the men returned to their duty and did good service afterwards. The Dutch fleet came out at last, and was defeated by Duncan at the Battle of Camperdown.

8. Bonaparte in Egypt.—Very soon after this battle, the French made peace with the Austrians, and Pitt tried once more to make peace with the French, though again the two governments failed to agree, and the war went on. Bonaparte sailed with an army to Egypt. On his way he took possession of Malta. He then went on to Egypt, which was spoken of as part of the Sultan's dominions, though it was in reality governed by some warlike soldiers called Mamelukes. Bonaparte tried to take them in by telling them that the French were true Mussulmans. They did not believe a word of it, and they fought hard for their independence. These fierce horsemen could not stand up against the guns of the disciplined French army, and they were defeated with great slaughter. The battle was named the Battle of the Pyramids, from the huge pyramids standing near, which had been raised in the days of the Pharaohs, to be the tombs of those ancient kings. 'From the tops of the pyramids,' said the French general to his men, ' forty centuries are looking down upon you.'

9. The Battle of the Nile.—When Bonaparte was on his way to Egypt, Nelson, who had been made an Admiral since the Battle of St. Vincent, was sailing up and down the Mediterranean in search of him. When he reached the coast of Egypt, he found that the French army was no longer on board the ships which had brought it. Nelson at once attacked the ships, which were anchored in a long line near the shore. He broke through their line, placing half of his own ships between them and the shore, and placing half outside. The battle raged far into the night. Nelson was wounded and carried below. A surgeon ran up to attend to him. 'No,' said the Admiral, 'I will take my turn with my brave fellows.' His wound proved but a slight one. Whilst he was lying in his cabin, he heard the sailors on deck calling out that the French Admiral's ship was on fire. Wounded as he was, he went on deck, and gave orders to send out boats to help the Frenchmen to escape from the burning vessel. In the end the French were completely beaten.

10. Irish Difficulties.—England could overpower the French at sea. There was one country which it was easy to keep down, but where it was very hard to do good. After the time of William III. the native Irish were treated with very great cruelty. There was an Irish Parliament which sat at Dublin, and no one who was not a Protestant was allowed to be a member of it. The laws made by it were very oppressive to the Irish Catholics, and it was no wonder that they hated bitterly those who ruled them so ill. These laws, however, were gradually put an end to, but the Protestants of English origin who ruled Ireland had no feeling of kindness towards the Catholic Irish, and did not care to help them. Soon after the American War was over, the Parliament at Dublin insisted upon making itself quite independent of England, which it had not been before. Pitt, when he became Minister, saw that the best thing to be done for Irishmen was to help them to be richer than they were. They were not allowed to trade with England without paying duties as if they had been foreigners. Pitt therefore proposed to give to Ireland freedom of trade with England so that they might become better off than they had been. Pitt, however, was unable to give to the Irish all that they thought they ought to have, and the Irish Parliament rejected his proposal. They did not understand the proverb which says, 'Half a loaf is better than no bread.' Even after the French Revolution began, Pitt tried hard to do something for Ireland. The Catholics were now allowed to vote for members of Parliament, though they were not allowed to sit in it, any more than they were in England. Pitt at last sent over Lord Fitzwilliam to be Lord Lieutenant. He was to ask the Irish Parliament to make a law allowing the Catholics to become members of Parliament and to hold offices in the State. Unluckily some of the Irish Protestants came over to England and complained to the king. George III. thought it would be very wicked to allow Catholics to have any power, and that if they had it they would use it to hurt the Protestant Church. Most of his subjects in England thought so too, and Pitt was obliged to recall Lord Fitzwilliam, and the plan about the Catholics had to be given up.

11. The Irish Rebellion of 1798.—It was a most unhappy ending to Pitt's first attempt to do good to Ireland. He was himself wiser than the English king or the English people. To the Irish it seemed useless to hope for anything good from England. Even some Irish Protestants were now ready to join the Irish Catholics, and a society was formed which bore the name of the United Irishmen. These men invited a French fleet and army to come to their help. The fleet and army actually arrived, but the general who was to command the army did not come. The rest of the expedition waited for him in Bantry Bay. A storm drove it out to sea, and not a single French soldier landed. In 1798 the Irish rose in rebellion. The rebels committed many cruelties, burning houses and murdering the people. The Irish Protestants who took the side of the English Government were as cruel as the rebels, and killed all they met without mercy. Things seemed to be as bad as they had been at the time of the Long Parliament. The rebels formed a great camp at Vinegar Hill. By this time an English force was ready to attack them, and their camp was taken. There were more brutal massacres on both sides. At last the rebels were put down. Then followed scenes of the utmost horror. Soldiers and officers and magistrates did as they pleased. Irishmen were treated with barbarity on the mere suspicion of having had something to do with the rebels. One

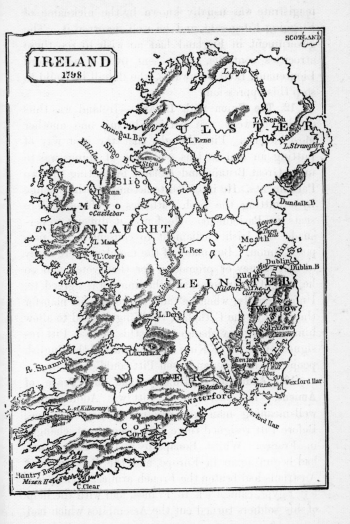

IRELAND
1798

SCOTLAND

L. Foyle

R. Bann

Donegal Bay

L. Erne

ULSTER

L. Neagh

Belfast

L. Strangford

Blackwater

Killala B.

Sligo B.

Sligo

Sligo

Dundalk B.

L. Conn

Mayo

Castlebar

CONNAUGHT

L. Mask

L. Ree

L. Corrib

Boyne

Tara Hill

Meath

R. Shannon

L. Derg

R. Shannon

LEINSTER

Dublin

Dublin

Dublin B.

Kildare

Kildare

The Curragh

Wicklow

Arklow

Carnew

Limerick

R. Suir

Kilkenny

Carlow

Wicklow Hd.

Enniscorthy

New Ross

Vinegar Hill

Wexford

Wexford Har

R. Shannon

MUNSTER

Waterford

Waterford

Waterford Har

L. of Killarney

McGillicuddy's Reeks

CORK

Cork

Bantry Bay

Mizen Hd.

C. Clear

magistrate was usually known by the nickname of Flogging Fitzgerald, and he well deserved it. The government in England had no wish to see these atrocities continue. Pitt sent over a new Lord Lieutenant, Lord Cornwallis, who did all he could to stop this oppression.

12. **The Union with Ireland.**—Ireland was thus divided between two parties, hating one another most bitterly. Pitt thought that the best way of putting an end to this evil state of things was to unite Great Britain and Ireland by uniting the two Parliaments. He intended to accompany this change by admitting the Irish Catholics to offices and to seats in Parliament. He found it difficult to persuade the Irish Parliament to consent to the proposed union. But many of the members were ready to take money or promotion for their votes, and so he bought their votes, and the union was agreed to. Unfortunately, when he came to propose his plan for the relief of the Catholics, the King refused to allow him to make any change. On this refusal Pitt resigned office. The King had the mass of the English people on his side, and even Pitt could do no more.

13. **Addington's Ministry and the Peace of Amiens.**—The successor of Pitt was Addington, a well-meaning man who was not a very wise one. Before Pitt resigned there had been great changes in France. Whilst Bonaparte was in Egypt, war had begun again in Europe, and the Russians and Austrians had beaten the French armies. Bonaparte left Egypt, came back to France, and with the help of his soldiers turned out the Assemblies which had

governed the country. He then proposed to the
French people to set up a form of government of which
he was to be the head, with the name of the First
Consul. This proposal was accepted, and from that
time the French allowed Bonaparte to rule them as
he pleased. He led an army into Italy, beat the Austrians, and made a treaty of peace, by which it was
arranged that France should extend as far as the

COPENHAGEN.

Rhine. England was now the only country at war
with France. It made matters worse that the states
on the Baltic were preparing to resist England,
because English ships of war stopped their trading
vessels, to see if they had any goods on board intended for the use of the French Government.
Admiral Hyde Parker was sent with a fleet to the
Baltic. Nelson was his second in command, and

when the fleet arrived near Copenhagen, Parker directed Nelson to attack the Danish fleet. What followed has been told by the poet Campbell.

> Of Nelson and the North,
> Sing the glorious day's renown,
> When to battle fierce came forth
> All the might of Denmark's crown,
> And her arms along the deep proudly shone.
> By each gun the lighted brand,
> In a bold determined hand,
> And the Prince of all the land
> Led them on.
>
> Like Leviathans afloat,
> Lay their bulwarks on the brine,
> While the sign of battle flew
> On the lofty British line.
> It was ten of April morn by the chime
> As they drifted on their path,
> There was silence deep as death,
> And the boldest held their breath
> For a time.

For some hours the battle raged fiercely. The Danes fought bravely. Admiral Parker, who remained at a distance, thought that it would be impossible to beat them. He hoisted a signal to Nelson, ordering him to stop fighting. Nelson, who had some years before lost the sight of one eye, put his telescope to his blind eye, and declared that he could not see the signal. He ordered his ships to go on with the battle.

> Again! again! again!
> And the havoc did not slack,
> Till a feeble cheer the Dane
> To our cheering sent us back;
> Their shots along the deep slowly boom,

Then cease — and all is wail,
As they strike the shattered sail;
Or, in conflagration pale,
Light the gloom.

Out spoke the victor then,
As he hailed them o'er the wave,
' Ye are brothers ! ye are men !
And we conquer but to save.
So peace instead of death let us bring,
But yield, proud foe, thy fleet,
With the crews, at England's feet,
And make submission meet
To our king.'

Nelson sent the wounded Danes on shore and told
the Crown Prince, who ruled Denmark in his father's
place, that he should consider this the greatest
victory that he had ever gained, if it led to friendship between England and Denmark. When he
landed, the people received him with shouts, to thank
him for his kindness to the wounded.

14. **The Expedition to Egypt and the Peace of
Amiens.**—About the same time that the battle of
Copenhagen was fought, an expedition was sent to
Egypt, to drive out the French who had been left
behind by Napoleon. The French were defeated, and
sent home to their own country. Not long afterwards, in 1802, a peace was signed at Amiens
between England and France, and fighting came to
an end for a little time.

CHAPTER XL.

FROM THE PEACE OF AMIENS TO THE BEGINNING OF THE PENINSULAR WAR.

(1802–1808.)

1. End of the Peace of Amiens.—The Peace of Amiens did not last long. Bonaparte had no intention of satisfying himself with ruling over France, even with the new countries which had been added to it. He seized upon part of Italy, sent troops into Switzerland, and interfered with the Dutch. The English Government had promised to give back Malta to the knights, but they now refused to do so unless the French would give up meddling with other countries. Bonaparte was very angry, and scolded the English ambassador. Before long the war began again.

2. Projected Invasion of England.—Before the Peace of Amiens there had been many people who disliked the war with France. Scarcely any one had a good word for Bonaparte now. He had begun by seizing 10,000 English travellers who had gone to enjoy themselves in France. He shut them up in prisons, in which they remained for years. Then he made preparations for the invasion of England. All classes were roused to resist him. The merchants and tradesmen of London declared their readiness to do all that it was possible to do in defence of their country; and the same readiness to support the Government spread over the country.

When news came that a French army was being
collected at Boulogne, and that boats were being
built to carry it across the Straits of Dover,
60,000 volunteers offered to come forward to
defend their homes. A few weeks later the number
had risen to 300,000. A little later it had almost
reached 380,000. Bonaparte had come down to
Boulogne to review his army. He looked across
the Channel. 'It is a ditch,' he wrote, 'that will
be leaped over when we shall have the boldness
to make the attempt.' He did not intend, however,
to send his boats laden with soldiers across the sea
without protection. He had a plan in his head by
which he hoped before long to have a fleet in the
Channel to guard the passage. In the meanwhile
the English volunteers were busily drilling. The
King reviewed the London regiments in Hyde Park.
Pitt became an officer of volunteers, and exercised
his men diligently.

3. Pitt's Second Ministry.— Naturally enough,
there was a strong wish in the country to have a
better Prime Minister than Addington. After some
time Addington resigned, and the King sent for
Pitt. Pitt proposed that a ministry should be
formed composed of the best men of both parties.
Both Whigs and Tories were equally ready to defend England against invasion, and why should they
not all work together ? Pitt proposed that Fox
should join the ministry. He had been bitterly
opposed to Pitt, but Pitt was ready to be reconciled.
Fox, too, was ready to be reconciled. The King
would not hear of employing Fox, whom he had

never forgiven for joining North in the Coalition Ministry. The others who had been Pitt's colleagues in his last ministry refused to join him now if Fox was to be excluded. One of these was Lord Grenville. ' I will teach that proud man,' said Pitt, ' that I can do without him.' Pitt became Prime Minister, but he had to fill the other offices with men most of whom were not at all fit for such important posts.

4. **Napoleon's Plan for invading England.**—Not long after Pitt became Prime Minister, Bonaparte changed his title. He was now Napoleon, Emperor of the French. The Pope came all the way to Paris to crown him. Napoleon took the crown himself and placed it on his own head. His plan for bringing a fleet into the Channel was now ready to be carried out. He had persuaded the King of Spain to join him in the war against England. By Napoleon's orders a French fleet came out of Toulon, passed the Straits of Gibraltar to Cadiz, picked up a Spanish fleet which was there, and sailed off to the West Indies. Napoleon expected that the English fleet would follow it there, and would lose time, whilst the French and Spanish ships returned to Europe, and joined another French fleet which was at Brest. All of them together were to sail up the Channel, and guard the Straits of Dover whilst his army crossed. The first part of his expectation was fulfilled. Nelson, with only thirteen ships, crossed the Atlantic in pursuit of the thirty ships of the enemy. When he heard that they had left the West Indies he came after them. He did not catch

them, but another British admiral with fifteen ships fell in with them, took two Spanish ships, and so frightened the rest, that they went off to Cadiz, and never even tried to come near the Channel.

5. **The Battle of Trafalgar.**—Napoleon was greatly disappointed. He fancied that the failure was owing entirely to the cowardice of his admiral, and he ordered him to put out to sea again. The poor man assured the Emperor that he should certainly be beaten. His sailors had long been shut up in harbour, and they had not been in the constant habit of managing their ships in the rolling seas as the English sailors had. Napoleon would take no excuse, and the admiral set out with a heavy heart. Nelson came up with him off Cape Trafalgar. He ordered the signal to be made which told the British fleet that ' England expects that every man will do his duty.' The French and Spaniards fought well, but they had no chance against the trained British crews. In the midst of the fight Nelson was shot by a man in the rigging of a French ship. He was carried below to die. The enemy's force was almost entirely destroyed. Never again during the war did a French or Spanish fleet put to sea. Yet so deeply was Nelson beloved in England, that it was doubtful when the news arrived whether joy for the victory or sorrow for the loss was greatest. The Battle of Trafalgar was for England what Cromwell would have called ' a crowning mercy.' Never again has an English fleet had to fight a battle against a European navy. Our ancestors fought and died that England might be free and unconquered.

6. Pitt's Last Days.—Not long after England lost her greatest sailor, she lost her greatest statesman. As soon as Napoleon saw that his chance of invading England was over, he led his army to attack Austria and Russia. He forced an Austrian army to surrender at Ulm, entered Vienna in triumph, and defeated the combined Austrian and Russian armies at Austerlitz, forcing the Austrians to make peace with him. Pitt had hoped much from this alliance. His health was no longer what it was, and the last bad news crushed him. In January 1806 he died.

7. The Ministry of all the Talents.—The ministry of all parties which Pitt had wished for came into office after his death. The King allowed Fox to have office. Lord Grenville was Prime Minister. This Government was known as the Ministry of all the Talents. It did not last long, but it lasted long enough to do one great thing. As far as England was concerned, it put an end to that horrible slave trade which Pitt and Wilberforce had denounced in vain. Fox died a few months after Pitt, but he lived long enough to know that English ships would no longer be allowed to carry black men across the Atlantic into slavery. The other ministers were not successful. Napoleon got into a war with Prussia, and won a great victory, after which nearly the whole of Prussia submitted to him. Then he attacked the Russians. For some time it seemed doubtful whether he would succeed in beating them or not. They called on England for help. The English ministry had sent away its soldiers on useless expeditions, and had none to spare. The

Russian army was beaten, and the Emperor of Russia at once made peace with Napoleon. The peace is known as the Peace of Tilsit. Before that happened the Ministry of all the Talents had ceased to govern. It proposed to allow Catholics to be officers in the army and navy. The King not only refused to allow this, but ordered the ministers to promise that they would never even propose to do anything for the Catholics again. On their refusal he turned them out of office.

8. State of the Continent after the Peace of Tilsit. —The next ministry was headed by the Duke of Portland, who was an invalid. The real leader was Mr. Perceval, who was determined to keep the Catholics out of all kinds of offices. As the English people agreed with him in this, he was able to do as he wished. Amongst the new ministers was George Canning, who had been a great admirer of Pitt. He was resolved to do all that could possibly be done to resist the power of Napoleon. Since Napoleon had made peace with Russia, no one on the Continent dared to say a word against him. He did exactly as he liked, pulled down kings and set them up at his pleasure, and forced the people whom he had conquered to pay him enormous sums of money. As he could no longer hope to be able to invade England, he tried to overpower it by injuring its commerce. He ordered that no one wherever the French power reached —that is to say, as far as the borders of Russia— should use any goods brought in by English vessels. In consequence of the superiority of the English fleets, the inhabitants of all the western and central countries of Europe had no chance of getting any goods from beyond the sea except in English vessels, as their own vessels would be stopped by the English ships. Coffee and tea, sugar and cotton, became very much dearer in all these countries. English merchants tried to smuggle them in, and whenever Napoleon's officers found them they seized them. The consequence was that the poor grew even more angry with Napoleon than the kings and great men had been before. Every poor man who found that he had to pay much more than he had been accustomed to pay for his cup of coffee, or for his shirt, hated Napoleon. It would not be many years before this universal hatred would rouse millions of people in Europe against Napoleon, and would pull him down from his power.

9. The Seizure of the Danish Fleet.—One of Napoleon's designs was to seize the Danish fleet, which was a very good one, and to use it against England. Canning heard of this, and at once sent a fleet and army to Copenhagen. As soon as they arrived, a messenger was sent to the Crown Prince, or eldest son of the King, who governed Denmark in his father's name, to ask him to give up the Danish ships. He was told that if he did so the British Government would give them back at the end of the war. He refused, and Copenhagen was attacked. At last the Danes were forced to give up their ships. Napoleon was very angry. He could not imagine how Canning had found out the secret. In England a great many people who did not know what Canning knew were very much displeased, because they thought it an unjust thing to take the fleet from the Danes. When the fleet returned, George III. spoke to the gentleman who had carried the message to the Crown Prince, and asked him whether the Crown Prince was upstairs or downstairs when he received him. 'He was on the ground floor, please your Majesty,' was the gentleman's reply. 'I am glad of it for your sake,' said the King; 'for if he had half my spirit, he would certainly have kicked you down stairs.'

CHAPTER XLI.

FROM THE BEGINNING OF THE PENINSULAR WAR TO THE PEACE OF PARIS.

(1808–1814.)

1. **Spain and Portugal.**—Napoleon was not content with his victories. His army had never marched beyond the Pyrenees, and he disliked nothing so much as to be at peace. First, he picked a quarrel with Portugal, and sent an army which seized Lisbon. Then he looked out for an opportunity to get possession of Spain. It happened that Charles IV. King of Spain, and his son Ferdinand had quarrelled. Napoleon sent for them both to Bayonne, pretending that he would make up their quarrel. When they arrived, he persuaded the king to give up his crown, and at the same time seized the young man and sent him into confinement in a distant part of France. Then he sent his own brother Joseph to

Madrid, to be king of Spain. The Spaniards were
disgusted by this treatment. They rose in insurrec-

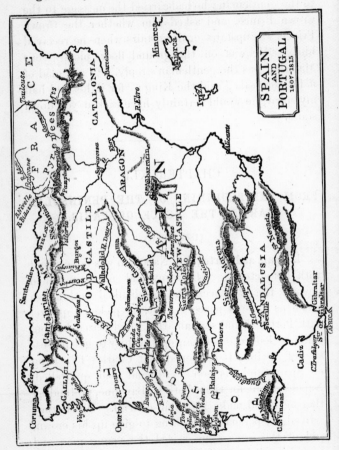

tion, and proclaimed Ferdinand king. They sent to
England for help. Canning at once took up their

cause, and sent them guns and gunpowder and money. He also sent an army to Portugal, under Sir Arthur Wellesley, who afterwards became the Duke of Wellington. He had fought well in India, but nobody knew yet how very great a man he was. The war which now began in 1808 is known as the Peninsular War, because it was fought in the peninsula formed by the two countries of Spain and Portugal. Wellesley beat the French in Portugal, at Vimiero, and drove them into Lisbon. An. arrangement was made by which the French army was to be allowed to go back to France, leaving Portugal free. Soon after this Wellesley returned to England, though part of his army remained behind. About the same time a French army had to surrender to the Spaniards at Baylen, in the south of Spain. The Spaniards fancied that their troubles were nearly at an end.

2. **Napoleon in Spain.**—The Spaniards had plenty of trouble before them. Each separate Spaniard was ready to fight and to die for his country. But they did not fight well when they were together in an army. The men were without discipline, and did not trust their generals. The generals did not deserve to be trusted. They thought it was so easy to win victories that they did not take any pains to win them. The consequence was, that they were always beaten whenever they fought battles. Napoleon no sooner heard that his soldiers had been taken prisoners than he resolved to come himself to Spain. At the head of an army he marched into the country, beat the Spaniards, and entered Madrid in

triumph.   The English general, Sir John Moore, was advancing through the north-west of Spain. He hoped that the Spaniards would gather round him to fight the French.   The Spaniards did nothing of the sort.   When Moore reached Sahagun he heard that Napoleon was coming to attack him with a much larger army than his own.   He had to retreat, and fortunately for him Napoleon went home to France, and left one of his generals to follow the English.

3. The Battle of Corunna.—Sir John Moore reached Corunna with difficulty.   He had hoped to find the English fleet there to take his army on board.   But a mistake had been made, and the fleet had gone to another harbour.   Before it could be fetched, the French arrived, and a battle had to be fought, to drive them off, in order that the tired soldiers might get safely on board.   The French were beaten, and the men got safely away, but their brave commander was killed.   He was buried on the field of battle by his sorrowing companions.   The story has been told by a poet named Wolfe:—

> Not a drum was heard, not a funeral note,
>   As the corpse to the ramparts we hurried;
> Not a soldier discharged his farewell shot
>   O'er the grave where our hero was buried.
>
> We buried him darkly at dead of night,
>   The sods with our bayonets turning,
> By the struggling moon-beam's misty light,
>   And the lantern dimly burning.
>
> No useless coffin inclosed his breast,
>   Not in sheet nor in shroud we wound him,
> But he lay like a warrior taking his rest
>   With his martial cloak around him.

Few and short were the prayers we said,
  And we spoke not a word of sorrow,
But we steadfastly gazed on the face that was dead,
  And we bitterly thought of the morrow !

We thought as we hollowed his narrow bed,
  And smoothed down his lonely pillow,
How the foe and stranger would tread o'er his head,
  And we far away on the billow !

  .   .   .   .   .   .

But half of our heavy task was done,
  When the clock struck the hour for retiring,
And we heard the distant and random gun
  That the foe was sullenly firing.

Slowly and sadly we laid him down,
  From the field of his fame fresh and gory ;
We carved not a line and we raised not a stone,
  But we left him alone with his glory !

4. Oporto and Talavera.—The next year Wellesley
was sent back again with a fresh army to Portugal.
Landing at Lisbon, he marched swiftly to Oporto,
and drove the French out. Then he returned and
pushed on towards Madrid. At Talavera he met the
French army. He had a large Spanish army with
him as well as his own. But the Spaniards were
jealous of him and would not fight. The British
soldiers had to do everything themselves. At last
they won the victory. The Spaniards gave no help.
Before long other French armies approached, and
Wellesley, who was made Lord Wellington on account
of the victory, had to go back to Portugal. It
seemed as if all this fighting had been useless. In
reality it was of the greatest use. It taught Wellington that he could not depend on the Spaniards,

and he never again trusted their promises to help him, or marched anywhere at their request.

5. Walcheren.—Napoleon was by this time engaged in another war with Austria. The people of the North of Germany was longing to rise against his tyranny, but his armies were too strong for them, and he had put French soldiers into all the strong fortresses in those parts. The English Government had an army to dispose of, and if it had been sent to the north of Germany it might have given great assistance to the Germans. Instead of this, Lord Castlereagh, who was the minister who managed the war, sent it to the Scheldt, to attack Antwerp. The command of the army was given to Lord Chatham, the eldest son of the great minister. He was not a good soldier, or a wise man. The command of the fleet was given to Sir Richard Strahan. Instead of sailing quickly up to Antwerp, the commander stopped near the mouth of the river, and landed the men on the Island of Walcheren. The French soldiers from all parts hurried to Antwerp, and made the place too strong to be taken. Walcheren is a low flat island, and a fever broke out amongst the English soldiers, which destroyed a great number of them. At last the expedition came back without doing anything, and people in England laid the blame on the general and admiral. Some clever fellow wrote that

> My Lord Chatham, with his sword drawn,
> Stood waiting for Sir Richard Strahan;
> Sir Richard, longing to be at 'em,
> Stood waiting for the Earl of Chatham.

6. Wellington's Difficulties in Spain. —Wellington had difficulties enough in Spain. He had but few soldiers to oppose to the hosts of the French. If the French armies could have joined together, they must have driven him out of the Peninsula. Yet he did not despair. He did not trust merely in his own skill, great as it was, so much as in the righteousness of his cause. He knew how terribly cruel and oppressive Napoleon was, and he felt sure that, sooner or later, his cruelty would provoke all Europe to rise against him. How soon that day would come he could not tell, but he felt that it was his business to wait patiently till the time came. In Spain, the French armies, numerous as they were, were already in difficulty. The Spaniards could not fight great battles, but they could form small groups of men, each having his gun in his hand, and firing at small parties of Frenchmen. Then too there were always a number of French generals in Spain, and they despised Joseph, whom Napoleon had made King of Spain, because he was not a soldier, and, therefore, they would not do as he ordered them. They were also very jealous of one another, and never liked to help one another, for fear that the other might get the credit of any victory that was gained. All this helped Wellington very much, because, if he had two or more generals against him, he could calculate that they would not agree what to do. Perhaps the treatment which Wellington received from the ministers at home was worse for him than the opposition of his enemies. Canning ceased to be minister about this time, and Mr. Perceval became Prime

Minister. The ministers did not think it possible that Wellington would ever succeed in conquering Spain, and were always talking of ordering him to come home. With all this to endure, he had need of the most wonderful patience. His patience was as great as that of Washington, and it was this even more than his being a great general which enabled him to win in the end.

7. Torres Vedras.—In the year in which the Battle of Talavera was fought Napoleon had beaten the Austrians. He did not himself come into the Peninsula the next summer, but he sent his best general, Massena, with orders to drive the English into the sea. Wellington knew that he had not a large enough army to fight him, though he had now got a number of Portuguese, who were put under English officers, and made excellent soldiers. He quietly prepared means to stop him. At Lisbon he had a good port, where the English ships could come and take his army away if he were forced to leave the country, or could bring food for his men as long as he chose to stay. He therefore threw up three lines of fortifications from the river Tagus to the sea. The first one was intended to stop Massena for a time. The second one was intended to stop him if he passed the first. The third one was intended to protect the soldiers if they had to embark, though Wellington did not expect to have to use it for that purpose. These fortifications are known as the Lines of Torres Vedras, from the name of a village near them. When Massena reached Portugal, Wellington met him near the frontier, and retreated slowly. He had given ᴏrders that all cattle were to be driven away and the crops destroyed, in order that the French might find nothing to eat. When Massena saw Wellington retreating, he thought that everything was going well, and that he would soon drive the English to their ships. He had not the slightest idea that there were any fortifications in the way. When at last Wellington's army went behind the first line, the French were taken by surprise. Massena took some time to think whether he would attack the lines at all. The more he thought of it the less he liked the idea. Week after week passed by, and he did not venture to attack. All this while provisions were running short in the French camp. At last the half-starved Frenchmen had, unwillingly, to retreat. No less than 45,000 of them died of hunger and disease, or were cut off by the Portuguese if they straggled from their ranks. Wellington followed up the retiring enemy, and by the next spring there was not a Frenchman left in Portugal.

8. The Regency.—Whilst Wellington was struggling with the French, the old King at home ceased to have any further knowledge of joy or sorrow. The madness, with which in the course of his reign he had been from time to time afflicted, came down upon him like a dark cloud in 1811. He remained insane the rest of his life. He lost his eyesight too, and the blind old man was an object of affectionate pity to his subjects during the nine years which he had still to live. His strong will was broken down for ever. His place was taken by his eldest son, a selfish and unprincipled man, who was now known as the Prince Regent, and afterwards as George IV. That year was marked by some fighting in Spain. At Barossa and Fuentes d'Onoro in the spring, and at Albuera in the summer, the British gained victories; but the main object of Wellington was to capture two strong fortresses, Ciudad Rodrigo in the north, and Badajoz in the south, which shut up the two great roads from Portugal into Spain. If the French held these they might again invade Portugal. If Wellington could gain them he might invade Spain. The invasion of Spain seemed to him now likely to be possible. Napoleon, not content with the enormous power which he exercised over all western Europe, was threatening Russia, and Wellington knew that if Napoleon engaged in war with Russia he would have no soldiers to spare to send to Spain.

9. The Guerillas.—The year 1812 was the one which saw the beginning of the ruin of the great oppressor. Spain swarmed with armed men, moving about separately or in small bands. These men were called Guerillas, which is a Spanish word meaning men who fight in small companies, and not in great armies. They shot down the French wherever they found them straggling, slipping away easily amongst the hills or woods, where every path was known to them. The French found it as difficult to lay hands upon them as a man finds it difficult to catch gnats which sting him. If a French soldier had to carry a letter, even a short way, he needed an escort of at least 200 men to see him safely through Spain. An important despatch to the Emperor had to be guarded by more than 1,000 horsemen. The Guerillas seized money or provisions going to the enemy's army, and stole the horses or the guns. Wellington knew that a great part of the French army would be so occupied in keeping off the Guerillas that the whole of it could not be gathered into one place to fight him.

10. The Capture of Ciudad Rodrigo and Badajoz.— Wellington was thus able to attack the two great fortresses which stopped his road into Spain. In the first month of the year he set out for Ciudad Rodrigo. He knew that if he did not take it in a short time he would not be able to take it at all, because a large French army would arrive to drive him off. He had no proper tools for digging trenches. The English Government kept their general ill-supplied in almost everything that he ought to have had. Yet the town was taken after great slaughter, and the soldiers disgraced themselves by brutal violence when they burst into the place. Three months later Badajoz was also attacked. Again the British soldiers had to rush upon almost certain death, because there was no time to wait. Rank after rank, as the men charged up the slippery breach, which was guarded with a row of sword-blades fixed in a beam, was mown down by fire from the French guns like grass before the scythe. After a terrible slaughter the town was at last taken. When Wellington heard of the number of the dead, ' the pride of conquest yielded to a passionate burst of grief for the loss of his soldiers.' Sad to say, the soldiers who were living were raging madly about the streets in drunken fury, slaying and wounding the miserable inhabitants, plundering and destroying whatever came into their hands.

11. The Battle of Salamanca.— Happily British soldiers would not now behave like wild beasts. Wellington had none others to lead. Before long he came up with a French army at Salamanca. The French general moved his troops in an awkward way across the field of battle. ' At last,' said Wellington, ' I have him.' He ordered his men to advance, and gained a complete victory. He had gained no such victory before. He went to Madrid, where the Spaniards received him with the greatest honours. King Joseph fled before him. Wellington, however, did not quite conquer Spain in this year. He carried his army to Burgos, and laid siege to it. But the French armies gathered round him, and he had to go back to Portugal. Yet even this failure, as it seemed, was the beginning of success. The French armies had to leave the south of Spain, in order to meet Wellington in the north, and the south of Spain was thus set free from their presence.

12. Napoleon's Russian Campaign.—Whilst Wellington was fighting at Salamanca and Burgos, Napoleon was marching through Russia. The Russians retreated before him. There was one tremendous battle, after which he reached Moscow. He expected that the Russians would make peace when he had taken Moscow, but instead of making peace they set fire to Moscow. Napoleon and his army had nowhere to shelter themselves against the bitter cold of the Russian winter which was coming on. Even if they had been able to keep themselves warm at Moscow, they had not provisions enough to feed on till summer came, as they had been so sure that the Russians would submit that they had not brought large stores with them. There was no help for it. They had to go back for hundreds of miles. Soon the snow began to fall, and the bitter frosty wind swept over the level plains. For a time they struggled on. Then they began to give way. The hard frost was bad enough to bear when they were on the march, but it was terrible at night, when they had to lie down on the snow round large fires of wood which, large as they were, were not enough to warm them. Every morning when they started some of their comrades were left behind frozen to death. Others lagged behind, worn out with cold and fatigue, and dropped dead upon the snow. Fewer and fewer they grew as they struggled on, with pale and hunger-stricken faces. Of 400,000 men who had entered Russia, only 20,000 came out. Napoleon's grand army was destroyed.

13. The Uprising of Prussia and the Battle of Vittoria.—The pursuing Russian army advanced into Prussia. Prussia and its king resolved to rise against Napoleon. From one end of the land to the other the cry arose for deliverance. From field and city the volunteers poured forth, to be drilled and disciplined, that they might fight worthily for their Fatherland. Napoleon came amongst them with a new army, for the most part composed of young lads. His extraordinary military skill enabled him to beat the Russians and Prussians in two great battles. Then the Austrians joined his enemies,

One other battle he succeeded in winning. But the number of his enemies and their fierce hatred were too much for him to bear up against. At Leipzig, in a tremendous battle lasting for three days, he was utterly defeated, and with the small remnants of his army he made off for France before the year was over. Germany was free. That year Wellington had struck down Napoleon's lieutenants in Spain as surely as their master had been struck down on the plains of Northern Germany. He had now a finer and more numerous army than he had ever had before. As he crossed the little stream which separated Spain from Portugal, he stood up in his stirrups and waved his hand, crying out, 'Adieu, Portugal!' He marched along the road that led to France. At Vittoria he came upon the French army, in which was King Joseph himself. Joseph had abandoned Madrid, to fight one last battle for the throne which had brought nothing but misery to him. He was utterly defeated. There was a long siege of St. Sebastian. At last it was taken, and then Spain was as free as Germany.

14. Napoleon's Last Struggle.—In the first months of 1814 Napoleon struggled hard at least to maintain his power in France. He fought with even more than his usual skill. In the north the united armies of Russia, Prussia, and Austria pushed on. They were often beaten, but they pushed on still. They were too many to be overcome. At last they reached and entered Paris. Napoleon abdicated, and was sent to the Isle of Elba, off the coast of Italy, where he might continue to call him-

self Emperor.   The Peace of Paris restored peace
to all Europe.   Lewis XVIII., the brother of the
King Lewis who had been executed, came back to
be King of France.   In the south, Wellington had
reached Bordeaux after further victories.   His last
battle where he defeated the French was fought at
Toulouse.

THE DUKE OF WELLINGTON.

15. Wellington's Military Career.—The English
general was now Duke of Wellington.   He had
rendered services to his country which no honours
could repay.   When there were few men in Europe
who did not despair, he did not despair.   He was
hopeful, because he believed that wrong-doing and
cruelty could not prosper for ever.   He fought not
for glory but for duty.

C C

CHAPTER XLII.

FROM THE PEACE OF PARIS TO THE DEATH OF GEORGE III.

(1814—1820.)

1. The American War and the Return of Napoleon.—The army which had served Wellington so well, and which as he said 'could go anywhere and do anything,' was not allowed to rest. It was sent to America. Unhappily England was at war with the United States. Fortunately the war came to an end after it had lasted two years. In 1815, the year after the end of the great war, the Peninsular army was really wanted in Europe when it was not to be had. Napoleon escaped from Elba and landed in France. The restored king had governed so unwisely that Napoleon was welcomed by the soldiers and by a great part of the people. He entered Paris in triumph, and was once more Emperor of the French.

2. The Battle of Waterloo.—The other nations of Europe were not likely to be so well pleased. They knew that Napoleon had always picked quarrels with them before, and that if he had time to get together a large army he would probably pick a quarrel with them once more. They did not want to run the chance of being conquered again, and they knew that if they were conquered by him he would show them no mercy. They therefore declared that they would have no peace with him. England, Prussia, Austria, and Russia joined in this declaration. Of the four, England and Prussia were first ready. An English army under Wellington, and a Prussian army under Blucher, appeared in the Netherlands. Napoleon dashed across the French frontier to attack them whilst they were still separated. He beat the Prussians and drove them back, fancying that they would retreat towards their own home, and that the English, who were not nearly as many as his own troops, would be left alone to resist him. He attacked Wellington at Waterloo. For some hours the English army had to resist the charges of the French. They held out bravely, though most of them had never been in battle before. Yet unless they were succoured they would hardly hold out to the end. In the afternoon help came. The Prussians were seen marching to their aid. Napoleon found that he had two armies to meet instead of one. The whole French army fled in utter rout. Napoleon was once more deposed, and gave himself up to the captain of an English ship. He was carried to St. Helena, and there he was kept in safety till he died, that he might no more trouble the nations which he had afflicted so long. Lewis XVIII. was again set upon the throne of France.

3. General Distress.—England was now at peace. She had done her duty to Europe. Those who do their duty must not expect that it will bring no hardships with it. For a man to do his duty means that he is ready to give up many things that are pleasant, and to suffer much which is unpleasant. It is so with nations as well as men. There was

terrible suffering after the war. Millions of pounds
had been spent and lost to the country in supporting
the war. This and other causes brought about the
ruin of manufacturers and farmers. The ruin of
manufacturers and farmers brought sharp distress to
the labourers and the artisans. Poor men were more
ignorant then than they are now, and they broke out
into riots, as if rioting would give them work, or
earn them money.

4. Romilly as a Criminal-Law Reformer.—The
Government was frightened. Mr. Perceval, the
Prime Minister, had been murdered some years before, and had been succeeded by Lord Liverpool.
Lord Liverpool was a man of kind disposition, who
left the business of governing very much to the
other ministers, and the other ministers were still
frightened lest what had happened in France at the
Revolution should happen in England. They did
not like changes to be made, and thought it best
to keep everything as it was. One man in the
House of Commons, Sir Samuel Romilly, thought
that the cruel laws which had come down from the
old England of the Plantagenets and Tudors ought
to be altered. It was law that any one who picked
a pocket of more than five shillings, or carried off
goods to the same amount from a shop, should be
hanged. Some years before Romilly had induced
Parliament to agree to abolish the hanging of pick-
pockets, but the House of Lords refused to abolish
hanging for those who robbed a shop. Romilly again
tried to persuade the House of Lords to be merciful,
but they were stubborn, and the hangings still went on.

5. Agitation in the Country.—Amongst the artisans of the north of England a demand arose for Parliamentary Reform. They saw how much was amiss, and they thought that if every man had a vote, and there was a fresh Parliament every year, things would mend. They forgot that the greater number of men in England could neither read nor write, and that it might be dangerous to subject the Government to the control of those who were so very ignorant. In London a crowd marched into the City, but it was easily driven back and its leaders secured by the Lord Mayor and a few citizens. All this frightened the Government. They obtained from Parliament new laws to enable them to put down rebellion. There was no rebellion to be feared, though the working-men knew that they were miserable, and wanted to be better off. A large number of men collected at Manchester, and set off towards London to ask for relief. Some of them had blankets rolled up on their backs, perhaps to keep them warm by night, so that their procession is known as the March of the Blanketeers. They never got further than Macclesfield. Some were driven home again, some grew tired, and went home of their own accord. In Derbyshire a man named Brandreth, who was half mad, headed about twenty men with pikes and guns, broke into several houses to search for arms, and shot one unfortunate man. His numbers increased to a hundred. They were met by a party of soldiers. Most of them ran away, but some were taken. Three of these were hanged, and others sentenced to various punishments. The Government and Parliament did all that they could do to put down these disturbances, but as yet they had no thought of setting their minds to find out their cause, or to relieve the people from their miseries.

6. The Manchester Massacre.—For some time the conflict between the Government and the working-men of the north went on. It was announced that a great meeting would be held in St. Peter's Field at Manchester to petition for Parliamentary Reform. The Government was afraid that large numbers of men, when they came together, would not be content with merely preparing a petition. It was known that many of them had been drilled by old soldiers. According to their own account of the matter, they only wanted healthy exercise, and to be able to march to and from the meetings in good order. It is no wonder that the Government thought that they intended to fight. The meeting was to be addressed by a man named Hunt, a vain empty-headed speaker with a fluent tongue, who was very popular at that time. The magistrates determined to arrest Hunt, and instead of waiting till the meeting was over they sent soldiers to seize him in the midst of the multitude. The soldiers, who were not from the regular army, but yeomanry, chiefly composed of master-manufacturers, could not get through the thick crowd. They drew their swords and cut right and left. The regular soldiers, the Hussars, were then ordered to charge. The mass fled in confusion, leaving the wounded behind them. Six persons were killed and many more were wounded. The Manchester Massacre, as it was called, took place in 1819. It had an unexpected effect upon thoughtful men all over the country. Till then there had been little disposition amongst well-educated persons to favour the demands of the artisans. Nobody who knew anything about politics could think that it would be wise to give every man a vote in those days of ignorance. But no one who thought seriously could doubt that the crowd at Manchester had been grievously wronged. When they were attacked by the soldiers they had committed no offence against the law, and had simply come to listen to speeches in a peaceable and orderly way. The Government most unwisely declared the magistrates to have acted rightly, before they had had time to inquire whether they had or not. Parliament was on their side, and made new laws, known as The Six Acts, to stop seditious meetings. But many people, therefore, who had hitherto supported the Government, were so disgusted that they began to turn their minds to consider whether there might not be some way in which things might be altered for the better.

7. **Death of George III.**—The year after the Manchester Massacre the poor blind, mad old king died. His son, the Prince Regent, became king, under the name of George IV.

CHAPTER XLIII.

REIGN OF GEORGE IV.

(1820–1830.)

1. The Cato-Street Conspiracy. — When many people are dissatisfied it often happens that there are some who think that the easiest way to have right done is to murder those whom they think to be guilty. So it had been in the time of the Gunpowder Plot, and so it was again now. A man named Thistlewood formed a plan with some others for killing all the ministers as they were at dinner together. The plot is known as the Cato-Street Conspiracy, because the conspirators met in Cato-Street, a small street near the Edgware Road. The plot was however found out, and the plotters seized, though they succeeded in killing one of the policemen sent after them, and in wounding three others.

2. George Canning; Foreign Policy.—In 1822 two men entered the Government who did very much to change its character, and to lead it in a better way. They were George Canning and Robert Peel. Canning became Foreign Secretary, that is to say, the minister who has to manage all the arrangements with Foreign States. The kings and emperors of the Continent were much more frightened lest there should be rebellions in their dominions than even the English Government had been, and they agreed to send troops to put down any rebellion which might happen, even in states which were not their own. An Austrian army had marched into Italy to put down a rebellion which had resulted in establishing a parliament in Naples, and soon after Canning came into office a French army marched into Spain to put down a rebellion which had had the same result at Madrid. The French restored the government of the cruel Ferdinand VII., and Ferdinand VII. then wanted to send Spanish soldiers to Portugal, because Portugal had established a parliament. Canning sent British soldiers to the help of the Portuguese, and the Spaniards left Portugal alone. Without going to war Canning did much to help the weak against the strong. There had been a long struggle in America, in which the Spanish colonies, Mexico, Peru, Chili, and others had been striving to free themselves from Spain. Canning came forward to treat them as independent states, as they really were. In the east of Europe, too, a bitter conflict was being waged. Greece was striving to set itself free from the brutal Turks. Most of the governments of Europe did not like this, and thought that the Greeks were setting a bad example of rebellion. Canning was unable to do anything for the Greeks, but he let them understand that he wished them well.

3. Peel; Reform of the Criminal Law.—Peel had become Home Secretary almost at the same time that Canning had become Foreign Secretary. He had to look after the affairs of the people at home. He set himself at once to do useful work. He took up the task which Romilly, who was now dead, had begun, and persuaded Parliament to do away with a great number of laws inflicting the punishment of

death for very slight offences. At the beginning of
the century there were no less than two hundred
crimes which were punished by hanging. Any one,
for instance, who stole fish out of a pond, who hunted
in the king's forests, or who injured Westminster
Bridge, was liable to be hanged. The House of
Commons had again and again voted that men
should no longer be put to death for such things,
but the House of Lords had been obstinate. Peel
insisted that a less punishment than that of death
should be imposed on those who had been guilty of
at least a hundred of these small crimes. The
House of Lords gave way, and it became known
that there was at last a man in the Government who
could be trusted to make wise improvements.

4. **Huskisson's Commercial Reforms.** — Another
member of the Government, Mr. Huskisson, began
to diminish the payments made when foreign goods
were brought into the country. It was a commence-
ment of freedom of trade. People began to see
that they would be better off by making trade with
foreign nations as easy as possible, instead of making
it as hard as possible. What was done was indeed
only a beginning, but this, and all the other useful
things that the Government was now doing, helped
to put an end to all that ill-feeling which had caused
such trouble a few years before. There were now no
Manchester Massacres or Cato-Street Conspiracies,
because Government and Parliament were doing
their best to help the people, instead of merely
doing their best to keep them down.

5. **The Catholic Association.** — There had been

formed in Ireland a society known as the Catholic Association. Its object was to obtain for Catholics the right of holding offices and sitting in Parliament. At its head was Daniel O'Connell. He was a most eloquent speaker, and he had a good cause. The Catholic Association became so powerful in Ireland that many people in England were frightened lest it should bring about a rebellion. A law was passed to put an end to it, but the law was so badly made that the Association was able to go on just as if there had been no law at all. Fortunately there were men in Parliament who could understand that what the Association asked ought to be granted. The House of Commons passed a Bill for giving to the Catholics their rights. Canning was in favour of this. Peel was against it. The House of Lords rejected the Bill, and nothing more was done for some years.

6. The Representative System.—Another matter about which there had been much discussion was Parliamentary Reform. There were many great towns in England, such as Birmingham, Manchester, and Leeds, which sent no members to Parliament. There were many little villages which sent two members apiece. Of course the villagers did not really choose the members to please themselves. They had to give their votes to the man who was recommended to them by the great landowner on whose estates they lived. Sometimes even there were no villagers to vote. One borough sending members to Parliament was only a ruined wall in a gentleman's park. Another was a grassy

mound. Another had for some centuries been under
the sea. In Scotland matters were even worse. In
the county of Bute there were only twenty-one
electors. On one occasion only one of these appeared at the time of election. He voted for himself, and so became a Member of Parliament. The
noblemen and gentlemen who were able to make the
voters elect whom they pleased considered the votes
of these men as their own property. If they were
in want of money they got it by selling the post of
Member of Parliament to any one who would pay
them for it. There were places where there was a
large number of electors, and where they really
chose whom they liked. But they very often liked
to choose those who bribed them most highly.

7. Parliamentary Reform. — Before the French Revolution attempts had been made to alter this state of
things. When the French Revolution came it was
impossible to induce Parliament to listen to any plan of
reform. Because the French had violently done away
with their bad government, Englishmen were afraid
to improve their good one. They were too frightened
to be reasonable, and they fancied that if they put
an end to a few rotten boroughs, as the little villages which returned members to Parliament were
called, they would somehow or another pull down
the king's throne, and bring a Reign of Terror into
England. By the time which we have now reached
this feeling had passed away. Men of ability and
education were ready to ask whether things might
not be improved. A majority in the House of Commons had already resolved to do justice to the

Catholics. But it was easier to do justice to the Catholics than to reform Parliament. There were so many members who found it easy to get into Parliament by getting the favour of a Duke or Lord, who would not find it easy to get in if they had to get the votes of the inhabitants of a large town. Besides this there were others who objected to the change for better reasons. Even Canning, who was in favour of the Catholics, was against Parliamentary Reform. He thought that if noblemen and gentlemen were no longer able to name members of Parliament, there would be fewer men of real intelligence and ability elected. Whilst this feeling prevailed, there was no chance that the House of Commons would listen to any scheme of Parliamentary Reform, unless some one was found to propose it, who would be content to ask for only a slight change at first. Nobody who asked for universal suffrage, or for anything like it, would get any one to follow him. Fortunately a young man, Lord John Russell, took the matter up. Even before the death of George III. he had persuaded the House of Commons to disfranchise four boroughs where the votes were openly sold; that is to say, to take away from them the right of electing members of Parliament. As usual, the Lords refused to assent to the change. After that Lord John Russell got one little Cornish village disfranchised. He proposed to give the right to Leeds. The Lords gave it to Yorkshire. After this some time passed before anything more was done.

8. The Canning and Goderich Ministries.—In

1827 Lord Liverpool died. As soon as it was known
that he was too ill to remain at his post he resigned.
Canning became Prime Minister. Great things
were expected from him. He had not been three
months in office when he was taken ill and died.
Canning was succeeded by Lord Goderich, whose
ministry only lasted for a very short time. During
that time important news arrived from the East.
The Greeks had for some years been fighting for
their independence against the Turks. Some Englishmen went to their help; amongst others the
great English poet Lord Byron, who died of a fever
caught in an unhealthy swamp. The Turks, not
being themselves able to conquer them, sent to
the Egyptians for help. An Egyptian army landed
in Greece, and committed great atrocities, killing
the people, and destroying everything that it was
possible to destroy. A fleet composed of English,
French, Austrian, and Russian ships was sent to
Greece, and destroyed the Turkish fleet at Navarino.
In consequence of this, the Egyptian army left
Greece, and the war came to an end. Not long
afterwards Greece became an independent state.

**9. The Wellington Ministry and the Repeal of the
Test and Corporation Acts.**—The Duke of Wellington,
followed Goderich as Prime Minister. Peel was again
Home Secretary, an office which he had given up
when Liverpool resigned. The new Ministers agreed
to a Bill proposed by Lord John Russell for the relief
of the Dissenters. By the laws made in the time of
Charles II. they were forbidden to hold offices in
towns or under the Government. Lord John Russell

had taken up their cause. He proposed that the law should be repealed, and he accomplished his object without difficulty.

10. The Clare Election.—The Ministers had given way about the Dissenters, but they had made up their mind not to give way to the Catholics. But they had not been long in office before they discovered that it would be very difficult to resist much longer. There was an election in Ireland in the county of Clare. Though Catholics could not sit in Parliament, they were allowed to vote for members. O'Connell was elected. As he was a Catholic he was by law unable to sit in the House of Commons. Yet it was certain that whenever Parliament was dissolved, almost every county in the three provinces of Leinster, Munster, and Connaught would elect a Catholic. In the fourth province, that of Ulster, Protestants were as numerous, perhaps more numerous, than the Catholics. Protestants and Catholics spoke angrily of one another, and it seemed very likely that they would take arms against one another. The cruel massacres and outrages which had desolated Ireland in 1798 might come again in 1829.

11. Catholic Emancipation.— Both Wellington and Peel had been all their lives against the Catholics. The majority of the English people probably agreed with them. They were afraid that if the Catholics got power they would use it to hurt the Protestants. Wellington, however, had seen what war was, and he had no wish to see a civil war break out in Ireland. Anything, he thought, would be better than that. He resolved to give way. A Bill was brought into Parliament and passed into a law, that from that time Catholics should have equal rights with their Protestant fellow-subjects. It was one of the few reforms which have been made against the popular feeling in England. Perhaps if Parliament had been reformed and the great towns had got their right of voting, it might not so easily have been carried.

12. The New Police.—Another improvement of a different kind was owing to Peel. The police in London, whose business it was to take up thieves and other criminals, did not do their duty. Peel introduced much better policemen, who were well disciplined. The example was afterwards imitated in the rest of England. The nickname of ' Peeler,' which is sometimes used for a policeman, is derived from Peel's surname, and the other nickname of ' Bobby,' from his Christian name Robert. In June 1830 King George IV. died.

13. Roads and Coaches.—Together with the political improvements which were being introduced, there were others which produced great advantages of another kind. Trade and manufactures had grown so much that the canals which had been made in the beginning of the reign of George III. were no longer sufficient to convey the goods which had to be carried from one part of the country to another. It was true that the ordinary roads were much better than they had formerly been. Telford had taught roadmakers that it was better to go round a hill than to go over it. Macadam had suggested that, by breaking up stones, a hard surface could be made in which carriages could pass without sinking in the mud up to the axle-trees, as used to be the case, and had made travelling much easier than it had once been. Coaches flew about the country at what was then thought the wonderful rate of ten miles an hour instead of crawling along at the slowest possible pace. But the new coaches would not carry heavy goods, and more than one person had hit upon the idea that a steam-engine might be employed to do the work. Of many attempts not one succeeded till George Stephenson took the matter in hand.

14. Railways and Locomotives.—George Stephenson was born in Northumberland, a poor collier's son. He learnt something about machinery in the colliery in which he was employed, and after he was grown up he saved money to pay for instruction in reading and writing. He began as an engineer by mending a pumping-engine, and after making some other engines he tried to make a locomotive. The new engine was not successful at first, but he improved it till it did all that it was required to do. It dragged trucks of coal from the colliery more easily and cheaply than horses could do. Some years later the first real railway was made between Stockton and Darlington. As yet however Stephenson's engines did not go very fast. The next railway to be made was one between Liverpool and Manchester. Stephenson made it go over Chat Moss, a bog over which a man could not walk. When the railway was made, the proprietors began to be frightened at the idea of using steam engines. Stephenson persuaded them to offer a prize for the best locomotive. Four inventors sent engines to be tried. Stephenson's, which was called ' The Rocket,' was the only one which would move at all. The other inventors asked to be allowed to try again, but they did not succeed on the second day any better than they had on the first. ' The Rocket ' set off at the rate of thirty-five miles an hour. After that nobody doubted that the line must be worked by steam, and before long there was scarcely a town in England which did not want to have a railway. Yet there were exceptions. The people of Northampton, for instance, preferred to stick by the old ways, and that is the reason why travellers from London to Northampton have to change carriages at Blisworth and go by a branch line which was made after the inhabitants of Northampton had repented of their folly, too late to bring the main line of the London and North-Western Railway through their town.

CHAPTER XLIV.

REIGN OF WILLIAM IV.

(1830–1837.)

1. The End of the Wellington Ministry.—In 1830 George IV. died. His brother William IV. was the new king. He had only been on the throne a few weeks when there was another Revolution in France. The king, Charles X., tried to govern against the

wishes of the people. There was an insurrection in
Paris, and the king was forced to fly from the
country. His distant cousin, Louis Philippe, became
king of the French. This news caused a good
deal of excitement in England. People began to

WILLIAM IV.

think that if foreign nations could do so much,
Englishmen might try to get rid of the rotten
boroughs, and to send members to Parliament who
would really represent the people, instead of repre-
senting the great landowners. The Whigs were in
favour of Parliamentary Reform. Many of them

were themselves owners of boroughs, but they were ready to give them up for the good of the nation. A new Parliament was elected in which there were many more Whigs than in the old one. They would perhaps have been contented at this time without making any very great change, if the Duke would have agreed to do something. But the Duke declared that there ought to be no reform at all. Whilst this dissatisfied the Whigs, the Tories were still angry with him because he had displeased them by what he had done for the Catholics. The majority of the House of Commons declared against him, and he resigned office.

2. The Reform Bill.—The next ministry was composed of Whigs and of the followers of Canning. The Prime Minister was Lord Grey. He and his colleagues resolved to bring in a Reform Bill. The bill was introduced into the House of Commons by Lord John Russell. Neither friends nor enemies expected him to propose so great a change as he did. Sixty small boroughs returning 119 members were to be disfranchised entirely. Forty-six more were to return only one member instead of two. Most of the seats thus at the disposal of the ministry were given, in almost equal proportions, to the counties and the great towns, a few being reserved for Scotland and Ireland. Both in towns and counties a large number of persons were to be allowed to vote who had never had a vote before. If the bill passed, the government of the country would be controlled by the middle classes, and no longer by the great landowners, as had been the case before. Inside the House of Commons the Tories were strong. When the House was asked whether it approved of the Bill or not, the majority which approved of it was only stronger than the minority which disapproved of it by a single vote, and after this a majority voted that it should be altered in an important particular. The Government resolved to withdraw the Bill and to dissolve Parliament, in order that the electors all over the country might say what they thought.

3. The Reform Bill rejected by the Lords.—There was very little doubt what the electors would think. Even under the old system of voting there were the counties and large towns which voted as they pleased, and in times of great excitement the towns of a middle size would refuse to vote as they were bidden, whilst some of the very small towns were under the influence of Whig landowners. From one end of the country to the other shouts were heard of ' The Bill, the whole Bill, and nothing but the Bill.' The new House of Commons, unlike the last, had an enormous Whig majority. The Reform Bill was again brought in and was carried through the House of Commons. The House of Lords rejected it.

4. Public Agitation.—The news was received with a torrent of indignation. Meetings were everywhere held to support the Government, and in some towns there were riots and disturbances. In the House of Commons, Macaulay, a young man, afterwards famous as the historian of the reigns of James II. and William III., called on the House of Commons to stand forward to prevent the excitement degenerating into deeds of violence. ' In old times,'

he said, ' when the villeins were driven to revolt by
oppression, when a hundred thousand insurgents
appeared in arms on Blackheath, the king rode up
to them and exclaimed " I will be your leader," and
at once the infuriated multitude laid down their
arms and dispersed at his command. Herein let us
imitate him. Let us say to our countrymen " We
are your leaders. Our lawful power shall be firmly
exerted to the utmost in your cause ; and our lawful
power is such that it must finally prevail." ' Outside
Parliament there were men who thought that
nothing but force would bear down the resistance of
the Lords. At Birmingham a great meeting was
held by a society called the Birmingham Political
Union, at which those who were present engaged to
pay no taxes if the Reform Bill were again rejected.
At Bristol there were fierce riots, houses were burnt,
and men were killed.

5. The Reform Bill becomes Law.—Fortunately
the Government and the House of Commons were as
earnest as the people. A third Reform Bill, slightly
altered from the former ones, was introduced as soon
as possible, and carried through the Commons. Some
of the Lords thought that they had resisted enough.
It was known too that the king had consented to
create new peers who would vote for the Reform
Bill. Upon this many peers stayed away from the
House, and in the spring of 1832 the Bill was
accepted by the Lords and became law.

6. Abolition of Slavery, and the new Poor-law.—
After so great a change the two parties began to
take new names. Instead of Whigs and Tories,

people began to talk of Liberals and Conservatives. The liberals had a good deal of work to do. When the slave-trade had been abolished, the negroes who were in the West Indian Colonies remained as slaves. A law was now passed to set them free, and a large sum of money was voted to recompense their masters for the loss. Then too there was a change in the English Poor-law, intended to prevent money being given to those who were idle. It was thought right that no one should be allowed to starve, but that people who would not work if they could, must not be living upon the money of those who are industrious.

7. Dismissal of the Government, and Peel's first Ministry.—Besides these a good many other right and wise things were done. For this very reason the Government became less popular than they had been. There are always a large number of people who have an interest in things remaining as they are, and they usually grow very angry when improvements are made. Besides the people who disliked the Government because it did right, there were also people who disliked it because it made mistakes. The Conservatives, too, were growing in favour. Peel, who led them in the House of Commons, was a prudent man, and many persons began to think that he could manage things better than the ministers could. Then the ministers disagreed amongst themselves. Some of them resigned. At last Lord Grey resigned, and Lord Melbourne, one of the other ministers, became Prime Minister. The king soon afterwards dismissed Lord Melbourne, and made Sir Robert Peel Prime Minister. Peel dissolved Parliament, and a great many more Conservatives were elected than had been chosen to the last Parliament. But they were not enough to form a majority, and Peel resigned. Lord Melbourne came back into office.

8. Lord Melbourne's Ministry.— Lord Melbourne's ministry was not very successful. Its members were not good men of business, and the Conservatives were nearly as numerous as the Liberals in the House of Commons, and much more numerous in the House of Lords. People in the country were not very enthusiastic in favour of the ministry. Nevertheless, they did some good things. They reformed the municipal governments of the towns, so that the mayors and aldermen would be elected by the greater part of their fellow-citizens, instead of being elected only by a few. Other things they did; but whilst the Conservatives thought they did too much, there were some Liberals who wanted much more to be done, and thought they did too little. In 1837 William IV. died.

CHAPTER XLV.

FROM THE ACCESSION OF VICTORIA TO THE FALL OF THE MELBOURNE MINISTRY.

(1837–1841.)

1. State of the Country.—William IV. left no son to succeed him. His niece, Queen Victoria, as-

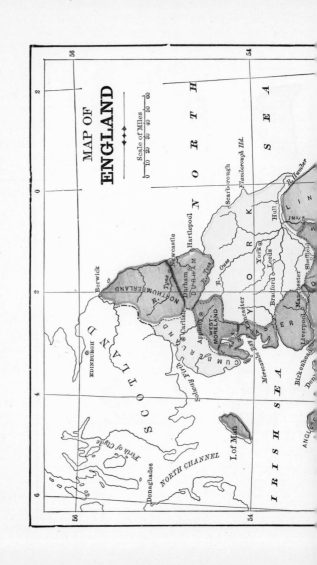

MAP OF
ENGLAND

Scale of Miles
0 10 20 30 40 50 60

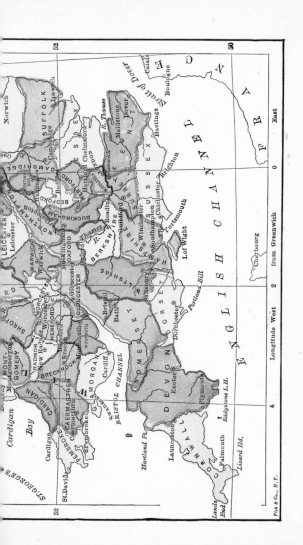

cended the throne. She was young, and was popular
from the first. There were difficulties enough before the Government, and the Government was not
competent to meet them. Lord Melbourne was an
easy-going man, who disliked the idea of taking

PORTRAIT OF THE QUEEN.

trouble. Often when he was asked how some difficult thing could be done, he asked lazily, 'Can't you
let it alone?' There were large masses of people in
England in misery. Both the agricultural and the
manufacturing poor were in great distress. Wages
were low and the price of food was high. Soon

after the end of the war with France, Parliament
had passed a Corn Law, imposing a heavy duty on
foreign corn. It was thought that if corn came in
from abroad it would be sold cheaply, and then the
farmers and landlords could not get enough for their
corn to enable them to make a livelihood, and that
the land would go out of cultivation. In this way
bread was made very much dearer than it would
have been if foreign corn had come in. Besides
this, there was no care taken for the health of the
poor. There were no inspectors to see that the factories were airy enough for the workers to breathe
properly in. The hours of labour were very long,
and women and children were put to work much too
hard for their strength. In the collieries, especially,
women and children had to drag about heavy carts.
In the country the cottages of the labourers were often
very unhealthy and over-crowded. Very few knew
how to read and write, so that they had no chance
of learning how to join together to help themselves.

2. **The People's Charter.**—When people are dissatisfied, the first thing they think of usually is that
if they had political power they could set everything
right. So it was now. Large numbers of men supported what was called 'The People's Charter,' and
were therefore called Chartists. It had six points,
(1) universal suffrage for all men, (2) division of the
kingdom into equal electoral districts, (3) vote by
ballot, (4) annual Parliaments, (5) permission for
every man to be elected whether he had property
in land or not, (6) payment to members of Parliament. Of these, two, the third and the fifth,

have now become law. At that time both the
gentry and the shopkeepers were very much alarmed
when they heard what a number of Chartists there
were. Some of these Chartists talked of getting
what they wanted by force, and that frightened a
good many people. The Chartists were, however,
certainly right in wanting to be represented in
Parliament. The Reform Bill had arranged the
right of voting so that the shopkeepers had votes,
but very few, if any, of the working men. Still it
was probably as well that the working men had to
wait some years for their votes, and that many in-
justices were removed first, so that when they did
get power they did not come to it angrily as they
would have done at that time.

3. Post-Office Reform.—It was not likely that
Lord Melbourne's ministry would have done much
to relieve the general suffering. But one reform it
effected which has given happiness to millions. One
day a young man named Rowland Hill was walking
in the north of England. As he passed a cottage a
postman arrived with a letter. A girl came out, took
the letter, and gave it back to the postman. In
those days the charge for postage was very great, a
shilling or two being an ordinary charge, as the payment rose higher with the distance. The receiver
of the letter, not the sender, had to pay, though he
need not take in the letter unless he liked. In this
instance Rowland Hill felt compassionate towards
the girl, paid the postage, and gave her the letter.
When the postman was gone she told him that she
was sorry that he had done it, as there was nothing

written in the letter. Her brother had gone to London, and they had agreed that as they were too poor to pay the postage, he should send her a plain sheet of paper folded up. She would always return it, but as long as these sheets of paper came regularly, she would know that he was in good health. This story set Rowland Hill thinking, and he considered that it would cause much happiness if postage were reduced to a penny whatever distance the letter went. The number of letters would so increase that a large number at a penny would bring in more than a small number at a shilling. It would be necessary to charge the penny to the sender, by making him buy postage stamps, as when the number of letters became very great the postman would not have time to stop at every door to collect pennies. This idea was much laughed at at first, but at last the Government took it up. First of all postage was reduced to fourpence, and after a little while to a penny. The system of low payments and of postage stamps has since been adopted by every country in the civilised world.

4. Education.—Soon after the Reform Bill a beginning was made in helping the spread of education with the money of the nation. A sum of 20,000*l*. was given to help two private societies which had been doing their best to educate. Two years after the Queen's accession the sum was increased to 30,000*l*. It was proposed that this should be employed by the direction of some members of the Government, and that a school should be set up to train the teachers. There was such a resistance to this proposal that it had to be altered a good deal. But enough was done to make a beginning, and from that time it began to be understood that it was the duty of the Government to see that the people were taught.

5. The Queen's Marriage.—The marriage of the Queen called forth afresh expressions of loyalty

PORTRAIT OF PRINCE ALBERT.

from every part of the kingdom. Her cousin, Prince Albert of Saxe Coburg, who became her husband, was a man of varied learning and accomplishments. What was of greater importance, he brought with him an affectionate devotion to his young wife, which caused him through his whole life to throw away all thoughts of personal ambition, and a prudence and tact which made him her. wisest counsellor. He never considered anything to be beneath his notice, and always did his best to understand thoroughly whatever was worth understanding at all. Once a man came to the palace to fit up a new glass chandelier. Prince Albert saw him and talked to him. When the man came away he said that the Prince seemed to know more about chandeliers than he did himself. The Prince knew more about many things than Englishmen were aware of, and he took great pains to encourage whatever he thought would be for the good of the people.

6. Lord Palmerston and the Eastern Question. — Soon after the Queen's marriage there was very near being a war between England and France. The minister who managed Foreign Affairs was Lord Palmerston. He had had the same office in Lord Grey's ministry, and had then done all that he could to help the nations in Europe which were trying to be governed by kings with parliaments instead of being governed by kings without parliaments. His attention had latterly been chiefly directed to the East of Europe. Turkey was growing weaker every year, because the Sultan did not know how to govern properly. The Turks had conquered that part of Europe more than four hundred years before, just as the Normans had once conquered England. But they did not unite with their subjects as the Normans did with the English. Their subjects were Christians and they were Mahometans. The poorer Turks were honest and brave, and would bear suffer-

ing so patiently that they astonished Europeans
who went amongst them; but the rich Turks who
governed thought only of becoming wealthy, and
did not mind what they did to grow richer than they
were. Besides this, all Turks were very ignorant, and
did not care to learn how to govern properly. Their
great enemy was Russia. The Russians had taken
from them one province after another. Lord Palmerston was afraid lest Russia should gradually go
on till it conquered all Turkey, and he thought that
Russia would then be so powerful as to be dangerous
to other European states, and especially to Turkey.
The only way of stopping this that he could think
of was to keep the Turks in possession of all that
they had got, in hopes that some day or other they
would find out that it was to their own advantage to
govern well.

7. **Mehemet Ali driven out of Syria.**—Whilst
Turkey was growing weak, the ruler of Egypt,
Mehemet Ali, had been growing strong. He was a
resolute man with a well-disciplined army, and some
years before he had conquered Syria from the Turks.
The Sultan sent an army to drive him out, but he
beat the Turkish army, and would have gone on to
take Constantinople, if he had been allowed. Lord
Palmerston was so anxious to save Turkey that he
persuaded Russia, Austria, and Prussia to sign a
treaty to stop the Egyptians. As the French did
not agree to this, they were left out of the treaty.
They were so angry that a war very nearly broke out
between France and England. Happily the ill-
humour cooled down. Mehemet Ali was driven out

of Syria, and the Turks had one more chance of trying whether they could govern decently.

8. The Fall of the Melbourne Ministry.—At last the Melbourne ministry came to an end in 1841. Having done so little for so many years, it suddenly announced an intention of doing very great things indeed. It was going to lower the duties on corn. The ministers did not gain anything by their proposal. People thought that they offered to make corn cheap, not because they cared about cheap corn but because they wanted to remain in office. There was a dissolution of Parliament, and in the new Parliament there was a great majority against them. They resigned office, and Sir Robert Peel became Prime Minister.

CHAPTER XLVI.

THE MINISTRY OF SIR ROBERT PEEL.

(1841–1846.)

1. Commercial Free Trade.—Peel was at the head of the Conservative party, but he was bent on improving all that he saw to be amiss, though he took some time to find out all that was wrong. He and his followers were determined that the duties on corn should continue to be paid. He made some alteration in the way in which they were to be paid, but he did not mean to do any more. He thought that trade would flourish much more if the duties were lowered or taken off a great many articles of commerce. Every year he took off duties, and it was found that the more taxes he took off the more was the amount of money paid in the taxes which remained. Manufacturers became richer when they could buy articles to use in their factories without having to pay duties on them. The whole people was better off than before, and after this there was much less misery than there had been.

2. The Invasion of Afghanistan.— Peel had not been long in office when bad news arrived from India. Gradually since the day when Clive won the Battle of Plassey, the English had conquered India. Their dominions now reached as far as the Sutlej, one of the five rivers which form the great stream of the Indus. Some way to the eastward was the mountainous country known as Afghanistan. The Afghans by whom it was inhabited were hardy and warlike. There was a panic amongst the English in India. It was believed that the Russians, who were making conquests in central Asia, meant to invade India some day, and that Dost Mahomed, the ruler of Afghanistan, was their friend. It was determined to invade his territory, to dethrone him, and to set up another ruler in his stead. The British army defeated the Afghan troops, took the fortresses, and reached Cabul in safety. Dost Mahomed himself won a victory over some Indian cavalry in the British service, and then delivered himself up as a prisoner.

3. The Rising of the Afghans.—A British force remained to occupy Cabul. Sir William Macnaghten had charge of all political arrangements. He fancied

E E

that all difficulties were at an end. Suddenly an
insurrection broke out in Cabul. Some of the most
notable of the British officials were murdered. Still
there were British soldiers enough to attack the
Afghans with every chance of success. Unhappily
their commander, General Elphinstone, could not
make up his mind to run the risk. He waited to
see what would happen, and before long his position
was hopeless. Food was failing, and the number of
the enemies was increasing. Macnaghten and
Elphinstone entered into negotiations with the
Afghans. The Afghans offered to give them food if
they would give up the forts by which the British
were protected. The forts were given up, and the
Afghans learnt by this to despise their enemies.
Akbar Khan, Dost Mahomed's son, invited Macnaghten to a conference, and treacherously shot him
dead with a pistol which Macnaghten had given him
the day before. The British officers, instead of re-
solving to fight to the last, entered into a treaty
with the murderer, in which he engaged to protect
the army on its way back to India.

4. The Retreat from Cabul.—The retreat began
sadly. It was winter, and amidst those lofty mountains snow and ice lay thickly on the path. Akbar
Khan did what he could to protect the retreating
soldiers, but he could not do much. Crowds of
fierce Afghans were posted on the rocks and on the
steep sides of the hills through which the army had
to struggle, shooting down the fugitives as they
passed. Amongst the soldiers were English ladies,
some with children to care for. When they reached

the end of a narrow pass through which they had to go, scarcely a thousand men were left out of four thousand who had started from Cabul. To save the women and children they were delivered up to Akbar Khan, who promised to treat them kindly. He kept his word, and no harm happened to them. The men had to march on to death. They reached another narrow pass. The cruel Afghans were already on the rocks on either side, and shot them down without mercy. Very few lived to reach the other end. Those few pushed on, hoping to reach Jellalabad, where there was a British garrison. When they were still sixteen miles from Jellalabad only six were alive. The pony on which one of these, Dr. Brydon, rode was so worn out, and he himself was so utterly fatigued, that he lagged behind. The other five pushed on and were slain by the Afghans. Believing that the last Englishman had been killed, these Afghans went off to tell the tale. Weary and unnoticed Dr. Brydon came on slowly. At last he reached Jellalabad. He was the one man who arrived to tell the tale of the great disaster.

5. Pollock's March to Cabul.—Jellalabad held out against all the Afghan forces that could be brought against it. A fresh army under General Pollock came to its succour. Then Pollock advanced to Cabul. The prisoners were recovered. The place in which Macnaghten had been murdered was destroyed. Then Pollock returned. Dost Mahomed was sent back and allowed to reign without further interference.

6. The Anti-Corn-Law League.—At home something was done to lighten the toil of those who were least able to bear it. A law was made forbidding the employment of women and girls in mines and collieries. By another law, it was forbidden to make children work in factories more than six and a half hours a day. Yet the great evil remained unredressed. Bread was dear, because a duty had to be paid on corn brought in from foreign countries. There were a few men in Lancashire who resolved to devote themselves to the work of procuring the abolition of the Corn Law in order that the food of the people might be brought in free of duty. First of these was Richard Cobden, a Sussex man, who had established himself in Manchester. He and his friends, of whom the principal was John Bright, established the Anti-Corn-Law League. It was a society formed for the purpose of lecturing and printing pamphlets with the object of instructing the public on the evils which arose from the Corn Law. The League was soon busily employed, but it had many difficulties before it. Many of the working class were suspicious of it, because it originated with master manufacturers, and they thought that the demand for the repeal of the Corn Laws was a trick to make them forget the People's Charter. Naturally many of the landowners were against them, because they thought that they would be ruined if foreign corn was allowed to come in freely, and because they believed that if they were ruined all England would suffer, and in this they had the farmers on their side. Yet there were not a few amongst the landlords who were ready to take their chance of being ruined, as soon as they were convinced that the whole nation, and especially the poor, would suffer by the maintenance of the Corn Law. Nevertheless the League persevered. It had a good cause, and it set forth its cause with plain and convincing arguments. It converted many persons, and it half converted Peel. What converted him entirely was the Irish famine.

7. The Irish Famine.—In Ireland the greater part of the population lived upon potatoes. The potato disease, unknown before, appeared, and made the greater part of the crop unfit for food The mass of the Irish people found starvation before them. The Government tried to do what it could to provide work and pay for the hungry millions. Bountiful subscriptions were collected and sent over. But all that could be done was not enough. Masses of Irishmen emigrated to America. In the face of such suffering Peel felt that food could no longer be kept artificially dear. He proposed to the other ministers that food should now be allowed to come in without paying duty. The ministers would not agree to this. Lord John Russell wrote a letter on behalf of the opponents of the Government, declaring that the Corn Laws must be abolished. On this, Peel urged his fellow ministers, not merely to let corn come freely into Ireland for a time, but to ask Parliament to abolish the Corn Laws altogether. When Parliament met, Peel proposed their abolition. Most of his own followers were desperately angry. A new party known as that of the Protectionists was formed. They treated Peel as a deserter who had come into office to uphold the Corn Laws, and who remained in office to abolish them. The Protectionists however could not get a majority in the House. A certain number of Peel's followers were convinced by his arguments, and he had the support of the Liberals who had hitherto been his opponents. The Corn Laws were abolished, and free trade in corn was introduced. The food of the people was no longer to be taxed.

8. The End of Peel's Ministry.—Peel's ministry did not last much longer. The first time that the Liberals differed from him, the Protectionists joined them against him, and Peel was left in a minority. He resigned office. He had done a good deed, but he was generous enough to remember that, if his had been the hand to accomplish the work, the thought of doing it had come from another, and in the last speech which he made as Prime Minister he reminded the House of Commons that his success was due to Richard Cobden.

CHAPTER XLVII.

FROM THE BEGINNING OF LORD JOHN RUSSELL'S MINISTRY TO THE END OF THE CRIMEAN WAR.

(1846—1856.)

1. The European Revolutions.—The new Prime Minister was Lord John Russell. He had not been long in office when troubles burst out over nearly the whole of the European continent. The year 1848 was one of general alarm. There was a revolution in France. King Louis Philippe was forced to fly, and a Republic was set up. In Italy the kings and princes were forced to allow Parliaments to meet, and to make war on Austria, which ruled over a great part of Northern Italy. In Austria itself and in Prussia Parliaments were set up after insurrections.

2. The Chartists in London.—In England the Chartists thought that now was the time to gain what they had so long demanded in vain. Their leader was Feargus O'Connor, a member of Parliament. He and the leading Chartists determined to gather in enormous numbers on Kennington Common, where Kennington Park now is, and to carry with them a petition to Parliament on behalf of the Charter. They thought that Parliament would not venture to refuse to grant a request made by so large a number of men. They forgot two things: first, that it was against the law to go in procession to Parliament in such numbers; and, secondly, that the great bulk of the English people was thoroughly resolved that Parliament should not be bullied into changing the laws. The Government declared the plan of the Chartists to be illegal, and invited any one who would, to come forward as a special constable, that is to say, to act as a policeman for the day. Thousands of men did as they were asked, and the Chartists discovered that the numbers of those who were against them -were far greater than the numbers of those who were on their side. There were about 200,000 special constables. Besides, the Duke of Wellington had soldiers ready to act in case of necessity. At Kennington there were not more than 25,000 people, and many of these only came to see what was going on, without caring the least about the Charter. The procession of Chartists never tried to cross Westminster Bridge. The great petition was put into a cab and carried to the House of Commons. Feargus O'Connor told the House that it was signed by 5,700,000 persons. The House took the trouble to have the signatures counted, and found that there were less than 2,000,000. On examining the signatures further, it appeared that whole pages were full of signatures written in one hand, and that many who had signed it had written, instead of their own names, those of Prince Albert, the Duke of Wellington, and other celebrated persons. Others had written down ridiculous names, such as Pugnose, Wooden-legs, and Bread-and-Cheese. It was evident that all these did not care much about the Charter. Yet it must not be forgotten that there were a great many people who did care about it, and that the working men had gained by their peaceable and orderly conduct a fair right to ask that they should have some part in electing members of Parliament, and that their opinions about the government of the country might be heard.

3. The Death of Peel and the Great Exhibition. Russell's Government.—The time for giving votes to the working men was not yet come. The minds of Englishmen were taken up at home with seeing that the Protectionists did not get power to bring back the corn laws. People were better off than they had been before, and as one of Peel's followers said,

'they knew the reason why.' But they did not feel
very enthusiastic in favour of the Government, and
it is probable that if Sir Robert Peel had lived he
would before long have been back in office. Unhappily one day he fell from his horse in the Park,
and was so injured that he died shortly afterwards.
The year after Peel's death Englishmen could think
of nothing but the Great Exhibition in Hyde Park,
where the produce of the world was to be seen in
the enormous glass house which was afterwards en-
larged and removed to Penge Hill. It was a useful
undertaking, which had been first thought of by
Prince Albert, and it served its purpose in teaching
English manufacturers that they might improve
their own work by studying the work of foreigners.
Many people thought it would do more good than
that. They fancied that because crowds of foreigners
came to see London and the Exhibition, there would
be no more wars. These people were soon to be
disappointed. Two or three years before, the kings
and princes of Europe had put down the people who
had risen against them, and had in most places
abolished the Parliaments that had been set up.
Shortly after the Exhibition was closed, Louis Napoleon, the nephew of the former Emperor, who had
been elected President of the French Republic, put
down the Republic, and marched soldiers into the
streets of Paris to shoot any men who resisted him.
He then asked the French people to name him President for ten years. They did so, and not long
afterwards they named him Emperor. He arranged
that they should elect a Parliament, but he took

care that the newspapers should not print anything that he did not like, and that the ignorant people should be told freely what a great and wise man he was. In this way he managed to do pretty much as he pleased for some years.

4. The Derby Ministry.—Not long after the close of the Great Exhibition Lord John Russell's ministry resigned, and the Protectionists came into office. Their leader was the Earl of Derby, and their chief man in the House of Commons was Mr. Disraeli. They dissolved Parliament, but the majority of the new Parliament was against them. They gave up Protection, and declared that they would accept Free Trade. It was of no use; the majority would not support them, and they had to resign.

5. The Coalition Ministry and the Eastern Difficulty.—They were succeeded by a ministry known as the Coalition Ministry, because it was formed of two sets of men, the Liberals and the followers of Sir Robert Peel. The Prime Minister was the Earl of Aberdeen. They had not been long in office when fresh troubles arose in the East. The Emperor of Russia, Nicholas, was of the same religion as most of the Christian subjects of Turkey. He and all his subjects would have been glad to set them free from the rule of the Sultan. He was also a man with a very strong will, who governed his own subjects very harshly, and who wanted to make his power felt outside Russia. He proposed to the English Ambassador at his Court that part of the Christian provinces of Turkey should be set free and placed under his protection, and he offered to let England take Egypt and Candia too if it liked to do so. Such a proposal was sure to shock the English Ministers. They did not wish to see Russia gaining any more power in Turkey than it had had before, and they did not think it honest to settle the question by an agreement which would have allowed them to rob Turkey in the south if they would shut their eyes whilst Russia robbed it in the north.

6. War between Russia and Turkey.—After a time Nicholas resolved to do alone what the English Government would not help him to do. He required the Sultan to give him the right of protecting all the Christians of Turkey. If this had been granted, Nicholas would have been far more powerful than the Sultan. As soon as a dispute arose between the Sultan and his Christian subjects, a Russian army would have marched in to take the part of the Christians. The Turks naturally refused to give way, and Russia then sent troops to occupy the Danubian Principalities, which are now known as Roumania. England and France, Austria and Prussia, joined in supporting Turkey, though they wished if possible to prevent war. Nicholas insisted on his demand, and the Turks insisted on refusing it. Turkey declared war against Russia. The Turks defended themselves well on land, but their fleet in the Black Sea was destroyed by the Russians. Then the combined English and French fleets entered the Black Sea, to defend the Turks. From that moment it was certain that there would be war between Russia on the one side and England and France on

[THE CRIMEA AND THE NEIGHBOURING COUNTRIES]

the other. In the beginning of 1854 war was declared. Austria and Prussia remained neutral.

7. The Invasion of the Crimea and the Battle of the Alma.—An English and French army was sent to Varna, in Bulgaria. The Turks, however, defended themselves so well on the Danube that this army was not needed there, and before long the Russian troops left Roumania. In the English Ministry there was one man who was not content with this success. Lord Palmerston urged his colleagues to put an end to the power of Russia in the Black Sea. He was supported by the Emperor of the French. It was therefore determined to attack the great fortress of Sebastopol, in the Crimea, where the Russian navy was safe under strong batteries of guns. Orders were given to Lord Raglan, the English general, and to Marshal St. Arnaud, the French general, to invade the Crimea, taking with them a small Turkish force. They landed to the north of Sebastopol, with 64,000 men in all. As they marched southwards, they found the Russian army drawn up along the top of a hill beyond the river Alma. They crossed the stream and marched up the hill. There was not much skill shown by the generals on either side, but in the end the Russians were driven off, and the victory was won.

8. The Beginning of the Siege of Sebastopol.— Some people have thought that if the conquerors had pushed hurriedly on, Sebastopol would have been taken. Instead of that they waited, and, marching round the head of the harbour, they attacked Sebastopol on the southern side. Even then some have thought that the allied armies might have forced their way in with a rush. But they did not try it, and prepared for a regular siege. Sebastopol was not to be taken in that way so easily. There was inside it a vast store of guns, and of everything needed for defence. What was more than this, there was a man of genius, General Todtleben, inside it. He set to work and fortified the place. The guns of the allies were not enough to beat down the fortifications.

9. The Balaclava Charge and the Battle of Inkermann.—Then came the fight at Balaclava. The Russians attacked, and were driven back. An order was sent to Lord Cardigan, who commanded the light cavalry, to retake some guns which had been captured by the Russians. He misunderstood it, and thought that he was directed to charge into the midst of the whole Russian army. The poet Tennyson has told the story how, when Cardigan gave the order, the brave men rushed to their death, knowing that all they could do would be in vain. They would not set an example of disobedience. Very few escaped. As a French general who was looking on said, 'It is magnificent, but it is not war.' Thousands more were to perish because the generals did not know how to lead their men, and the Ministers at home did not know how to provide for them. At Inkermann there was a great battle. The few English troops were surprised in the early morning by the thick columns of the Russian army. They held out for some hours, till the French came to their help. The Russians were driven back, and the allied armies were saved from destruction.

10. Winter in the Crimea.—The battle of Inkermann had been fought in the beginning of November. It has often been called a soldiers' battle. The English private soldiers and the officers of the English regiments were more intelligent, and more ready to act on their own responsibility, than the Russians were. But there was no skill in the general who commanded the army. He had foreseen nothing, and he provided for nothing. Neither he nor the Ministers at home had provided for the winter. They had hoped to be inside Sebastopol before that came, and instead of that they were still outside, on the bleak hill-side. It was not all the fault of the general or the Ministers. It had been long since England had engaged in a great war, and all the lessons of the last one had been forgotten. Wellington's skill and the bravery of his troops were remembered, but not his patient labour in providing all things necessary for the subsistence of the troops. The Ministers had indeed sent many things, but they had not sent enough. A storm swept over the Black Sea, and wrecked vessels laden with comforts for the soldiers. The storm brought bitter cold to the men on shore. They had but tents to protect them against frost and snow, and the tents were often blown down, leaving them without shelter. The men fell ill by hundreds, and medicine and medical comforts were sent out from England. But there were constant blunders. The sick and wounded were sent to one place, the medicine was sent to another. Men at home who had to provide the proper things were so eager and excited to do what was right that they usually ended by doing what was wrong. Once a large amount of coffee was sent out to keep the soldiers warm. Those who sent it forgot to have it roasted, and they did not send out any machines for roasting it in the Crimea. Another time a large quantity of boots was despatched. Unfortunately they were all made to fit the left foot.

11. The Hospital at Scutari.—With great difficulty the sick were sent away to a hospital at Scutari, near Constantinople. When they arrived there there were doctors to cure them, but no nurses to attend to them. There had been no nurses in the Peninsular War. Sidney Herbert, the Minister who had the charge of the war, saw that the best doctors could do but little without the help of women, and he asked Miss Florence Nightingale, who had taught herself how the sick should be nursed, to go out with other ladies who would volunteer to help the poor men at Scutari. She at once agreed to go. With her help the hospital was brought into order. Many a sick man's life was spared, and many a dying man went peacefully to his rest through the gentle help thus offered. What she did was a token for good in every way. One of the best things that are happening in this time in which we live is the discovery of the many ways in which women can help men in the work of life. In Queen Elizabeth's time the great poet Shakspere told about the lives of many good and beautiful women. Even Shakspere himself could never have imagined Florence Nightingale. Good women in his days were gentle and kind to their husbands and brothers. Now they can go out into the world and be gentle and kind to the poor, the sick, and the afflicted.

12. **The Palmerston Ministry.**—At home Englishmen looked on at all the misery and confusion in the Crimea with growing anger. They thought that somebody must be to blame, and they could not clearly make out who the somebody was. As soon as Parliament met, the Government was attacked, and forced to resign. From every side there were calls upon Lord Palmerston to be Prime Minister. It was known that his whole heart was in the war, and that he was a man of strong common sense and of resolute character. The arrangements for the army were gradually brought into order. Perhaps things would have improved even if Palmerston had not been there to direct them. Officials were beginning from many failures to learn their duties. The winter too was passing away, and their work was easier than it had been. But it was something to have a man at the head of the Government who knew both how to work himself and to make others do the same.

13. **The Fall of Sebastopol and the End of the War.**—During the summer which followed, the siege of Sebastopol was pushed on. The English army was in good condition. Officers and men were learning their work. But the French army was more numerous than ours. It occupied the best positions, from which the town was most easily

F F

attacked. One assault was made, from which both French and English were driven back. Then came another. The English attack failed, the French was successful. Sebastopol was taken. Through the next winter the English army increased in numbers and improved in discipline. But there was no more fighting. The Emperor Nicholas had died in the hard winter which did so much harm to the English and French armies. Now that Sebastopol had been taken, his successor, Alexander II., was ready to make peace. In the spring of 1856 peace was made. The fortifications of Sebastopol were destroyed, and Russia obliged to promise not to have a fleet in the Black Sea. The chief object of the war had been to show Russia that she must not settle the affairs of the lands governed by the Sultan in her own way, and this had been gained. There was, however, a belief in England that the Turkish Government would improve, and govern those countries better. This was, however, a mistake. The Sultan and his Ministers did not improve, or learn how to govern, and after a few years there were fresh troubles in Turkey.

CHAPTER XLVIII.

THE INDIAN MUTINY.

(1857, 1858.)

1. Troubles in India.—In the year after the Crimean War was ended the attention of men was fixed on a country still farther to the East than Turkey. In 1857 exactly a hundred years had passed since Clive had won the battle of Plassey. The religion of the Hindoos, who form a great part of the natives of India, teaches many things which seem very strange to Englishmen. Among other things they are taught that they will be defiled if they eat any part of a cow. By this defilement they will meet with much contempt from their fellows, and will suffer much after their death in another world. The bulk of the army in India was composed of Hindoos, and it happened that an improved rifle had lately been invented for the use of the soldiers, and that the cartridges used in this rifle required to be greased, in order that they might be rammed down easily into the barrel. The men believed that the grease used was made of the fat of cows, though this was not really the case. There was, therefore, much suspicion and angry feeling among the native soldiers, and when ignorant men are suspicious and angry they are apt to break out into deeds of unreasoning fury. The danger was the greater because a great many of the native princes were also discontented. These princes governed states scattered about over India, though they were not allowed to make war with one another. Many of them had governed very badly, had ruined their subjects by hard taxation, and had spent the money they thus obtained in vicious and riotous living. The English Government in India had interfered with some of these, and had dethroned them, annexing their territories to its own, and ruling the people who had been their subjects by means of its own officers. The consequence was that some of the princes who had been left in possession of authority thought that their turn would come next, and that they too would be dethroned before long. These men were therefore ready to help against the English, if they thought that they had a chance of succeeding.

2. The Outbreak of the Mutiny.—The place at which the soldiers broke out into open mutiny was Meerut. They fired at their English officers, killed some of them, and massacred such Englishmen as they could meet with. Then they made off for Delhi. At Delhi lived an old man whose ancestors had been the chiefs of the Mohammedans who had once conquered India, and who had successively ruled India under the title of the Great Mogul. Their descendant was without power and authority, but he was allowed to live in state, in a magnificent palace, and had a large allowance of money, to support him in every luxury. The mutineers placed him at their head, and called him the Emperor of India. Happily the Governor-General of India was

Lord Canning, George Canning's son. He knew
how to oppose the mutineers, and he sent for a large
body of English troops which happened to be on
its way to China. Till they came he must look to
India itself for help. In the north-west of India lay
the Punjab, a province recently conquered, and the
best English troops were there. The Punjab was
governed by Sir John Lawrence, one of the best and
wisest of the English statesmen in India. He at once
disarmed the Sepoys in the Punjab. Then he sent
forth an army to besiege Delhi. That army was not
composed of British troops only. The Sikhs, or
natives of the Punjab, were a fierce, warlike race.
Not many years before they had fought hard for independence. Now they were reconciled to British
rule through the wise government of Lawrence and
those who served under him. They despised the
natives of the plains on the banks of the Ganges,
and they were eager to serve against the mutineers.
They formed a great part of the army which Lawrence
despatched to the siege of Delhi. But though the
Sikhs and the English alike fought well, Delhi was a
large city, and it was long before it could be taken.

3. Cawnpore.—The mutiny spread to Lucknow.
Lucknow was the capital of Oudh, which had lately
been annexed to the British dominions. The few
Englishmen who were in the town were driven into
an inclosed house and grounds known as the
Residency, with their wives and children. There
they held out against the raging multitude outside
till help might come. Worse things than this
happened at Cawnpore. There were there about a

thousand British men, women, and children. The old commander, Sir Hugh Wheeler, thought that he might trust a native named Nana Sahib, who lived near, as Nana Sahib had been particularly friendly to him. He did not know that Nana Sahib hated the whole British race, because the English Government had refused to acknowledge his right to an inheritance to which he laid claim. Wheeler retired into a hospital round which was a low mud wall. He had with him more than five hundred women and children and less than five hundred men Nana Sahib arrived, but he came not to help Wheeler, but to put himself at the head of the mutineers. The mutineers again and again made a rush at the low mud wall. Again and again they were beaten off, but swarms of them were firing all day, and many of the defenders fell under their bullets. The poor women and children had to crouch for shelter under the wall, with no roof over their heads to guard them from the scorching rays of the Indian sun. There was but one well from which water could be drawn, and those who went to draw water there did it at the peril of their lives. The mutineers took care to direct their bullets upon it, and many a man dropped slain or wounded as he strove to fetch a little water to cool the parched mouths of wife or child. At last Nana Sahib, finding that he could not get in by force, offered to let the garrison go safely away if the hospital were surrendered. The offer was accepted, and all who still lived were taken down to the river and placed on board large boats, to float down the stream. The treacherous mutineers never meant that they should escape with their lives. They gathered on the bank, and shot them down. Some of the women and children who were still alive were carried to a house, where for some days they were kept alive. The murderers were sent in, and they were all massacred. Their bodies were thrown into the well from which their brothers and husbands had sought for water in the days of the siege. Of the whole number which had been with Wheeler at the beginning, only four men escaped to tell the miserable tale.

4. **Clemency Canning.**—It was no wonder that such news as this put all Englishmen in India into a fury of wrath. The tale was bad enough in itself, but even more horrible things were told and believed than any which really happened. The talk was everywhere of revenge. Even here in England, men whose lives were spent in deeds of kindness could not refrain their tongues from uttering words of cruelty, not merely calling out for the death and destruction of the actual murderers, but of the populations of whole cities, in which, as in Nineveh of old, there were many thousand persons so young and innocent that they knew not their right hand from their left. No wonder that men in India were even fiercer still. One man remained cool amidst the wild outcry. Lord Canning, Clemency Canning as he was called in derision by those who were asking for blood, resolved that there should be punishment, but nothing more, and that as far as it was possible to make a distinction the innocent should not suffer with the guilty. He bore the scorn of thousands.

Let his name be held in honour. It requires truer bravery to stand alone in resisting a multitude eager to do evil, than it did to stand ready for death behind the mud wall of Cawnpore.

5. The Recovery of Delhi and the Relief of Lucknow.—Before long things began to look better. In the south of India there had been no mutinies. At last Delhi was taken, and reinforcements began to arrive. The Englishmen cooped up in Lucknow were in desperate straits. Sir John Lawrence's brother, the good and brave Sir Henry Lawrence, was slain. Unless help could reach them, they would be obliged to surrender from want of food. There would be another massacre like that at Cawnpore. As it was, the shot poured in amongst them, killing even the wounded in the hospitals. Mines exploded beneath the feet of the defenders, and the enemy rushed in like a tide. With a desperate effort the enemy was driven out. So it went on, day after day and week after week. Sickness and death were busy among the little band as well as the enemy's shot. Help was coming, though they knew it not. Havelock, a brave pious soldier, who prayed, and taught his men to pray, as the Puritan soldiers did in the days of Cromwell, was hastening to Lucknow with a small band, but one large enough for the purpose. He had fought his way steadily on, when another soldier, Sir James Outram, arrived. Outram was Havelock's superior officer, and might have taken the command from him, but he was too honourable a soldier for that. 'To you,' he wrote to Havelock, 'shall be left the glory of relieving

Lucknow, for which you have already struggled so much. I shall accompany you, placing my military service at your disposal, should you please, and serving under you as a volunteer.' This happy band of brothers fought on to accomplish their mission of mercy. In Lucknow it was known that they were on the way, but it was hard to believe that they would come in time. At last the good news was told. Some one had heard the bagpipes of the Highlanders sounding the pibroch—the music of their own country— beyond the ranks of the foe. Havelock and Outram were there indeed, and the sorely tried garrison was saved.

6. Sir Colin Campbell in India.—Havelock had succoured the garrison of Lucknow, but he had not men enough to beat off the enemy, and he soon afterwards fell ill and died. Before that, Sir Colin Campbell, an old Scotch general, had been appointed Commander-in-Chief in India. Campbell had more men at his disposal than Havelock had had. Bit by bit Northern India was reconquered. There were terrible punishments, and peace was at last restored. The task of governing India was even more difficult than it had been before. Future generations will be able to say how that task has been accomplished.

CHAPTER XLIX.

FROM THE END OF THE INDIAN MUTINY TO THE PASSING OF THE SECOND REFORM BILL.

(1858—1867.)

1. **The Reform Bills which did not Pass.**—Before the Indian Mutiny was suppressed Lord Palmerston's ministry had come to an end. There was an attempt in Paris to murder the Emperor Napoleon, and a foreigner living in England was supposed to have had something to do with the plot. Whether he had or not, he was acquitted by an English jury. On this the French grew very angry with England, and called on us to alter our laws. No nation likes to be told what it ought to do, and Lord Palmerston was charged with having been too civil to the French Government. He was beaten in the House of Commons, and he resigned. A Conservative Government took office, with Lord Derby at its head and Mr. Disraeli as its leader in the House of Commons. This Ministry did not last long. For some years there had been a growing feeling amongst many of the statesmen on the Liberal side that there ought to be a new Reform Bill, which would allow the working men to vote, and several attempts had been made to get such a Bill passed. But most people in the House of Commons did not care about a Reform Bill, and people outside the House did not care much about it either. Their minds were too

much taken up with other matters. They had had the European revolutions to think of. Then had come the establishment of the Empire in France, and after that the Crimean War and the Indian Mutiny. Now that all these things were over, the Conservatives thought that they would bring in a Reform Bill too, but they did not succeed any better than the other party. The Liberals said that it was a bad Reform Bill, and beat them in the House of Commons. Then there was a new Parliament, and the new House of Commons declared against them. Lord Palmerston became Prime Minister a second time. He did not himself care for a Reform Bill, but, as some of his colleagues did, he let them bring one in. The new House of Commons did not care much more about it than the old one had done, and so the Reform Bill came to nothing, and as long as Lord Palmerston lived no new one was brought in.

2. The French War in Italy.—Perhaps there was very little thought about the Reform Bill because every one was eagerly watching the things that were taking place in Italy. That country was cut up into little states, and most of the dukes and kings who ruled in those states ruled against the wishes of their subjects. The north-east of Italy, from Milan to Venice, was governed by the Austrians, and Austrian armies were ready to march to support any of the kings or dukes against their own subjects. No wonder that Italians began to think that they would rather form one nation, and be able to manage their own affairs, without being meddled with by the Austrians. Brave men had long been forming schemes to set Italy free, but the Austrians were too strong for them, and for years nothing was done. In the year 1848, the year of the European revolutions, Charles Albert, the King of Sardinia, who ruled over the north-west of Italy, declared himself ready to fight for Italian independence. He attacked the Austrians, but the Austrians were too strong for him, and he was beaten, and forced to resign his throne. His son Victor Emmanuel, who succeeded him, longed for the day when he might carry out his father's design. At last in 1859, two years after the breaking out of the Indian mutiny, he was able to do what he wished. Napoleon offered to help him. A French army, with the Emperor at its head, came into Italy, and defeated the Austrians in the two great battles of Magenta and Solferino. The Italians hoped that the Austrians would at last be driven out of Italy. It was perhaps as well for them that they had to wait a little longer. No one trusted Napoleon. He thought it a very fine and noble thing to help the Italians, but he wanted to get some advantage for himself. The Prussians threatened to join the Austrians, and the French made peace. The country about Milan was given to Victor Emmanuel. Venetia, as the country about Venice was called, was left to the Austrians.

3. The Kingdom of Italy.— It was difficult to say what was to be done with the rest of Italy. The Emperor's plan was that the dukes should remain where they were, and live in a friendly way with Victor Emmanuel. But the dukes had run away, and their people did not want to have them back.

The people asked that Victor Emmanuel should be their king, and so the central part of Italy was joined to the north-west. Savoy and Nice had to be given to France. A year or two later the new kingdom had a further increase. Garibaldi landed in Sicily with a thousand men, to attack the kingdom of Naples. The King of Naples did not know how to make himself popular amongst his subjects, and his kingdom fell like a house of cards. Victor Emmanuel now ruled in Naples as well as in Turin. The next question was whether the dominions of the Pope were to become part of the new kingdom. Many Catholics from other nations, especially Frenchmen and Irishmen, came to fight for the Pope. An Italian army attacked them and defeated them. Rome itself and the country round Rome was only saved to the Pope by the French Emperor, who insisted on keeping a French garrison at Rome. Victor Emmanuel ruled over all Italy except over Rome and Venetia.

4. The Volunteers.—The English Government had been very friendly to Italy all through these changes. Most Englishmen were glad to hear that there was another independent nation in Europe, and they were glad that, at all events, the French had not gained any part of Italy for themselves. In England there was a great suspicion of the French Emperor. He had all sorts of schemes in his head, and no one could tell what he was likely to do next. Lord Palmerston thought the best thing to be done was to prepare for the worst. Already, before Lord Palmerston came into office, young men engaged in

all kinds of employments had offered to form volunteer regiments, to be ready to resist invasion if it
came. Every encouragement was given to them,
and the Rifle Volunteers were established as a per-
manent part of the British army.

5. The Commercial Treaty with France.—In
Palmerston's ministry the Chancellor of the Exchequer, that is to say, the minister who had to
make all arrangements about taxation, was Mr.
Gladstone. Year after year he tried to carry out
the work which Peel had left uncompleted, of improving the system of taxation by removing burdensome duties. He did not like to see the growing
risk of a quarrel between England and France, and
he gladly forwarded a plan for inducing the Emperor
of the French to agree to a commercial treaty, by
which English goods should be admitted into France
upon payment of no more than a low duty, and French
wines and other articles should be admitted in the
same way into England. The treaty was arranged by
Cobden, who went to Paris to talk it over with the
Emperor. He and Mr. Gladstone hoped that if the
two nations traded with one another more, they
would be less inclined to quarrel.

6. The Civil War in America.—Whilst the treaty
with France was being made, events beyond the
Atlantic drew the attention of every one in Europe.
The United States of America were divided into two
parts. In those of the South some millions of black
slaves worked for their masters, mostly in producing
sugar and cotton. In the North there were no
slaves. There was a vast amount of rich, wild land

open to emigrants from both sections, and sometimes slaveowners thought they would be better off if they could go to fresh soil further west, and carry their slaves with them. The free states were willing that they should keep their slaves where they were already, but not that they should take them anywhere outside the slave states which already existed. In 1860 there was an election of a new President, the officer who stands at the head of the American Republic for four years. This time Abraham Lincoln was elected, a man who was determined not to allow the fresh land outside the slave states to be cultivated by slaves. The Southern States declared themselves independent, and formed a government of their own under the name of the Confederate States. The Northern States kept the old name of the United States, and resolved that the Confederates should not be allowed to separate. A terrible war followed, which lasted for four years.

7. **The Blockade Runners and the Privateers.**— English feeling took different sides. The upper classes and the merchants were mainly on the side of the South. The Northern navy was strong, and blockaded the ports of the South, to prevent any goods being carried in. Many merchants in England fitted out quick steamers as blockade runners, to carry arms and powder and shot and other stores to the Confederates. In time the Confederates thought that it would be an excellent thing if they could buy from their English friends armed ships, and have them sent out from English ports. The English merchants did as they were asked, took

the money, and sent out these ships to plunder and
to burn the merchant vessels of the United States.
One of the most famous of these was the *Alabama*.
It did an enormous amount of damage, for which
England had afterwards to pay, as the English
Government had not stopped the vessel's sailing, as
it ought to have done.

8. The Cotton Famine.—To one part of England
the American War brought terrible suffering.
Masses of men in many of the large towns in the
north depended for their daily bread upon making
cotton goods. The cotton used in this manufacture
came at that time almost entirely from the Southern
States. There was no possibility of bringing it from
those states, as the blockading ships of the North
would have stopped it on the way. All that could
be done was done to get together supplies of cotton
from Egypt and India and other parts of the world.
That which came from these sources was not nearly
so good as the American cotton had been, and even
of the bad cotton there was not enough. The cotton
famine, as it was called, stopped the mills, or caused
them to work at short time. Thousands of persons
ready to work to earn their livelihood were thrown
out of work through no fault of their own. In many
a house there was want and hunger. That want and
hunger were nobly borne. Not only were the sufferers patient under their misfortune, but they were
not to be tempted to speak evil of the Northern
States, whose blockade was the cause of their misery.
They believed that the slaveowners of the South
were in the wrong, and that if the war went on long

enough the men of the North would win, and that when they won they would set free the slaves. The working men of the north were right. After four years of hard-fought war, the North won the victory, and the slaves were set free. The English working man had done something for himself without thinking of himself at all. He had shown that he was capable of standing up for that which he believed to be a righteous cause, however much he might suffer through it. It was impossible to deny to such men as these the rights of citizens. They were surely worthy of having votes to send members to Parliament to make the laws, after showing that, under the most trying circumstances, they knew how to obey the laws. A Parliamentary Reform which should reach them could not now be long in coming.

9. The Last Days of Lord Palmerston.—It was well known that Lord Palmerston would not hear of Parliamentary Reform. Mr. Gladstone, however, declared in its favour, and Mr. Gladstone was likely to have great influence soon. In 1865 a new Parliament was elected. Before it met Lord Palmerston died. He was eighty years of age, and kept brisk and active to the last. He was the most popular man in England, always cheery, and ready to speak a friendly word to every one. But there was work now to be done which needed the hands of younger men.

10. The Ministry of Earl Russell.—The successor of Lord Palmerston was not a young man. Earl Russell, who had once been the Lord John Russell who had advocated Parliamentary Reform not long after the Battle of Waterloo was fought, and who had had much to do with the first Reform Bill, became Prime Minister, to advocate a second Reform Bill, the object of which would be to give votes to the working men, as the first Reform Bill had given votes to the tradesmen. Mr. Gladstone was the chief person in the House of Commons. A Reform Bill was proposed, but the House of Commons did not care about it, and would not have it. The Ministers at once resigned office. They thought that it was so important to reform Parliament that they would not keep in office unless they could do this. Lord Palmerston had stayed in office after proposing a Reform Bill, but they cared about reform, and Lord Palmerston did not.

11. The Conservative Ministry and the Second Reform Bill.—A Conservative Ministry came into office. The Prime Minister was Lord Derby, but the most important minister was Mr. Disraeli. All at once it appeared that though the greater number of the members of the House of Commons did not care about Reform, the working men did. There were meetings held in different parts of the country in its favour. In London a large body of men made up their minds to hold a meeting in Hyde Park, to make speeches about Reform. The Government tried to shut them out. They broke down the railings and held their meeting. The Government found out that it had no right to shut them out. Mr. Disraeli saw that the working men were now in earnest, and that they were determined to have reform. He determined to be the person to give it to them. When Parliament met he presented a Reform Bill, which did not satisfy anybody. When that would not do he presented another Reform Bill, which was accepted. When it became law everyone who had a house of his own in a town of any size had the right of voting, and almost everyone who lived in the country who had a house which was at least of a moderate size. The working men had got what they wanted. They would now be consulted on the making of the laws.

CHAPTER L.

FROM THE PASSING OF THE SECOND REFORM BILL TO THE END OF LORD BEACONSFIELD'S MINISTRY.

(1867–1880.)

1. **Irish Troubles.**—The year in which the Reform Bill was passed was one of trouble in Ireland. An association was formed, the members of which were known as Fenians, for the purpose of separating Ireland from England. This association had many friends in America, where many Irish were living. An attempt was made to rise in insurrection in Ireland itself. The insurrection was not likely to succeed, as the Irish had scarcely any arms, and no discipline. It happened that when the

Irish collected in the hills it began to snow, and they were unable to remain in the open country. The attempt was easily put down. At Manchester some Fenian prisoners were being carried in a prison van, when some Irishmen rushed at the van, to set them free. A shot was fired, and a policeman was killed. Some of the Irishmen were tried for murder, and hanged.

2. The Irish Church and the Gladstone Ministry. —These things had a great effect on many of the Liberals, and especially on Mr. Gladstone. He thought that it was not enough to keep the Irish down by force, and that it would be right to find out whether the Irish had anything to complain of, in order that it might be remedied. The first thing which he proposed to do was to take away the income of the Protestant Church. The greater part of the Irish people was Catholic, and had to support their priests out of their own pockets, whilst the Protestant clergy were paid by money which the law required Irishmen to pay, whatever their religion might be, and were also treated with more honour by the Government than the Catholic priests were, as if their Church had been the Church of the country. Mr. Gladstone proposed to put an end to this, and to allow both the Catholic and the Protestant clergy to be paid voluntarily by their own congregations. Mr. Disraeli, who was now Prime Minister, as Lord Derby had become too ill to attend to business, objected to this, but the House of Commons agreed with Mr. Gladstone. Parliament was dissolved, and the new Parliament was on

Mr. Gladstone's side. He therefore became Prime Minister.

3. The Irish Church Act and the Irish Land Act. —The first thing that the new ministry did was to pass a law to take away the money from the Irish Protestant Church. The next thing that it did was to pass a law about Irish Land, and to try to do what was just between landlords and tenants. Some years afterwards there were great complaints in Ireland that enough had not been done. But, at all events, the law was an honest attempt to remedy what was wrong.

4. The Education Act.—Many changes too were made in England. The greatest of these was the introduction of a new system of education. For many years the Government had been enabled by Parliament to do more and more for education. It had given large sums of money to certain Societies, which subscribed money to pay for schools on condition that the children were properly educated. A law was now made to enable the people who lived in a district to set up a school to be paid for by themselves. These schools, which are known as Board Schools, would teach a great many children who had not been taught by the Societies. Parents too, who neglected to send their children to school, were to be made to do so.

5. The Ballot Act.—Another new thing was the introduction of voting by ballot at elections. Before this, every man who voted had to give his vote openly, and many persons were afraid to vote as they thought right for fear of offending either their employers or the people amongst whom they lived. Now no one knows how they vote. It was thought at the time that the ballot would prevent voters from taking bribes. This, however, has not been the case, and we can only hope that men will some day be ashamed of taking money for their vote. Not much more than a hundred years ago noblemen and gentlemen took money or something that was worth money for their vote in Parliament, and perhaps a hundred years hence some writer will be able to speak of it as a wonderful thing that there had been a time when some people took money for their votes at elections.

6. **The Franco-German War.**—Whilst these things were being done in England, great events were taking place on the Continent. In 1866 there had been a war between Prussia and Austria, in which Prussia was completely successful. Italy had helped Prussia, and obtained the country about Venice at the end of the war, so that Austria was now entirely excluded from Italy. The French grew extremely jealous of Prussia, and in 1870 the Emperor Napoleon picked a quarrel with the King of Prussia. In the war which followed, all Germany took part with Prussia. The Germans invaded France, and defeated the French armies in several great battles. The Emperor Napoleon was taken prisoner, and France again became a Republic. Then siege was laid to Paris. After bearing much hardship, the great city was starved out and surrendered. France had to give up some of her provinces. The King of Prussia became the German Emperor and the little States

of Germany united together to form the German Empire. The Italians, too, took possession of Rome, and there was now at last a United Italy under one king.

7. The End of the First Gladstone Ministry.— In England the Gladstone Ministry had been very busy, and, as often happens, people got tired of seeing so many changes made. Some of the Ministers, too, behaved rudely to those who had business with them, and when, in 1874, a new Parliament was elected, it had a large Conservative majority. Mr. Disraeli became Prime Minister. and remained in office for six years.

8. Mr. Disraeli's Ministry and the Turkish Disturbances.— After some time there were fresh troubles in Turkey. Some of the Christian inhabitants rose against their oppressors, and in one place the Turks massacred men, women, and children. The European States sent ambassadors to Constantinople, to see what could be done, but though they gave some good advice to the Sultan, the Sultan, as is always the case, refused to take it. All the States except Russia thought there was no more to be done. Russia declared war against the Sultan, to make him do what he had been advised to do. The war lasted about a year. The Russians had great difficulties, and lost a great number of men, but in the end they beat the Turks thoroughly. They made a treaty with the Sultan, by which a great part of the provinces of Turkey in Europe were taken away from the Sultan and given to the people who lived in them. Mr. Disraeli, who had now become Earl of Beaconsfield, thought that Russia would make the people in these provinces obey its orders, and would in this way become too powerful. He and the English Government insisted that Russia should consult the other European States and make a new treaty, and he was prepared to go to war if this were not done. This made him very popular in England, though there were many people who did not wish to have a war with Russia. At last Russia gave way, and the different States sent Ambassadors to Berlin, where a new treaty was drawn up, by which, though many of the Christian peoples were set free, some, who had been taken away from under the rule of the Sultan by the Russian treaty, were placed under it again. There have been more troubles since, and they are not likely to end as long as the Sultan continues to rule, because it does not seem possible to teach him to govern well, or to make him care to learn.

9. The End of the Conservative Ministry.—At this there were wars in other parts of the world. There was another invasion of Afghanistan and a war in Zulu Land. In 1880 there was again a new Parliament. This time the people thought that the Conservative ministry was too fond of war, and the new Parliament had a large Liberal majority. Mr. Gladstone became Prime Minister a second time.

10. Conclusion.—So far we have come in the story of England. What lies beyond we cannot tell; but this we can tell, that England has prospered most when she has most sought to do that which it was her duty to do. Each generation has been better

in something than the one before it, and it is for all
people to make the generation in which they live
better than the last one for the sake of their children
who will come after them. We need not be very
great or very learned to help in this work. Each
person, as he or she grows up, can do something.
Every time we choose the good and avoid the evil,
we set a good example to others. Thousands of
small right acts done come to a great deal when
they are taken together. Much of the grandest
work ever done by Englishman has blessed their
American descendents as well as their English ones,
and as we read what men of old have done for us,
we can fitly think of their deeds as the poet Brown-
ing thought when he was sailing off the Spanish
coast. His mind dwelt on Nelson and the old
warriors who had fought and died there for their
country. Trafalgar was in front and St. Vincent
behind. Then, as he turned to think of himself
the words that rose to his lips were

> Here and here did England help me ; how can I help
>   England ? Say
> Whoso turns as I, this evening, turn to God to praise
>   and pray.

THE END.

INDEX.